Pro iOS Geo

Building Apps with Location Based Services

Giacomo Andreucci

Apress·

Pro iOS Geo: Building Apps with Location Based Services

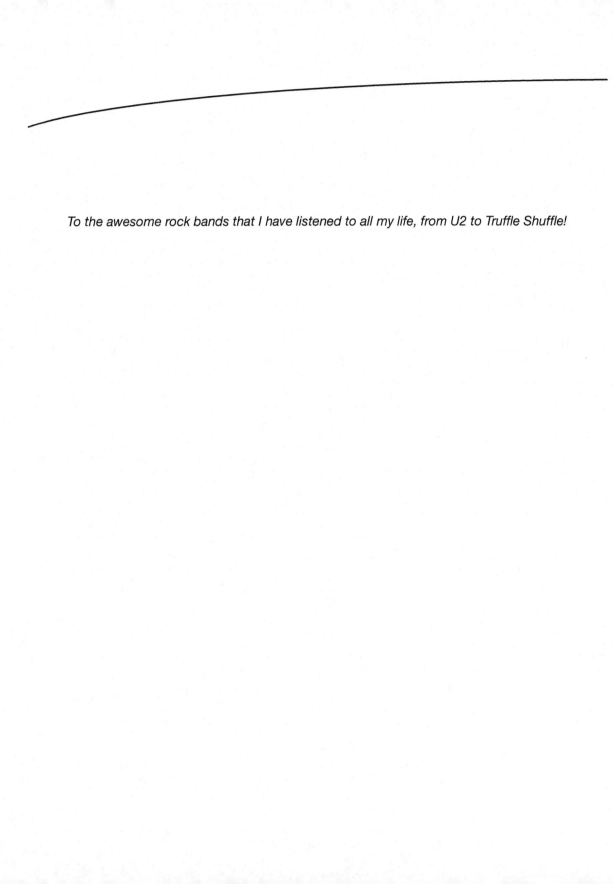

To the awesome rock bands that I have listened to all my life, from U2 to Truffle Shuffle!

Contents at a Glance

Contents

About the Author

Giacomo Andreucci has a Ph.D. in History and Geography at the University of Bologna, Italy. His main research interests embrace the use of new media in historical and geographical/cartographical research. He is also tech writer for the Italian publisher FAG for which he wrote books on Google Earth/Maps API, and SketchUp. More information about his books is available here: http://www.fag.it/autore_andreucci_giacomo_181.aspx.

About the Technical Reviewer

Nishant Pant is a software architect, mentor, and web and mobile developer with more than 15 years of experience in all aspects of software development. He is also the co-founder of Loqly, a platform for connecting local businesses with their customers.

Acknowledgments

Eric Racher proofread the text. I thank him for his patience and the quality of his work.

Introduction

Since its first release in 2007, iOS has offered geographic services: the (Google) Maps app was bundled with it by default. When the iOS SDK was released in 2008, developers were given the opportunity to implement geo components in their apps using the Map Kit Framework based on Google Maps services. Annotations (such as points of interest) could be overlaid on the maps provided by Google, and it became possible to use geocoding services and iOS geolocation to display data on the maps. In 2008 Google released its powerful Google Maps JavaScript API V3, which was optimized for use on mobile devices. This new API has since become the most widely used platform to implement maps services on the web, both for desktop computers and for mobile devices. In the meantime, competing platforms were created to deliver geo data through websites and web apps: Open StreetMap was (and still is) one of the most popular, even if it is less so than Google geo services. (Other competing platforms include Microsoft Bing Maps and Yahoo Maps.)

Thanks to these geo platforms, many iOS developers have featured geo functionalities in their apps, not only for iPod Touch and iPhone devices but for the iPad as well. The iPad is a very powerful device because it permits users to comfortably display and manipulate cartographic and geographic data, due to its dimensions and its geolocation capabilities. In the Apple App Store thousands of apps make use of online cartography and geo services, the majority of which rely on the Google Maps platform. Among those map-based apps, both free and commercial, some can display homes and apartments for sale within a certain distance from your current location, while other apps find parking lots, movie theaters, and restaurants (Figure 1).

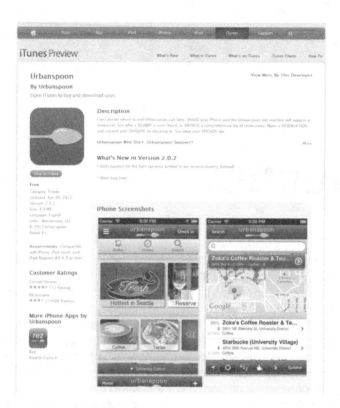

Figure 1. *Urbanspoon is an example of a successful geo app*
(http://itunes.apple.com/us/app/urbanspoon/id284708449?mt=8)

There are also guidebook-style apps that can give you information in real time about nearby monuments. These apps combine location data, maps, and StreetView imagery to create fascinating augmented reality experiences. Augmented reality apps are flourishing given the growing hardware capacities of mobile devices and the spread of broadband connections through 3G and 4G services. These apps can be used in many different fields, ranging from commercial guides to tourism or cultural initiatives supported by the public administration, institutions, museums, and so on. Additionally, social networks have been implementing geo services in their apps in recent years.

In this blossoming landscape, an important change took place in June 2012, when at the WWDC in San Francisco Apple announced its own new mapping platform, included in iOS 6 (Figure 2). This platform is going to take the place of Google Maps in native iOS apps. It was a commercial move to limit the power and earnings of Google in the iOS world. The iOS 6 default Maps app is indeed no longer based on Google services but on the new Apple Maps platform.

Figure 2. On June 11, 2012, at the WWDC in San Francisco, Apple announced its own mapping platform intended to replace Google Maps services

Similarly, the Apple Map Kit framework is no longer based on Google Maps but on the Apple maps platform and this affects all new native apps that are going to be developed for iOS. Apple's own mapping platform has become the reference point for any developer who wants to develop native iOS apps, while Google Maps remains the main mapping platform used in developing web apps for iOS since its powerful JavaScript API is still the best solution for the wealth and quality of services it offers.

The Purpose of This Book

The purpose of this book is to introduce the reader to the primary resources that are currently available for developing map-based services for iOS apps. As I have mentioned, the geo dimension can play different roles inside an app. The geo component might just be an accessory to a larger app (such as a social networking app that, among its functions, can show the location of friends in the vicinity) or it might constitute the main part of an app (such as an app whose only purpose is to show the nearest underground station).

In this book I will not focus on a specific genre of apps. Instead, I present a series of ideas and suggestions on how best to integrate and exploit the geo resources currently available for developers. However, in Parts 2 and 3 of the book (see the next section), I present a case study, which is the realization of a geo app, named "U2's Dublin." The purpose of this app is to show landmarks related to U2's rock band history implementing some geo functions we will be talking about extensively in the next chapters.

How This Book is Organized

As I will explain in more detail in the first chapter, it is possible to integrate geo services in an app in different ways, depending on the kind of app we are developing: a web app, a hybrid app, or a native app. This book deals with all three ways of creating an app.

After establishing the groundwork for building iOS map-based apps in Chapter 1 (Part 1), Chapters 2–6 (Part 2) focus on web apps. A greater amount of space is given to Part 2 because I believe that web apps are the easiest and most effective way to implement powerful geo services in an iOS app, which makes them easily accessible to other mobile platforms as well. The drawback to web apps is that they cannot be directly uploaded and distributed through the App Store. In the first section of the book I mainly focus on the Google Maps JavaScript API V3. Since web apps are the subject of this first part, it is necessary for the reader to have a basic knowledge of HTML5 and JavaScript.

Part 3 (Chapter 7) covers hybrid apps, which are web apps accessed through a browser window embedded in a native app. Hybrid apps are like web apps but they can be uploaded and distributed through the App Store. To develop hybrid apps, it is not necessary to know Objective-C; it is sufficient to know how to develop a web app and have basic knowledge of the Xcode environment.

In Part 4 (Chapters 8–10) I cover the new Apple Map Kit framework, which makes it possible to integrate mapping services in native iOS apps. The reader of this last part needs basic knowledge of the Xcode environment and Objective-C language.

This book is organized so that readers may choose to read the section or sections in which they are interested: knowledge of earlier chapters is not necessary for a thorough understanding of later sections. Nonetheless, I strongly recommend that everyone read the first chapter since it is a general introduction to developing geo and mapping functionalities for mobile devices. I also recommend that everyone read Appendix A of the book since it discusses Terms of Use and legal aspects related to the services mentioned in the book.

What You Won't Find in This Book (and Where to Find It)

As I mentioned earlier, readers must know certain languages depending on which sections of the book they are interested in. In this book I take that knowledge for granted and I do not provide introductions to the above-mentioned languages. The reader who is not familiar with the languages can easily learn them by consulting online resources or buying specific books. Regarding the languages necessary for the development of web apps, which are mainly HTML5 and JavaScript, I recommend the free courses at W3C Schools, http://www.w3schools.com/. For the Google Maps JavaScript API, I suggest bookmarking the official documentation site, which also hosts many tutorials, https://developers.google.com/maps/documentation/javascript/.

I also suggest reading the Apress title, *Learn HTML5 and JavaScript for iOS* by Scott Preston, Apress 2012.

For people interested in developing native apps it is a good idea to be familiar with the documentation hosted in the iOS Dev Center at the official Apple developers site (https://developer.apple.com/devcenter/ios/index.action). A good book to begin developing with iOS is *Objective-C for Absolute Beginners. iPhone, iPad and Mac Programming Made Easy* by Gary Bennett, Mitchell Fisher, Brad Lees, 2nd Edition, Apress 2011.

To grasp the concepts in the second and third sections of the book (hybrid and native geo apps), it is also necessary to have a working Xcode /iOS 6 development environment and to be enrolled in the iOS Developer Program (https://developer.apple.com/programs/ios/).

The Companion Site

In my blog I deal with topics related to online maps and mobile map design. The site also makes available all the code samples I have used in this book.
http://www.http://www.progettaremappeonline.it

Contacting the Author

If you have any questions or comments – or you spot a mistake you think I should know about – you can contact me at giacomo.andreucci@unibo.it.

Happy reading!

Part 1

Introduction

Chapter 1 lays the foundation for the rest of the book by comparing computer and mobile map-based apps, and highlighting the primary characteristics of mobile map, such as its key services and functionalities. You will also find out about the available options for building iOS map-based apps.

Getting started

Throughout most of history, maps were used mainly in static rather than dynamic form. For example, on ships they were placed flat on a surface to allow for easy readability. Measurements and other notations were drawn recorded on the map itself. With the growth of cartography in the first half of the 20th century, maps became easily portable and handy, showing up in road atlases and guidebooks. Paper maps thus became fully mobile. The advent of smartphones, tablets and other mobile devices equipped with broadband Internet connectivity, GPS, and other features brought about the introduction of mobile cartography (now made digital).

Thanks to their sensors, geolocation capabilities, elaboration power, and display quality, iOS devices can implement map-based apps that give users a unique geo experience. In this chapter I lay the groundwork for building iOS map-based apps. First, I focus on the main differences between computer and mobile map-based apps, highlighting the primary characteristics of mobile maps. I then present a list of key services and functionalities mobile maps can offer to make you more aware of the possible uses of this technology. To build a map-based mobile app it is important to respect some basic design and usability guidelines specific to this kind of app, so later in this chapter I provide a simple set of usability guidelines. Next, I introduce you to some options for building iOS map-based apps. These are web apps based on the Google Maps JS API, hybrid apps, and eventually native apps using the Apple Maps API. I complete the chapter with a brief section on testing, thereby providing you with a complete guide to getting started.

Comparing Desktop Computer Maps and Mobile Maps

Online desktop computer maps, like the maps you can use on maps.google.com, are usually accessed in relatively comfortable circumstances, for example, by a user seated at a computer. Users of these maps can view complex legends and show or hide the data levels available on the map. These are also the best conditions to enjoy thematic maps – that is, maps that display the spatial patterns of physical or social phenomenons, such as population density, life expectancy, etc. Here's an example of a thematic map showing housing data within determined areas (Figure 1-1).

Figure 1-1. Thematic map displaying the affordability of housing in local authority areas in UK in 2008
(http://www.hnm.org.uk/maps.html)

Thematic maps like this are best enjoyed on large desktop computer screens, while on small mobile devices they would be very cumbersome to use (Figure 1-2).

Figure 1-2. The same map displayed on an iPhone

Compared to maps viewed on a large screen, maps on mobile devices have certain limitations due to the technical characteristics of these devices, such as smaller displays, less computing power, and, in some circumstances, limited bandwidth. For example, you can see how the thematic map shown in Figure 1-1 appears clunky on an iPhone device, as shown in Figure 1-2.

These limitations are also related to where and how the mobile device is being used. In a mobility context, the available time to interact with the device may be shorter, the interaction with the map is less comfortable, etc. The user needs to access maps quickly and easily through an interface that does not require many finger movements or extra effort. Users of mobile devices may have less time to react, so geographical services have to be adapted to their specific conditions and limitations.

But mobile devices have also created new possibilities for map-based applications. Mobile apps possess a more "individual" character, meaning that they may be more related to the person using them. Mobile apps are indeed context-sensitive. The sensors that smartphones and tablets possess allow mobile apps to know the users' current and previous position data (coordinates, altitude, orientation, speed of movement) in addition to knowing what they have previously visited on the web, what they have searched for, and so on. Technically speaking, we can say that mobile applications are context aware. Users of these devices can take this "awareness" and become producers of new geodata rather than mere passive consumers. For example, GPS and other sensors allow users to georeference many types of data (that is, establishing their location in terms of coordinates), such as photographs, voice recordings, or routes followed while walking. Such a level of awareness is generally not available for geo services on a desktop computer.

Let's now take a closer look at what mobile maps have to offer.

Reviewing Mobile Geo Apps Services

Before you begin to develop your own mobile geo app, it's important to review the main types of geo services that existing apps can offer users. Here is a simple list of map-based services:

- **Navigation-mobility support services.** Included in this category are "You are here" services (real-time calculation of user position and visualization on a map), "You will go" and way-finding services (calculation of routes), navigation services.

- **Information-supply services.** This category includes all those services that allow users to visualize information layers on maps, such as Google Local (ex-Places) categories (restaurants, monuments, museums); in this category "event-calendar" services are also included to show all the current events (exhibitions, concerts) in a user-defined area. Augmented reality services also belong to this group – for example, a guidebook app that can show information layers on the monuments around the user's current position.

- **Information sharing.** This category includes those map-based services that permit users to produce geo information in order to share it. They can be simple services that enable users to share their position data with other users (like Google Latitude, Foursquare, Facebook, and many other social networks) or more complex applications that permit users to record many sets of geodata and share them online. An example: apps created by many municipalities which permit citizens to report urban problems, such as trash, bad road conditions, and abandoned buildings by geolocating them and referencing them with text, pictures, and videos. For example, Citizens Connect is a municipality app that empowers Boston residents to be the City's "eyes and ears" throughout the neighborhoods (Figure 1-3). Through this app, people can alert the City of Boston to neighborhood issues such as potholes and graffiti (http://itunes.apple.com/us/app/boston-citizens-connect/id330894558?mt=8).

Figure 1-3. *An example of an app whose strength lies in its information sharing functionalities*

One or more types of the aforementioned services can obviously be integrated into a single mobile app.

Let's now look at the main usability guidelines to follow while implementing the previously mentioned services.

Designing Guidelines for Optimal Usability of Map-Based Apps

Building a map-based mobile app requires some knowledge of basic design and usability guidelines specific to this kind of app. These guidelines are useful both for creating map-based apps from scratch and for converting already existing geo services into a mobile app. Before I get into the guidelines it is useful to consider the ways in which users commonly interact with maps on mobile devices – so you can avoid having to invent new ways that may confuse users.

Compared to computer users, mobile device users interact with maps in more ways: using physical buttons, touch screens, pens, and voice, or moving the device itself. When using a map-based app, users might employ a single interaction type (monomodal) or a combination of types (multimodal).

For instance, users can pan the map with the touch screen and start a search with vocal commands. The most common types of interaction users can perform while using a map-based app are the following:

- Panning: Users may define the visible portion of the map by dragging the map itself in different directions.

- Zoom: Users may zoom in and out, changing the scale of the map; when users zoom, new map data (with more or less detail) is usually loaded (Figure 1-4).

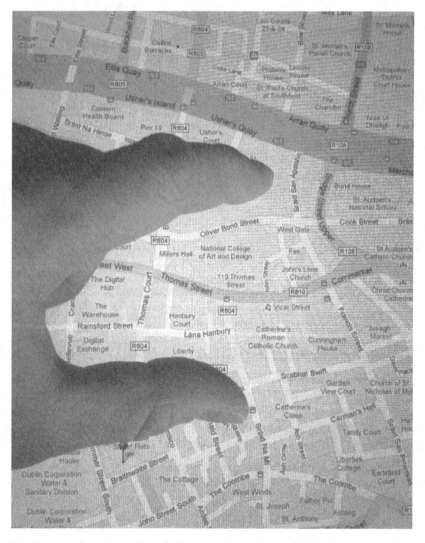

Figure 1-4. Example of user interaction: pinch-zoom performed on an iPad device

- Switching: Users may switch views or presentation styles: For example, they can switch from a view with map data to a view with aerial/satellite imagery or to a view with Street View data.

- Show/hide data layers: Users may show or hide data layers on the map – for instance, a traffic layer or a Panoramio photo layer.

- Focus: Users may click on a specific object on the map – for example, a placemark – and retrieve information connected to it. This information is generally displayed in a balloon or an information window.

- Search: Users can start a search by inputting search terms in a form; the results will be displayed on the map itself.

- Map settings setup: Users can define map settings like map language, map fonts, colors, 3D settings, and GPS activity.

The types of interaction I have just shown mostly relate to access to existing data, but other types of interaction allow users to produce their own geo content (if the app is designed for this purpose). For example, users might drag a marker onto a position on the map to create a new placemark. They might then enter text to fill some fields of the placemark, such as title or description. Typically, users must interact with dialog boxes to produce new geo information.

The developer has to take into consideration these basic types of interaction and be aware of the limitations users of a mobile app are subject to (scarcity of time, uncomfortable circumstances, to name a couple.). The developer is urged to find ways to make the tasks users have to perform as easy as possible. To meet users' needs, the developer can work in three strategic areas:

- Self-adaptability of the app: It is possible to build applications that automatically adapt to users' needs by exploiting the device's sensors.

- Usability of the app's GUI: The way in which buttons and menus are designed is essential to the effective use of the app.

- Usability of map contents: The maps and the geo data should be displayed in such a way that users can quickly and easily decipher them.

Self-Adaptability of the App

It is important to exploit the mobile device's capabilities in the best way possible. If, for instance, the device is equipped with a digital compass, then the map might automatically orient itself, without requiring user intervention. To give another example, if you create an app that shows the user's location, the app might automatically frame the user's current position when that person moves out of the visible area of the map. Creating apps with a good level of adaptability makes it possible for users to focus on essential tasks, without wasting time on settings. The developer can also make an adaptable app by recording the user's habits. For example, if a user generally prefers satellite imagery to default maps when using a certain app, the software itself might remember this setting so that the next time the user opens the app, it will display satellite imagery instead of maps.

Usability of the App's GUI

When designing an app's GUI, a simple but essential guideline to keep in mind is to be in tune with the look and feel of the operating system environment (iOS) and its already existing apps. It is necessary to integrate the GUI into a sort of ecosystem. It would be a frustrating user experience if a GUI displayed different buttons and menus from those interfaces to which the user is accustomed on that particular OS. It is more effective to show users something familiar, instead of trying to seduce them with new interfaces, buttons, and eye-candy menus that require a lot of time to learn how to use. Another important suggestion for a good GUI is to avoid long instructions.

This does not mean that developers shouldn't guide users when necessary, but these situations should be reduced as much as possible with simple, short, and clear instructions.

As far as GUIs are concerned, if we develop map-based apps for iPad devices, it is important to be aware of the capacities of iOS tablets regarding the manipulation of maps and geo data.

Thanks to their resolution (iPad 3 features a 2048-by-1536 pixel resolution), touch screen, Internet connection, GPS chip, and other sensors, iPads are powerful geo devices. They can be used to access maps and also to input geo data in various field more comfortably than is possible using the iPhone. Even if iPads are not usually associated with walking to view maps and access geodata, there are a growing number of people who use them while walking or traveling for their geo capabilities. In fact, by 2010 a Forbes's article reported an increasing availability of map-based apps for iPad devices (http://www.forbes.com/2010/07/14/navigation-gps-apple-technology-ipad.html). The article reported how iPad maps were being used in sports activities like hiking and sailing and how many cartography producers who had not previously released iPhone apps made their first entrance in the App Store with iPad apps (Figure 1-5).

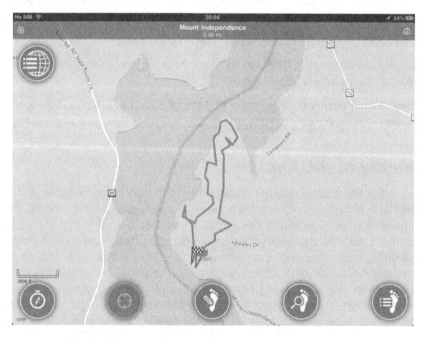

Figure 1-5. *OutDoors America: Example of a geo app running on an iPad device*
(http://itunes.apple.com/app/outdoors-america/id451136498?mt=8)

Usability of Map Contents

Cartography involves the art of reduction and the synthesis of information and these disciplines are well suited to the world of mobile devices, which is constrained by some relevant limitations. Some of these limitations are technological while others are due to the mobility context in which the user *acts*. As I mentioned before, in designing mobile apps it is crucial to avoid anything extraneous, anything that can create confusion or waste the user's time. Here I present a general list of things to avoid when displaying maps and related data layers:

- Avoid useless explanations and image captions. The user might need to be introduced to map data. For instance, a legend might be necessary to explain the symbols used. However it is important to reduce explanations to a bare minimum. For instance it is usually not necessary to explain that the areas in green on a map represent parks or other natural areas.

- Avoid showing a map view overcrowded with data and therefore difficult to decipher in a few seconds.

- Avoid the absence of key areas on the map. If the map is designed to show specific geo data in particular areas, it is important to guide users toward the areas instead of presenting a map where users must find interest data.

- Avoid filling balloons with too much information like large images or long text blocks, which strain users' eyes. Just as text on web pages should be brief, so should those in maps' balloon content; the balloon should open in the shortest time possible and should not occupy all the available visible space, thus completely covering the map.

- Avoid designing complex and overly elaborate icons, which are difficult to read and decipher; the icon's symbol should show a clear relationship with the content to which it refers.

- For icons, lines, and polygons, avoid using colors that are difficult to distinguish when these objects are overlayed on the map. The right choice of colors depends on the map type that we choose as the default map type for the app (for example, satellite images and standard map type).

- Avoid using acronyms and abbreviations that users are unlikely to know. If you must use these shortened forms, find a place to explain them.

- Avoid showing aerial/satellite/street View imagery (available with Google Maps API) or similar cumbersome layers as default map type when the app is opened, unless it is strictly necessary.

In short, it is better to start with a standard map type and permit the user to switch, if he prefers, to other map types, satellite images, etc.

After the review of usability guidelines it is now time to take a close look at the main developing options currently available to realize map-based apps for iOS.

The Primary Options to Develop Map-Based Apps for iOS

As I mentioned in the introduction, this book is organized in three parts, according to the three main available options to develop iOS map-based apps: web apps (Google Maps-based), hybrid apps (Google Maps-based) and native apps (Apple Maps-based).

Developing Web Apps with Google Maps

Google Maps-based web apps are apps developed using web technologies, mainly HTML5, CSS3, and JavaScript. Web apps are accessed directly through the iPhone or iPad's browser. Geolocation functionalities are managed through HTML5 and JavaScript. Maps and other geo data and services are implemented through Google Maps JavaScript API V3 and connected libraries. The Google Maps JavaScript API is by far the best available option for developing a map-based web app. None of the other platforms, such as OpenStreetMap or Microsoft Bing Maps, currently offer such a powerful set of geo data and services through a JavaScript API. The new Apple Maps platform is not even available to be implemented on a web app (it is only for native apps) and in any case it does not yet offer all the range of data and services that Google does. Paradoxically, a web app using Google Maps API V3 can offer certain types of services and data not available on native apps based on Apple Maps.

Developing web apps offers some other relevant advantages when compared to native apps. First of all, with mobile web apps you can reuse already existing map-based services available in the form of web apps for desktop computer users. All it takes is a few lines of code (Figure 1-6).

Figure 1-6. The desktop computer map wep app of the University of Missouri (left); the web app optimized for mobile devices (right) (http://search.missouristate.edu/map and http://search.missouristate.edu/map/mobile)

Compared to native apps, updating a web app is very easy and transparent. It is just a matter of updating the app's code on the web server and *voilà!* The user does not have to update anything but just reloads the web page. Moreover, every time Google updates its API and the geo data connected to that, changes are immediately reflected on the web app. Another advantage is that developers can use the HTML5 geolocation API to easily implement location-aware functionalities in their apps. By using HTML5 Javascript/jQuery it is also possible to develop GUIs very similar in their look and feel to native apps' GUIs. Many developers can develop map-based web apps, as it is only necessary to know web languages like HTML and JavaScript. These two languages are very easy to learn and can be used not only for mobile apps but also for every type of web content. Building native apps requires knowledge of the Objective-C language, which is more complex and tougher to learn than HTML and JavaScript. In addition, the usefulness of Objective-C is limited mainly to the Mac world, while HTML and JavaScript are more or less universal languages usable with countless operating systems and hardware combinations, so if one learns them he can then reuse his knowledge for many types of applications. Costs are also different: developing web apps is cheap, one basically needs just a text editor, an updated web browser and web server space. There are many free text editors while web server space can cost just a few dollars a year. Google Maps JS API are free for many uses. You can develop web apps on the platform you want, Mac, PC, etc. On the other hand, to develop native apps you need to use a Mac OS X computer and you have to pay to enroll in iOS developer program (99$/year). Costs can be relevant if you do not already have a Mac computer.

On the other hand, there are also disadvantages to map-based web apps: compared to native apps written in Objective-C, web apps can't make maximum use of the device's hardware, using all its capabilities and sensors. Web apps are generally slower and perform more poorly than native apps. Another con is that pure web apps cannot be directly uploaded and sold in the App Store and this excludes them from an enormous market: web apps are simply accessed in a web browser from their URL either directly or via a link.

Table 1-1 provides a list of the advantages and disadvantages of web apps.

Table 1-1. Web Apps: Pros and Cons

Pros	Cons
A developer only needs to know HMTL/CSS and JavaScript to create a web app.	A web app cannot access all hardware features of the device.
The app can be accessed directly from a URL from many kinds of mobile devices equipped with Internet connectivity and a browser supporting JavaScript and HTML.	A web app is generally slower and doesn't perform as well as an equivalent native app.
A mobile web app can be easily created from a desktop web app and vice-versa.	A web app cannot be directly distributed through the App Store.
Updating a web app is an extremely easy and quick procedure and is completely transparent for the users, who do not have to do anything.	A web app requires space on a web server.
Web apps are the basis of hybrid apps.	
A web app can take advantage of the HTML 5 Geolocation API to implement location-aware functionalities.	

Developing Hybrid Apps with Google Maps

Hybrid apps are basically web apps embedded in a native app shell. It is possible to convert a web app into a native app by using specific frameworks, like PhoneGap, or by using the iOS SDK. You don't need to know languages other than those required to build a web app. Using frameworks or the iOS SDK, you simply copy a few lines of code to embed an existing web app into a native app; the result is a native app that embeds a browser window pointing to the web app (Figure 1-7). By using a hybrid app, you have all the advantages of a web app while being able to distribute the app in the App Store like a native app. With frameworks like PhoneGap you can embed the same web app in native apps for other operating systems, like Android, Symbian, and Windows Phone, making it possible to reach new markets and platforms with very little effort.

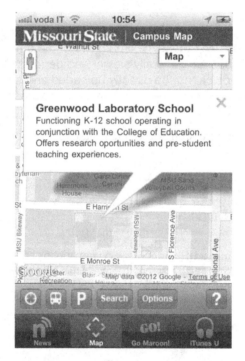

Figure 1-7. The hybrid app of Missouri State University, distributed in the App Store, embeds the web app seen in Figure 1-6 (http://itunes.apple.com/us/app/msu-mobile/id348991586?mt=8)

As I said earlier, the resulting app would be a web app in every way: Updating it would simply involve updating files on the web server. A hybrid app might still be affected by the typical limitations of web apps: it might not access all hardware features and it might be a little bit slower than a native app. Frameworks such as PhoneGap can improve interfacing with hardware features of the devices since they build a sort of bridge between the web app and the hardware layer. In any case, the app might not be as high performance as a truly native app (even if the gap is decreasing). Table 1-2 provides a list of the advantages and disadvantages of hybrid apps.

Table 1-2. Hybrid Apps: Pros and Cons

Pros	Cons
A hybrid app possesses all the advantages of a web app.	Hybrid apps have the same requirements as web apps: They must be hosted on a web server.
Compared to a pure web app, a hybrid app can be distributed through the App Store.	A hybrid app cannot exploit the device's hardware to the maximum, as a native app would do; for this reason, they are also generally slower than an equivalent native app.

Developing a Native App with Apple Maps

Later in the book I deal with native apps. Developing map-based native apps requires a basic knowledge of iOS SDK and Objective-C language. Since with iOS6 native apps' geo core is no longer based on Google Maps, I will give an introduction to the new Apple Maps platform, which is accessible from the Map Kit API (Figure 1-8). The Map Kit API relies on Apple standard and aerial/satellite 2D/3D imagery. The API currently offers fewer functionalities and data compared to the Google Maps JS API, but because Map Kit is the basic framework for developing map-based native apps for iOS, we cannot avoid dealing with it. Moreover, Apple is improving its map services and data, so it is probable that the gap with Google will be reduced more and more in the coming months.

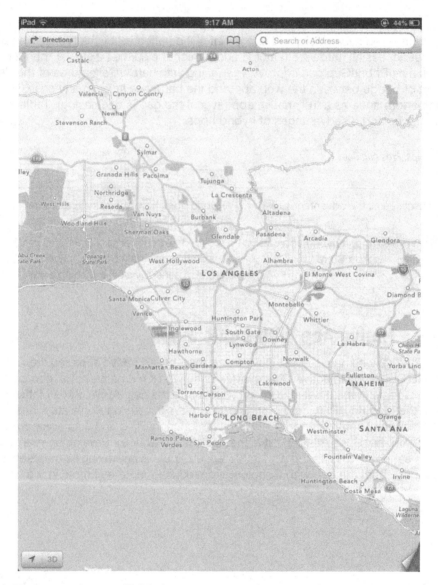

Figure 1-8. Apple Maps app running on an iPad device

One of the pros of main native apps is the possibility of distributing the apps through the App Store. In addition, it's no longer necessary to host the app on a web server, since a native app can reside on the user's device. (However, some datasets might have to reside on servers, depending on the type of app.) One of the cons of a native app, besides needing to know the iOS SDK and Objective-C, is the amount of time that's involved in getting the app approved by the App Store and then having the updates for the app itself approved and distributable. Table 1-3 provides a list of the advantages and disadvantages of native apps.

Table 1-3. Native Apps: Pros and Cons

Pros	Cons
A native app does not necessarily require space on a web server to work.	To develop a native app it is necessary to have knowledge of the iOS SDK and Objective-C language; it is also necessary to be enrolled in the iOS Developer Program to distribute an app through the App Store.
A native app can be distributed in the App Store.	Having the app approved in the App Store requires a certain amount of time; successive updates also have to be submitted to the approval procedures of the App Store, requiring more time. These time-expensive tasks might significantly slow the general development process.
A native app can take full advantage of the device's hardware.	A native app cannot directly take advantage of the services and capabilities offered by the Google Maps JS API, like Street View imagery, Google Places data, maps styling, and KML importing.

Having presented the primary options available for developing iOS map-based apps, I will make suggestions for the testing phase of geo apps.

Testing Map-Based Apps

As with any app, testing geo apps is a very important stage in the development process. Testing forces you to go beyond your schemes and ways of thinking and puts you in the user's shoes. Users can make you aware of problems and can even suggest possible solutions you didn't think of. Testing should occur in all stages of app development, not just at the end.

Some scientific literature suggest that users should have a say in how the app should be, right from the start. Once you've defined the app's objective at a general level, if time permits you should open a pre-design testing phase. This phase would consist of asking a sample of users how they expect the app to behave and what interface it should have. To avoid influencing the users in any way, take care not to show sketches or models. After this pre-design phase, set up testing activities for every step of development. You don't need a large number of testers to spot usability problems. Scientific literature says that a dozen users is sufficient to discover 80% of usability problems. More testers would be necessary only if you'd like to compare different design choices for the app, to understand which of them would be the most effective. In such a case, a sufficiently wide statistical base is necessary to make a viable comparison.

Testing Methodologies

Many methodologies and tools are available to test an app's usability. For example, you can use questionnaires to collect user data so as to understand users' previous skills and experiences with mobile apps. An interview-based method, on the other hand, can help you solicit critiques, suggestions, and recommendations. You might find it useful to ask users to draw sketches to describe their expectations and ideas. Another very useful technique consists of observing users' moves, gestures, and actions while they use the app. It would be better to observe them with a camera so as not to condition their behavior. The methods I propose here may not be the easiest to implement when creating a simple app with limited time or funds. However, it is often possible to find a dozen friends and acquaintances who are willing to test your application.

Once you have released the app, it is important to establish and nourish relationships with the users. To better the chances that your app will be a success, pay attention to comments and evaluations that users leave in the App Store, in forums, and in blogs.

Monitoring Tools

Monitoring tools, in particular the Google Analytics platform, permit you to freely monitor usage stats of web sites and web apps (https://developers.google.com/analytics/devguides/). With Google Analytics SDK for iOS (https://developers.google.com/analytics/devguides/collection/ios/) it is also possible to track native iOS apps user engagement data such as the number of active users of the app, where the app is being used, adoption and usage of specific features, and many other relevant metrics (Figure 1-9).

Figure 1-9. Example of a Google Analytics report for an iPhone application

A final word of advice regarding the maintenance and improvement of the app over time: Open a public bug-tracking system (many bug trackers are free) that can help you keep track of users' reported software bugs.

Summary

In this chapter I introduced the main characteristics of a mobile map-based app (also called a geo app). I then presented some guidelines regarding the usability of map-based apps including self-adaptability of the app, usability of the app's GUI and of map contents. After this I introduced the options that are currently available for the development of map-based apps for iOS: web apps based on Google Maps JS API, hybrid apps based on web apps, and native apps based on Apple Maps. I showed pros and cons for each of these options. Finally, I talked a little bit about the testing and monitoring phases of a geo app, giving some hints and suggestions. By the end of the chapter, you had enough information to select the best option for you to start developing the map-based app you've dreamed of.

Part 2

Web Apps

Chapters 2–6 focus on building web apps by using Google Maps JavaScript API V3 and connected services. In order to follow the topics it is necessary that the reader have a basic knowledge of HTML5 and JavaScript.

Chapter 2

Map-based Web App Basics: Hello World

In this chapter I lay the groundwork for building a map-based web app. Before I get into the heart of development work, I briefly cover the basic concepts and tools necessary to develop a map-based web app (using HTML/CSS and JavaScript), and I give an overview of Google Maps JavaScript API v3. Then I dive into web app development by proposing a Hello World app and commenting on its code.

Reviewing the Resources

To develop a map-based web app using HTML/CSS and JavaScript, you should be familiar with these basic concepts and tools:

- Mobile Safari
- iOS simulator
- Web servers
- Text editors
- Map-based apps

Let's quickly review these now.

Mobile Safari

The browser on iOS devices (iPhone, iPad, and iPod Touch) is Mobile Safari, which comes bundled with every iOS version. Other browsers are also available in the App Store, but they are less used than Mobile Safari. The browser's rendering engine is based on WebKit, the same engine used in the Safari desktop version, in Google Chrome, in Android Web browser, and in many other browsers.

Unlike the full version, Mobile Safari does not support Adobe Flash. To run and test the web apps we are going to talk about in this book we will need to use Mobile Safari on an iOS mobile device or via a simulator. When using Mobile Safari for developing web apps I suggest that you turn its debug option on to help with debugging the apps. To do this, click on your iPad or iPhone home screen, click on Settings, and then Safari. You will see a screen like the one shown in Figure 2-1. Make sure that JavaScript is enabled, and then open Advanced and set Web Inspector to On (Figure 2-2). To use the Web Inspector you have to cable connect your iOS device to a computer where Safari desktop version is installed. This way you can access your device directly from the Safari's Develop menu on your computer. Note that you have enable the Develop menu in Safari's Advanced Preferences on your computer.

Figure 2-1. Make sure that JavaScript is enabled

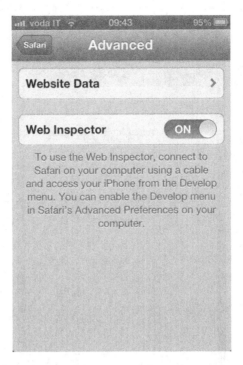

Figure 2-2. Set the Web Inspector to On

Simulator or Real Devices

To execute a web app in Safari Mobile we can use an iPhone or iPad device, or we can use the iOS simulator included in the Xcode development environment (https://developer.apple.com/xcode/). Note that running Xcode and its iOS simulator requires a Mac computer; you can't install it on a PC platform. Moreover, although the iOS simulator is a very handy tool, to properly evaluate geolocation functionalities of the web apps that you are developing, it is recommended that you use a real device-based testing. The simulator allows for easy emulation of both iPhone and iPad devices for testing native and web apps. You don't need to know Xcode to use the simulator, and it is possible to launch it as a standalone from its directory (for example, /Developer/Platforms/iPhoneSimulator.platform/Developer/Applications/iPhone Simulator.app). Once the simulator is running, you can simply open Mobile Safari and input the web address pointing to the web app (Figure 2-3).

Figure 2-3. The iOS simulator running a map web app

Web Servers

Whether you're using a real device or an iOS simulator, your web app code must be hosted on a web server to be accessible from a web browser. The iOS simulator can access both local web servers and Internet web servers. If you're using a Mac computer to develop web apps, you can take advantage of the Apache web server integrated in Mac OS X (see Mac OS X documentation). If you use another OS, you can install and configure one of the many free web servers available (if one is not installed by default). If you want to access a local web server using a real device, keep in mind that the iOS device has to be in the same local network of the computer that hosts the web server.

Editors

You may write HTML, CSS, and JavaScript code with a simple text editor, but there are also more advanced tools (not of all them are free, however) that can help you with color coding, auto indenting, and more. Among the most complete editors available are TextMate (http://macromates.com/), Coda (http://panic.com/coda/), and Vim (http://www.vim.org/index.php). You will also find editors included in an IDE (Integrated Development Environment) like Xcode and Eclipse. It is possible to edit HTML files directly using Xcode (you need to create an empty file in a project and then save it with an HTML extension), but it is better to use the Apple Dashcode tool (http://tinyurl.com/83zevh3) that comes bundled with Xcode. Dashcode is specifically designed for web app development.

Standalone App or Part of an Existing Website

Map-based web apps can be part of a (mobile) website and integrated in the site's template, or they can be designed to work as standalone apps. In this book I mainly consider map-based standalone web apps. Standalone web apps are also the basis for hybrid apps development.

Application Components

A map-based standalone web app is generally composed of several parts:

- HTML code that makes up the web page(s) of the app

- CSS code – the style sheets that will define app look and feel

- Images used for elements such as the app GUI and map controls

- JavaScript code to control the Google Maps JavaScript API and other functions.

HTML, CSS, and JavaScript code can be included in the same file or split into separate files. (The latter is the best solution, especially when there are many lines of code to manage.) Beyond these basic components, a web app might also include:

- External libraries, (for example, jQuery libraries)

- Geo data (for example, KML, GeoXml, and other geographic datasets that might be necessary to overlay on the map)

All this data should be put on the web server where the application is hosted, unless they can be referenced from other online locations. Note that basic map tiles or aerial/satellite imagery do not have to be put on the web server since they will be dynamically retrieved from Google servers through the Google Maps JS API.

SOME WORDS ABOUT THE GOOGLE MAPS JAVASCRIPT API

As you have probably noticed, I have mentioned the Google Maps JavaScript API several times. This powerful API constitutes the core of all the geo functionalities we will deal with. The Google Maps JavaScript API is a member of the wider Google Maps API family, which also includes the Google Earth JavaScript API, the Maps Image APIs, and web services, as shown in Figure 2-4.

Google Maps Developer Documentation

Google Maps has a wide array of APIs that let you embed the robust functionality and everyday usefulness of Google Maps into your own website and applications, and overlay your own data on top of them.

Discover what you can do with the Google Maps APIs

Maps JavaScript API
Embed an interactive Google Map in your webpage using JavaScript.

Google Earth API
Take your visitors anywhere on the Earth without leaving your web page.

Maps Image APIs
Embed a Google Maps image or Street View panorama in your web page without requiring JavaScript.
Static Maps - Street View

Web Services
Use URL requests to access geocoding, directions, elevation, and place information.

Maps for Business
Google Maps API for Business provides Enterprise-ready application support for your mapping needs.

Places API
Access information about establishments, geographic locations, or prominent points of interest.

Figure 2-4. The Google Maps API family (https://developers.google.com/maps/documentation)

The procedures I propose in this book rely on version 3 of the Google Maps JavaScript API, which is now the official JavaScript API. (Version 2 of this API has been officially deprecated as per Google's deprecation policy.) Complete documentation of JavaScript API V3 is available here: `https://developers.google.com/maps/documentation/javascript/`. You can find the changelog here: `http://code.google.com/p/gmaps-api-issues/wiki/JavascriptMapsAPIv3Changelog`. It is free to use the Google Maps JavaScript API upon acceptance of the service's terms of use. For more information, I recommend you read the Google Maps API TOS (`https://developers.google.com/maps/licensing`) and the FAQ, especially the information under the question, "Can I use the Google Maps API on a commercial website?" (`https://developers.google.com/maps/faq`).

Note that websites and applications using the Google Maps JavaScript API may generate up to 25,000 map loads per day for each service, at no cost. (For more information, visit this page: `https://developers.google.com/maps/faq?hl=it#usagelimits`). This usage limit is not easy to reach in most cases, however if you think that your web app will exceed this daily limit, you can purchase a Maps API for Business license that has no map usage limits for your app. Maps API for Business offers further options not available with the free API, including:support for a higher volume of geocoding requests, ability to use HTTPS to integrate maps into protected content and ability to control of advertising in the maps.

For a detailed comparison of the free Maps API (including the JavaScript API) and the Maps API for Business, visit `http://www.google.com/enterprise/earthmaps/maps-compare.html`.

Hello World

In this example I focus on coding in two steps. First, I will show you how to code a desktop computer web map based on the Google Maps JavaScript API, including commenting on its code, and then I will show you how to convert that map into a mobile iOS web app.

Since the study example we are going to create in the next chapters will be a geo web app for Dublin's U2 landmarks, naturally, we will center our Hello World map on Dublin (see Listing 2-1 and Figure 2-5).

Listing 2-1. helloworld-desktopversion.html

```
<!DOCTYPE html>
<html>

  <head>
    <title>Hello world</title>
    <style type="text/css">
      html {
        height:100%;
      }
      body {
        height:100%;
        margin:0px;
        padding:0px;
      }
      #map_canvas {
        height:60%;
        width:60%;
      }
    </style>
    <script type="text/javascript" src="http://maps.google.com/maps/api/js↵
?key=AIzaSyBa6jRCpFGLh691Ve_Srm5a7KPqi-HlrWO&sensor=false">

    </script>
    <script type="text/javascript">
      function initialize() {
        var coordinates = new google.maps.LatLng(53.344104, -6.267494);
        var myOptions = {
          center: coordinates,
          zoom: 14,
          mapTypeId: google.maps.MapTypeId.ROADMAP
        }
        var map = new google.maps.Map(document.getElementById("map_canvas"), myOptions);
      }
    </script>
  </head>
```

```
<body onload="initialize()">
  <div id="map_canvas"></div>
</body>

</html>
```

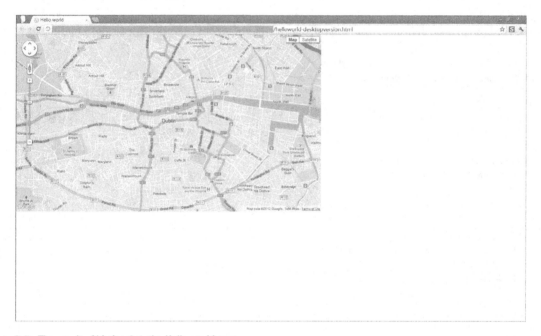

Figure 2-5. The result of Listing 2-1: the Hello world map

As you can see, I put all the code (HTML, CSS, and JavaScript) into a single HTML file, but I obviously could split it into three separate files. In the following sections I will comment on each segment of code.

Reviewing the HTML of Hello World

First, I declared the Doctype of the web page as HTML5 simply by writing

```
<!DOCTYPE html>
```

It is also possible to use other Doctype declarations, but I recommend you declare the web page as HTML5 since this will be the reference version of HTML we are going to use in building iOS web apps.

If you look at the HTML part of Hello World, you can see I created a div element in the body, setting its id property as map_canvas. This div element is the place where the map will be drawn. The map will take its size from that of its containing element, so it is also necessary to explicitly set a size for that div element. I did this through a style definition.

Reviewing the CSS of Hello world

Since the map's dimensions are those of the containing `div` element (named `map_canvas`), I specified these through a CSS declaration in the `<head>` tag of the page and gave them a height and width that is 60% of the total height and width of the body.

```css
<style type="text/css">
  html {
    height:100%;
  }
  body {
    height:100%;
    margin:0px;
    padding:0px;
  }
  #map_canvas {
    height:60%;
    width:60%;
  }
</style>
```

Note that I also had to set the height of the `html` and `body` elements (parents of `map_canvas`) to avoid problems that might arise in certain circumstances in determining percentage-based sizes. The map will take up 60% of the height of the HTML body.

Reviewing the JavaScript of Hello World

In this part of the app the code loads and initializes the Google Maps API. Let's look at loading the API script first and then initializing it.

Loading the API Script

The code to load the API must be included in a `<script>` tag as a value of the `src` attribute:

```
<script type="text/javascript"
src="http://maps.google.com/maps/api/js?key=YOUR_API_KEY&sensor=false">

</script>
```

The URL contained in the `<script>` tag points to the location of the JavaScript file that loads all of the symbols and definitions necessary for using the Google Maps API. The API key has not been a necessary parameter since version 3 of the API, so the API would also work without specifying it, for example:

```
src="http://maps.google.com/maps/api/js?sensor=false"
```

Even if it is not necessary to use an API key, I suggest you obtain one because this allows you to monitor your Maps API traffic and users.

Obtaining an API Key

An API key also ensures that Google can contact you in case your Maps API usage exceeds the usage limits. Please note that API key for JS API V3 is not the same key as JS API V2, so if you had one for the previous version you need to obtain another one for V3. Here are the steps to obtain an API key:

1. Browse to the home page of the API Console at
   https://code.google.com/apis/console and log in with your Google Account.

2. Click on the Services link from the left-hand menu. Activate the Google Maps API V3 service (Figure 2-6).

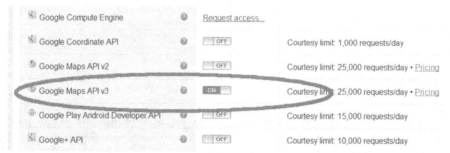

Figure 2-6. *Activate the Google Maps API v3 service*

3. Click on the API Access link from the left-hand menu. The API key you just registered is available in the Simple API Access section (Figure 2-7). You can copy that key and use it as a value for the src attribute in the loading string of the Maps JavaScript API.

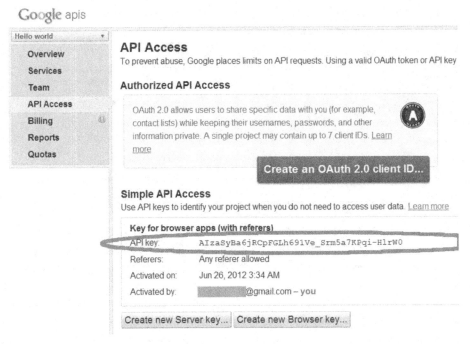

Figure 2-7. The API key

Note that an API key can be used on any site simply by copying the API key string. I strongly recommend that you limit the use of your key to domains that you administer, to prevent unauthorized uses on other sites. You can specify the domains that are allowed to use your API key by clicking the Edit allowed referrers in the Simple API Access section. From this section you can create new keys or delete the existing keys. You can also create more projects, each with its own API key.

As I previously mentioned, using an API key allows you to monitor Maps API usage in a very simple way: Go to the home page of the API Console at https://code.google.com/apis/console, and then click on the Google Maps API v3 service from the dashboard. (You can also click on the Services link from the left-hand menu, and then click on Google Maps API v3.) A page will be loaded showing traffic reports for your Maps API; the number of Maps API requests will be represented for a determined period of time as well as user demographics, referrers, and other useful data (Figure 2-8).

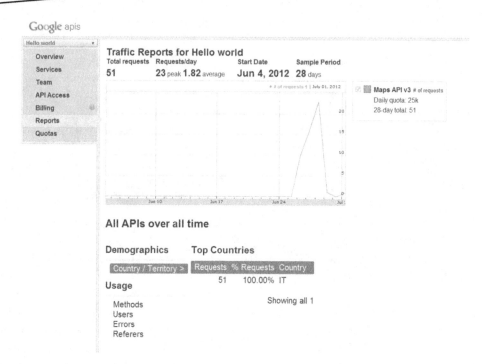

Figure 2-8. The API key traffic reports

Including Sensor Parameters

In the loading URL of the Google Maps JavaScript API, you must also include the sensor parameter, which indicates whether the application uses a sensor (such as a GPS chip) to determine the user's location. This property can be set to true or false: A value must always be set; otherwise, you get an error message when loading the API. It also possible to append a language parameter to the loading URL in order to choose the language to be used in the map, overriding the default map language based on the browser's preferred language setting. The map's language setting relates to elements such as place names, map controls, copyright notices, For example, to display a Maps API application in Russian in a browser with an English language setting, add &language=ru to the API loading URL, as shown below (Figure 2-9):

```
src="http://maps.google.com/maps/api/js?key=YOUR_API_KEY_&sensor=false&language=ru"
```

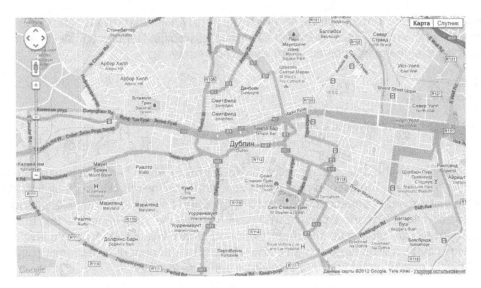

Figure 2-9. *The Hello World with the Russian language setting*

A list of supported country codes is available here:
https://spreadsheets.google.com/pub?key=p9pdwsai2hDMsLkXsoMO5KQ&gid=1

Loading Additional Libraries

You can specify additional libraries to load by appending the `libraries` parameter to the loading URL and setting it with the name of the desired library. A list of available libraries is here: https://developers.google.com/maps/documentation/javascript/libraries. (I will talk about libraries further in a later chapter.)

As an example, to load the `weather` library that contains functionalities for adding weather forecasts and cloud imagery to your map, you can write:

```
src="http://maps.googleapis.com/maps/api/js?libraries=weather&sensor=true_or_false"
```

Initializing the Map

To initialize the map I created a function called `Initialize` that will be triggered in response to the `onload` event of the body (that is, immediately after the page has been loaded): `<body onload="initialize()">`. Let's get deeper into the content of Initialize:

```
var coordinates = new google.maps.LatLng(53.344104, -6.267494);
```

You can see that I started by declaring a variable, `coordinates`, which is an instance of the `LatLng` constructor. LatLng defines a point in geographical coordinates. I set the variable with the coordinates (latitude and longitude in this order) on which I want the map to be centered. In this case, I used the coordinates of Dublin's city center (53.344104, -6.267494). To get the coordinates of a place, you can use one of many online services, like http://www.whatsmygps.com. Once I created the variable, to set the map center I declared a Map options object literal to contain map initialization settings (in this case, the map's center, zoom level, and map type):

```
var myOptions = {
  center: coordinates,
  zoom: 14,
  mapTypeId: google.maps.MapTypeId.ROADMAP
}
```

The first property inside the object literal myOptions is center to which I add the variable coordinates I had previously declared. The second property is zoom and it defines the initial resolution at which to display the map: zoom:0 corresponds to a map of the Earth fully zoomed out; higher zoom levels permit you to zoom in at higher resolutions. You have to know that map images within the Google Maps JavaScript API are broken up into map "tiles" and "zoom levels." At low zoom levels, a small set of map tiles covers a wide area; at higher zoom levels, the number of tiles dramatically increases. They are of higher resolution and cover a smaller area (Figure 2-10).

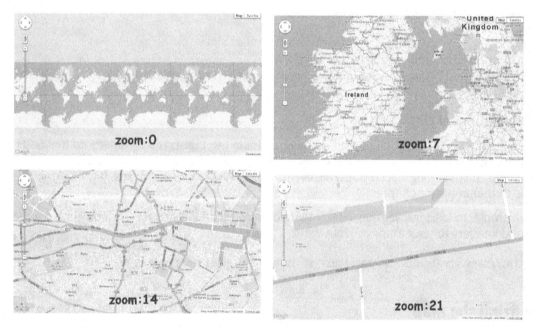

Figure 2-10. How the zoom parameter works (the map is centered on Dublin)

Along with center and zoom parameters, you must also set an initial map type with the property mapTypeId. Four map types are currently available:

- ROADMAP displays the default 2D tiles of Google Maps (this type is also called standard map type)

- SATELLITE displays aerial and satellite imagery tiles

- HYBRID displays aerial and satellite imagery tiles on which a tile layer for prominent features (roads, city names) is overlayed

- TERRAIN displays physical relief tiles representing elevation and water features (for example, mountains and rivers)

You can set a map type in this way: mapTypeId: google.maps.MapTypeId.ROADMAP (this sets the ROADMAP type). Note that you must always specify a map type; you cannot omit this property or leave the field empty.

After creating the object literal containing map options, I had to declare a variable instance (named map) of the constructor Map() that is the API's main class. Objects of this class define a single map on a page. (It is possible to create more than one instance of this class.) The code is as follows:

```
var map = new google.maps.Map(document.getElementById("map_canvas"), myOptions);
```

When I created the instance of Map(), I had to specify the div element in the page to be used as a container for the map (see previous explanations). I referred to the div element with the document.getElementById() method. I also had to pass in as argument of Map() the options defined within the myOptions object literal. These options will be used to initialize the map's properties.

The Initialize function is now complete and will be launched once the body element of the HTML page receives an onload event.

Adapting Hello World to iOS Devices

Now that I have shown you how to create a basic web app using the Google Maps JavaScript API, I am going to focus on how to adapt the Hello World app to iOS devices. It should look like the one in Figure 2-11.

Figure 2-11. Hello World as seen on an iPhone device

The map shown in Figure 2-11 is not very usable: It is not sized properly on the page, and the map type selector and Street View control are too small to be easily used on an iPhone and must be adapted. This task will not be difficult, since we can reuse almost all the previous code and add a meta tag that will do the job for us.

Setting the `<div>` Element

The first thing you can do to adapt the map is to set the `<div>` element containing your map to have width and height attributes of 100%:

```
#map_canvas{height:100%;width:100%;}
```

If you look at the map now, you can see that it fits the screen nicely, both in portrait and in landscape orientation (Figure 2-12).

Figure 2-12. The map fits the visible area of the browser, but controls remain too small

However, the controls remain too small to be used properly, and if you try to zoom in on the map, you encounter problems: While some elements, like bodies of water are zoomed in, others, like streets, remain very small in their dimensions, without being zoomed in. To solve these problems, there is a specific HMTL meta tag called `viewport`.

The viewport meta Tag

If you do not know anything about the concept of viewport in Mobile Safari, then I suggest you read the simple and easy explanations in the Safari Mobile official documentation (http://tinyurl.com/6otupzm). The viewport meta tag allows the web app to automatically adapt to the visible area of the browser window in the device that it is being used with. Since the visible area is different between iPhone and iPad devices but also within the same device family (the iPhone 4 visible area has doubled from that of the first version of the iPhone), we need the app to adapt automatically to the current available visible area. To do this, we set the viewport meta tag with these attributes:

```
<meta name="viewport" content="width=device-width, initial-scale=1.0,minimum-scale=1.0, ↵
maximum -scale=1.0"
/>
```

In the previous code I used the value device-width to set the width property of the viewport tag. This way, the viewport's size is automatically set to be the same as the available visible area on the device. I also set initial-scale=1.0 to show the standard dimension (not zoomed) of the viewport. I then set minimum-scale=1.0, maximum-scale=1.0 to lock viewport zooming: The web page will not have to be zoomed since zoom control will be delegated to the map itself. Now if you add the complete viewport tag to your Hello World HTML code, putting it in the head section of the page, and then save the file and run it on your iPhone, you will get a result like the one shown in Figure 2-13. You can see that map controls (map type and Street View controls) now are bigger and that the zoom works properly. The web app can be used in both portrait and landscape orientation.

> **Note**   The viewport tag is also correctly read by Android devices.

Figure 2-13. Map controls now have a bigger size and the map is usable in iOS devices

Other Useful meta Tags

Another useful meta tag to include in the code is named `apple-mobile-web-app-capable`. This tag sets the web app to run in full-screen mode. This is the syntax:

```
<meta name="apple-mobile-web-app-capable" content="yes">
```

If content is set to yes, the web application runs in full-screen mode once it is saved on the Home Screen and launched from there (Figure 2-14).

Figure 2-14. The app running in full screen mode

It also possible to set a custom icon to be used for the app on the Home Screen with the following `<link>` tag:

```
<link rel="apple-touch-icon-precomposed" href="iconURL"/>
```

Note that the `apple-mobile-web-app-capable` meta tag also works for Android devices. In this case, when saved on the Home Screen the app will get the custom icon but will not run in full screen mode.

Sizes for icons are indicated in the official documentation here: `http://developer.apple.com/library/ios/#DOCUMENTATION/UserExperience/Conceptual/MobileHIG/IconsImages/IconsImages.html#//apple_ref/doc/uid/TP40006556-CH14`. It is recommended that you specify the full image path in the URL.

A final useful meta tag named `apple-mobile-web-app-status-bar-style` sets the style of the status bar for a web app. This meta tag has no effect unless you first specify full-screen mode using the meta tag `apple-mobile-web-app-capable`. The syntax is as follows:

```
<meta name="apple-mobile-web-app-status-bar-style" content="black">
```

If content is set to `default`, the status bar appears normal. If it is set to `black`, the status bar has a black background. If it is set to `black-translucent`, the status bar is black and translucent.

Redirecting iOS Users with JavaScript

The Hello World example adapted to iOS devices can also be accessed from a standard computer. In this case, the map will be shown occupying all the visible area of the browser, and controls will be automatically adapted by the Google Maps JavaScript API: a zoom slider and a pan control will appear to permit users to navigate the map with mouse.

Thanks to JS API v3, which automatically detects if the map is being viewed on a computer or on a mobile device, you can maintain just one single web app without needing two different versions, one for computer and one for iOS. However, there are cases in which it is necessary to maintain two different versions of a web app. This happens if, for instance, the iOS web app has a very different design and additional functions than the desktop version. If you have a desktop computer web app and an iOS web app, you can add a few lines of code in the web app home page so that both versions can be accessed at the same time.

To do this, write a function that reads the User Agent string and then redirects the user to the mobile version if she/he is using an iOS (iPhone, iPad or iPod) device. (note that you must put the code at the beginning of the head element of the page):

```
<script type="text/javascript">
  var useragent = navigator.userAgent;
  if (useragent.indexOf('iPhone') != -1 || useragent.indexOf('iPad') != -1 ||
useragent.indexOf('iPod') != -1) {
    window.location = 'mobileversionaddress';
  }
</script>
```

Summary

In this chapter I introduced you to the basic concepts and tools necessary to develop a map-based web app using HTML, CSS, and JavaScript. I then showed the code (and commented on it) of a Hello World app that displays a map of the Dublin city center. This web app was not yet optimized for iOS devices, so I then illustrated the necessary steps to make it suitable for mobile iOS devices by using proper HTML meta tags. Before moving on to the next chapter, you should know how to load Google Maps JavaScript API v3 in a web page, center the map, setting the zoom level and map type, and adapt the map to iOS devices using meta tags.

Chapter 3

Map Controls and Styles

Map controls are UI elements connected to JavaScript functions that allow users to interact with a map in many different ways. Map controls can be positioned on the map itself or outside of it. In this chapter I talk about controls positioned on the map. I'll talk about more complex UIs containing controls positioned outside the map in the following chapter.

After talking about controls, I will show you how to use styles to customize the presentation of the map. Styles permit you to modify map features such as roads, parks, and rivers. Styles customization is a very powerful instrument that makes it possible to give a map a very specific look and feel, for instance in tune with a brand's color and style. Styles also allow you to hide specific features to make the map more usable and easier to understand.

Using Map Controls

Map controls are basically UI elements that allow user interaction with the map, such as zooming in or out, panning, and enabling or disabling Street View imagery. The Google Maps JS API comes with a handful of built-in controls but it is also possible to create new controls and add them to the app. Some of the built-in controls are activated by default both on computers and iOS devices (even if they do not always have a GUI element). Controls can be shown on the map itself or they can be placed outside the map – in a header or footer bar, for instance – using appropriate JavaScript methods to pilot them. In the following subparagraphs I show you the built-in API controls (activated by default and not activated by default), how to enable or disable them, and how to position them on the map.

Default Controls

Following is a list of controls that constitute the so-called Google Maps default UI. The default UI is useful in that it is automatically set up by the API. You can also disable default controls, which you will learn about shortly. These are the default controls the Google Maps JS API make available:

■ Zoom control: Represented by a slider (for large maps) or small "+/−" buttons (for small maps). This control allows the user to set the zoom level of the map. On computers and Android devices, the control is activated by default, but in iOS it is not shown and zooming is performed by a two-finger pinch.

■ Pan control: Displayed by default in the top-left corner of the map in non-touch devices, while in iOS (and Android) it is never shown and panning is accomplished by touching and dragging the map.

■ MapType control: Allows the user to toggle between map types (for instance, HYBRID, ROADMAP, and SATELLITE). This control is displayed by default in the top-right corner of the map and it has the shape of a horizontal bar if the screen size is 300px wide or more (as it is in iOS devices). Otherwise, it assumes the shape of a drop-down menu. This control also allows activation of 45° images (Figure 3-1).

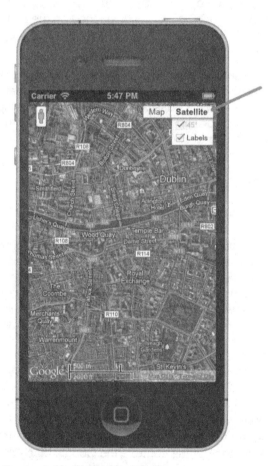

Figure 3-1. The MapType control is displayed by default

- Street View control: Displayed by default in the top-left corner of the map both on computers and on iOS and Android devices (Figure 3-2). It can be activated by dragging the orange icon, called Pegman, onto the map. This control works only in the areas where Street View imagery coverage is available. If the area is not covered, the icon assumes a gray color and cannot be dragged onto the map. To know which parts of the world are currently covered by Street View, consult the following link: `http://gmaps-samples.googlecode.com/svn/trunk/ streetview_landing/streetview-map.html`.

Figure 3-2. The Street View control is shown by default both on computers and mobile devices

■ Rotate control: Displayed by default both on computers and mobile devices. It allows you to rotate maps containing aerial 45° imagery. This is a new type of aerial imagery that Google introduced about two years ago and offers better views of urban areas, buildings, and monuments, since photos are taken at a 45° angle above the earth's surface (Figure 3-3).

Figure 3-3. *Trinity College complex (Dublin) with standard aerial view (on the left) and with 45° imagery activated (on the right)*

Please keep in mind that 45° imagery is not currently available worldwide. Check the current coverage here: http://goo.gl/AIWE. The 45° imagery is displayed by default when the user has activated the SATELLITE or HYBRID map type and zooms in at a high zoom level on a covered area. When the zoom-in reaches the activation point, 45° imagery is triggered and the following changes take place (Figure 3-4):

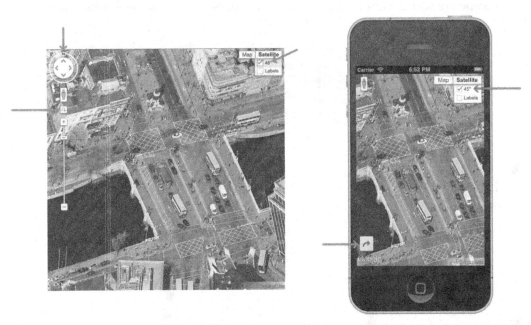

Figure 3-4. *View of 45° imagery controls when map is displayed on computers (on the left) and on iOS devices (on the right)*

- On computers, any existing Pan control will be changed to add a compass wheel around itself. This compass allows you to change the heading of any 45° imagery by dragging the wheel, snapping the direction to the nearest supported direction that contains 45° imagery; at the same time, a Rotate control will be displayed between the existing Pan and Zoom controls, allowing you to rotate through supported directions. This Rotate control is the only 45° imagery control that appears on iOS devices, and by default it is shown in the bottom-left corner.

- The satellite or hybrid imagery will be replaced with 45° imagery centered on the current location. By default, such views are oriented to the north. If you zoom out, you will return to he default satellite or hybrid imagery.

- The MapType control will show a submenu toggle control for displaying 45° imagery.

Non-Default Controls

Here are the built-in API controls that are not displayed by default on the map but that you can choose to display simply by adding a few code lines, as I will demonstrate later in this chapter.

- Scale control: Shows a mapscale. This control is not enabled by default on computers and iOS and Android devices. If enabled, it appears as in Figure 3-5.

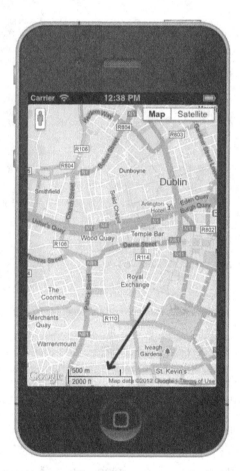

Figure 3-5. Scale control enabled on an iPhone device

- Overview Map control: Displays a small overview map that shows the current map viewport within a wider area. This control is not enabled by default on computers and iOS and Android devices. If enabled, it appears by default in the bottom-right corner of the map in its minimized state, as shown in Figure 3-6.

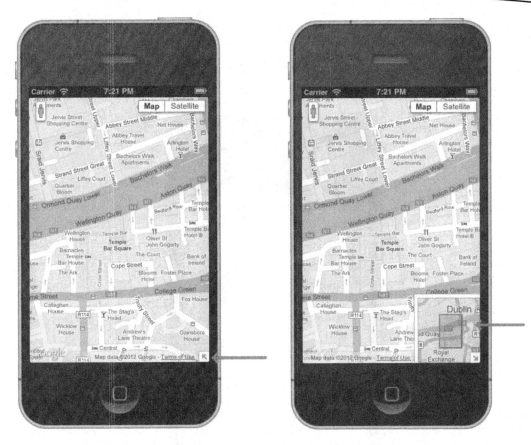

Figure 3-6. The Overview Map control shown on the left in its minimized state (default state) and on the right in its exploded state

As mentioned earlier, it is possible to completely disable the default UI and set up our choice of controls. Let's look at how to do this.

Enabling and Disabling Controls

To simultaneously disable all map default controls (Default UI), it is necessary to set the Map's `disableDefaultUI` property (within the `MapOptions` object) to `true`, as shown in the Listing 3-1. The resulting screen is shown in Figure 3-7.

Listing 3-1. How to disable the default UI

```
function initialize() {
  var coordinates = new google.maps.LatLng(53.344104, - 6.267494);
  var myOptions = {
    center: coordinates,
    zoom: 14,
```

```
    disableDefaultUI: true,
    mapTypeId: google.maps.MapTypeId.ROADMAP
  }
  var map = new google.maps.Map(document.getElementById("map_canvas"),↵ myOptions);
}
```

Figure 3-7. *The map displayed with the default controls disabled*

If instead you want to enable or disable single controls, you must set the boolean values of the respective fields within the MapOptions object: Set to true to make them visible or set to false to hide them. Below are the fields that permit you to enable or disable single map controls:

```
{
  panControl: boolean,
  zoomControl: boolean,
  mapTypeControl: boolean,
  scaleControl: boolean,
  streetViewControl: boolean,
  overviewMapControl: boolean
}
```

For example, if you wanted to add the Scale control to the maps, you would use the following code:

```
var myOptions = {
  center: coordinates,
  zoom: 14,
  scaleControl: true,
  mapTypeId: google.maps.MapTypeId.ROADMAP
}
```

Note that it was not necessary to disable the default UI because the property that you set was additional to the default UI behavior. If you wanted to show only the Scale control and hide all the other controls, you could disable the default UI and enable the Scale control (Figure 3-8) like this:

```
var myOptions = {
  center: coordinates,
  zoom: 14,
  disableDefaultUI: true,
  scaleControl: true,
  mapTypeId: google.maps.MapTypeId.ROADMAP
}
```

Figure 3-8. The map displayed with the Default UI disabled and only the Scale control enabled

Configuring Controls

Many of the mentioned controls are configurable, so that it is possible to modify their appearance or behavior. For instance, it is possible to choose whether the MapType control is to be shown in its default mode (horizontal bar) or as a drop-down menu. Controls are modified by defining control options fields within the MapOptions object upon creation of the map. For instance, options for modifying the MapType control are defined through the MapTypeControlOptions object literal fields. The MapType control may assume one of the following style options:

- google.maps.MapTypeControlStyle.HORIZONTAL_BAR displays buttons to select map types in a horizontal bar.

- google.maps.MapTypeControlStyle.DROPDOWN_MENU displays a drop-down menu through which a user can select map types.

- google.maps.MapTypeControlStyle.DEFAULT displays the "default" behavior that depends on screen size.

Let's put this notion into practice by setting a drop-down menu for MapType control instead of the horizontal bar shown by default on computers and iOS devices. To do this it is necessary to use the style option google.maps.MapTypeControlStyle.DROPDOWN_MENU. Here is the complete code (Listing 3-2):

Listing 3-2. How to set a drop-down menu for the MapType control

```
var myOptions = {
  center: coordinates,
  zoom: 14,
  mapTypeControl: true,
  mapTypeControlOptions: {
    style: google.maps.MapTypeControlStyle.DROPDOWN_MENU
  },
  mapTypeId: google.maps.MapTypeId.ROADMAP
}
```

Please note in the code that before setting a control option it is necessary to explicitly enable the control by setting its boolean value to true – in this case mapTypeControl: true. Figure 3-9 shows the drop-down menu for the MapType control.

Figure 3-9. The MapType control with drop-down menu style

Similarly to the MapType control, configuration options are also available for the Zoom control and may be shown in one of the following style options:

- google.maps.ZoomControlStyle.SMALL displays a mini-Zoom control, showing only + and – buttons.

- google.maps.ZoomControlStyle.LARGE displays the standard zoom slider. On iOS devices, this control displays as + and – buttons as in the previous style option.

- google.maps.ZoomControlStyle.DEFAULT select an appropriate Zoom control depending on the map's size and the device on which the map is running. On iOS devices no Zoom control will be displayed and zoom will be performed by a two-finger pinch.

The Zoom control style has to be defined inside the `zoomControlOptions` field. If you wanted to enable a small + and – Zoom control on an iOS app, you would write (Listing 3-3):

Listing 3-3. How to enable a small + and – Zoom control

```
var myOptions = {
  center: coordinates,
  zoom: 14,
  zoomControl: true,
  zoomControlOptions: {
    style: google.maps.ZoomControlStyle.SMALL
  },
  mapTypeId: google.maps.MapTypeId.ROADMAP
}
```

The + and – small Zoom control are shown in Figure 3-10.

Figure 3-10. Small Zoom control shown on an iPhone device

As with MapType and Zoom controls, it is possible to modify the style of the other controls. Here is a list of the names of the controls and the relative fields (object literals) to modify their styles:

- zoomControl/zoomControlOptions

- panControl/panControlOptions

- scaleControl/scaleControlOptions

- mapTypeControl/mapTypeControlOptions

- streetViewControl/streetViewControlOptions

- rotateControl/rotateControlOptions

- overviewMapControl/overviewMapControlOptions

For more information on style options available for the other controls, I invite you to consult the Controls section of the Google Maps JavaScript API documentation (https://developers.google.com/maps/documentation/javascript/reference).

You probably noticed that controls are configured when the map is created. However, you can also modify the presentation of controls dynamically by calling up the Map's setOptions() method and setting new controls options.

Positioning Controls

Each control has its own default position on the map, however it is possible to change the position to better fit your UI design purposes. Every control options object literal (for example, MapTypeControlOptions) contains a position property (of type ControlPosition), which permits you to define the position of the control on the map. Here is a list (from the API's official documentation) of currently available control positions:

- TOP_CENTER indicates that the control should be placed along the top center of the map.

- TOP_LEFT indicates that the control should be placed along the top left of the map, with any subelements of the control "flowing" towards the top center.

- TOP_RIGHT indicates that the control should be placed along the top right of the map, with any subelements of the control "flowing" towards the top center.

- LEFT_TOP indicates that the control should be placed along the top left of the map, but below any TOP_LEFT elements.

- RIGHT_TOP indicates that the control should be placed along the top right of the map, but below any TOP_RIGHT elements.

- LEFT_CENTER indicates that the control should be placed along the left side of the map, centered between the TOP_LEFT and BOTTOM_LEFT positions.

- RIGHT_CENTER indicates that the control should be placed along the right side of the map, centered between the TOP_RIGHT and BOTTOM_RIGHT positions.

- LEFT_BOTTOM indicates that the control should be placed along the bottom left of the map, but above any BOTTOM_LEFT elements.

- RIGHT_BOTTOM indicates that the control should be placed along the bottom right of the map, but above any BOTTOM_RIGHT elements.

- BOTTOM_CENTER indicates that the control should be placed along the bottom center of the map.

- BOTTOM_LEFT indicates that the control should be placed along the bottom left of the map, with any subelements of the control "flowing" towards the bottom center.

- BOTTOM_RIGHT indicates that the control should be placed along the bottom right of the map, with any subelements of the control "flowing" towards the bottom center.

Figure 3-11 shows the control positions on the map.

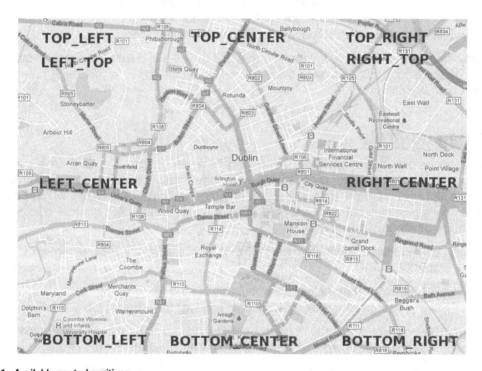

Figure 3-11. Available control positions

Set a new position for a control (for instance, setting the TOP_LEFT position for MapType control as shown in Listing 3-4):

Listing 3-4. How to set the TOP_LEFT position for the MapType control

```
var myOptions = {
  center: coordinates,
  zoom: 14,
  mapTypeControl: true,
  mapTypeControlOptions: {
    position: google.maps.ControlPosition.TOP_LEFT
  },
  mapTypeId: google.maps.MapTypeId.ROADMAP
}
```

Note that it is not an absolute positioning because the API will automatically flow controls so that they do not overlap other map elements, such as copyright information and logos. In flowing controls, the API will also consider the available screen space. This sometimes makes it difficult to precisely position controls on the map and can generate different behaviors in iOS according to the device's orientation. In Figure 3-12, I show what happens when I try to set the position BOTTOM_RIGHT for the MapType control. Since that position is already occupied by the link to Terms of Use and by copyright data that cannot be moved, the control flows toward the left to an unwanted position where it is also overlapped by the Google logo. Things get a little bit better when changing the device's orientation to Landscape, but the control is still not in the desired position (Figure 3-12).

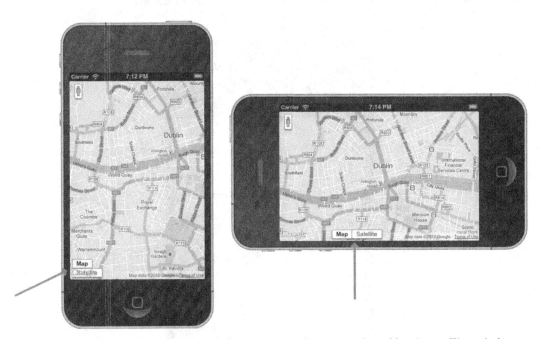

Figure 3-12. *When set in the BOTTOM_RIGHT position, MapType control is not correctly positioned on an iPhone device*

There is no way to avoid this behavior; the only thing to do is to set a different position for the control. For example, if BOTTOM_RIGHT does not work properly for the control, you could try with RIGHT_BOTTOM, which moves the control above BOTTOM_RIGHT position in order to avoid covering the Terms of Use and copyright information.

Now you know how to enable and disable built-in controls and how to position them on the map. In the next section I illustrate how to build custom controls and position them on the map.

Creating Custom Controls on the Map

The JavaScript API makes it possible not just to modify Google Maps built-in controls but also to create custom controls that can be used for the most varied purposes. You can use custom controls in place of built-in controls by repeating their functions, like a newly designed Zoom control. They can also be used to offer the users new functionalities, for instance to open a help window, to turn data layers on or off, and to take measurements on the map.

A custom control is no more than a UI element that can be positioned on top of a map at an absolute position (one of the positions shown in the previous paragraph). The control is stationary and does not move with the map when the map is panned or zoomed. This is very different from the so-called overlays, which are elements that move with the map, like markers, lines, and polygons (I will talk about them in a later chapter). Technically speaking, a control is based on a simple <div> element that contains UI elements (defined through CSS) and through which user interaction is handled. In Figure 3-13, you can see a set of custom controls at the top-right: two controls through which the user can select standard or satellite map type, as well as a third control, Home, that centers the map on a given coordinates set. You can see that the standard MapType control has been replaced and a new functionality, the Home control, has been added.

Figure 3-13. Example of a custom control

To understand how custom controls work, in the next pages I will explain how to build the above (Figure 3-13) set of three custom controls: one Home control to center the map on a given coordinates set (in the code it will be called homeControl), one control to select a standard ROADMAP map type (in the code it will be called roadmapControl), and one control to select a SATELLITE map type (in the code it will be called satelliteControl).

Creating the Container `<div>`

As I said previously, custom controls are usually created through `<div>` elements: for practical reasons, it is important that all the elements of a control be contained inside the same `<div>`. The control style is then easily managed through CSS while the user interaction can be handled by using events, like the click or touch on the control. In this case, first you have to create a `<div>` container that will contain the three `<div>` elements of the three controls. To do this, insert the following instruction inside the `initialize()` function:

```
var containerDiv = document.createElement('DIV');
```

Then, still inside the `initialize()` function, you need to name the function that will create the new controls and that will receive the container `<div>` as argument. I call this function `newControl()` and I recall it by declaring the variable `NewControl` (pay attention to the case):

```
var NewControl = new newControl(containerDiv, map);
```

You then have to declare the `newControl()` function that you can put outside the `initialize()` function:

```
function newControl(containerDiv, map)
{(redacted)}
```

Inside the function it is useful to set a padding for `containerDiv` to set it off from the edge of the map:

```
containerDiv.style.padding = '5px';
```

Defining the Three Controls

You can now proceed to define the three controls. Each control is composed of two parts, one interior and one exterior; each part is defined by a specific `<div>` element. The `<div>` of the exterior part sets the border aspect, background, and other attributes while the `<div>` of the interior part sets the control's text attributes.

Building the Exterior Part of the Controls

Let's look at the settings to define the exterior part of the first of the three controls, `homeControl` (Listing 3-5).

Listing 3-5. Defining the exterior part of the control

```
var exteriorHomeControl = document.createElement('DIV');
exteriorHomeControl.style.backgroundColor = 'white';
exteriorHomeControl.style.cssFloat = 'left';
exteriorHomeControl.style.borderStyle = 'solid';
exteriorHomeControl.style.borderColor = '#a9bbdf';
exteriorHomeControl.style.borderWidth = 'thin';
```

```
exteriorHomeControl.style.WebkitBorderRadius = '3px';
exteriorHomeControl.style.cursor = 'pointer';
exteriorHomeControl.style.textAlign = 'center';
exteriorHomeControl.title = 'Center the map on Dublin';
containerDiv.appendChild(exteriorHomeControl);
```

In Listing 3-5 you can see that it is necessary to create a <div> called exteriorHomeControl first. Then, through CSS, its aspect is defined: The control's background is set to white and the <div> is made floating on the left. It is important to make the <div> floating; otherwise, being <div> elements of block-level type, they would be piled and not lined. The border's aspect is defined in the aforementioned code; by using CSS 3 parameters, it is also possible to create rounded corners for the button. This way it is not necessary to use background images with rounded borders since they will be created through CSS thus diminishing the data the user has to download.

```
exteriorHomeControl.style.WebkitBorderRadius = '3px';
```

Please note that the above code only works for browsers based on a Webkit engine, like Safari, Mobile Safari, and Google Chrome. If you you want make the rounded corners visible on other browsers, you should add specific properties. Once settings are defined, exteriorHomeControl is appended to containerDiv.

Building the Interior Part of the Controls

It is now time to define the interior part of the control by creating a < div> named interiorHomeControl (Listing 3-6).

Listing 3-6. Defining the interior part of the control

```
var interiorHomeControl = document.createElement('DIV');
interiorHomeControl.style.fontFamily = 'Arial,sans-serif';
interiorHomeControl.style.fontSize = '16px';
interiorHomeControl.style.padding = '7px';
interiorHomeControl.innerHTML = 'Home';
exteriorHomeControl.appendChild(interiorHomeControl);
```

If you look at this code you see that interiorHomeControl has been appended to exteriorHomeControl, which in turn is appended to containerDiv. It is then possible to similarly define other control structures, as I show in the following code (Listing 3-7).

Listing 3-7. Defining the other two controls

```
// The exterior of roadmapControl is created and then formatted via CSS
var exteriorRoadmapControl = document.createElement('DIV');
exteriorRoadmapControl.style.cssFloat = 'left';
exteriorRoadmapControl.style.backgroundColor = '#6f8cce';
exteriorRoadmapControl.style.borderStyle = 'solid';
exteriorRoadmapControl.style.borderColor = '#6688c5';
exteriorRoadmapControl.style.borderWidth = 'thin';
exteriorRoadmapControl.style.WebkitBorderRadius = '3px';
exteriorRoadmapControl.style.cursor = 'pointer';
```

```
exteriorRoadmapControl.style.textAlign = 'center';
exteriorRoadmapControl.title = 'Map';
containerDiv.appendChild(exteriorRoadmapControl);

// The interior of roadmapControl is created and then formatted via CSS
var interiorRoadmapControl = document.createElement('DIV');
interiorRoadmapControl.style.fontFamily = 'Arial,sans-serif';
interiorRoadmapControl.style.fontSize = '16px';
interiorRoadmapControl.style.color = 'white';
interiorRoadmapControl.style.fontWeight = 'bold';
interiorRoadmapControl.style.padding = '7px';
interiorRoadmapControl.innerHTML = 'Map';
exteriorRoadmapControl.appendChild(interiorRoadmapControl);

// The exterior of satelliteControl is created and then formatted via CSS
var exteriorSatelliteControl = document.createElement('DIV');
exteriorSatelliteControl.style.backgroundColor = 'white';
exteriorSatelliteControl.style.cssFloat = 'left';
exteriorSatelliteControl.style.borderStyle = 'solid';
exteriorSatelliteControl.style.borderColor = '#a9bbdf';
exteriorSatelliteControl.style.borderWidth = 'thin';
exteriorSatelliteControl.style.WebkitBorderRadius = '3px';
exteriorSatelliteControl.style.cursor = 'pointer';
exteriorSatelliteControl.style.textAlign = 'center';
exteriorSatelliteControl.title = 'Satellite';
containerDiv.appendChild(exteriorSatelliteControl);

// The interior of satelliteControl is created and then formatted via CSS
var interiorSatelliteControl = document.createElement('DIV');
interiorSatelliteControl.style.fontFamily = 'Arial,sans-serif';
interiorSatelliteControl.style.fontSize = '16px';
interiorSatelliteControl.style.padding = '7px';
interiorSatelliteControl.innerHTML = 'Satellite';
exteriorSatelliteControl.appendChild(interiorSatelliteControl);
```

Connecting Controls to their Relative Functions

Once controls are set, it is possible to add listeners to them to handle events. To do this, the API makes available the addDomListener() method, which handles most of the browser's supported DOM events – for instance, a click or touch on a <div> element. To use this method, you need to specify a DOM element to which the listener is added, a type of event to listen to (for instance, a click event), and finally the function to be executed when the event is verified. In this case, I add the listener to the control's exterior part. In the following lines of code I show how to set the listener so that when the user taps the Home control button, the map is centered on a given set of coordinates:

```
google.maps.event.addDomListener(exteriorHomeControl, 'click', function () {
  map.setCenter(coordinates);
});
```

The setCenter() method centers the map on a given set of coordinates received as argument. (In this case, the coordinates have been set as a global variable at the beginning of the script because it is going to be used by different functions.) As far as `roadmapControl` and `satelliteControl` are concerned, in addition to the instructions for setting the respective map types, it is useful to add a condition to recognize, by using the `map.getMapTypeId()` method, the map type currently used and consequently set the appropriate formatting of the control. In Figure 3-14 you can see that when a control, for example, Map, is selected, its color and other formatting gets changed.

Figure 3-14. When a control (Map or Satellite) is selected, its formatting gets changed

Here is the code for the functions triggered when `roadmapControl` or `satelliteControl` are touched (Listing 3-8).

Listing 3-8. The functions connected to `roadmapControl` and `satelliteControl`

```
google.maps.event.addDomListener(exteriorRoadmapControl, 'click', function () {
  if (map.getMapTypeId() == 'satellite') {
    exteriorRoadmapControl.style.backgroundColor = '#6f8cce';
    exteriorRoadmapControl.style.borderColor = '#6688c5';
    interiorRoadmapControl.style.color = 'white';
    interiorRoadmapControl.style.fontWeight = 'bold';
    exteriorSatelliteControl.style.backgroundColor = 'white';
    exteriorSatelliteControl.style.borderColor = '#a9bbdf';
    interiorSatelliteControl.style.color = 'black';
    interiorSatelliteControl.style.fontWeight = 'normal';
    map.setMapTypeId(google.maps.MapTypeId.ROADMAP);
  }
});

google.maps.event.addDomListener(exteriorSatelliteControl, 'click', function () {
  if (map.getMapTypeId() == 'roadmap') {
    exteriorSatelliteControl.style.backgroundColor = '#6f8cce';
    exteriorSatelliteControl.style.borderColor = '#6688c5';
    interiorSatelliteControl.style.color = 'white';
    interiorSatelliteControl.style.fontWeight = 'bold';
    exteriorRoadmapControl.style.backgroundColor = 'white';
    exteriorRoadmapControl.style.borderColor = '#a9bbdf';
    interiorRoadmapControl.style.color = 'black';
    interiorRoadmapControl.style.fontWeight = 'normal';
    map.setMapTypeId(google.maps.MapTypeId.SATELLITE);
  }
});
```

Let's consider the first function shown in the above code, the one that is triggered when the user touches the control mapControl (Map button). First of all, it verifies if the map type is SATELLITE. If it is SATELLITE, the Map button will be highlighted and the map type changed to ROADMAP; otherwise, if the map type is ROADMAP, nothing will happen because the map type is already in the desired status. A similar function is applied to the control satelliteControl (Satellite button). In the aforementioned code, notice the usage of the method setMapTypeId(), which permits one to set the desired map type on-the-fly.

Now that the three controls have been defined inside the function newControl(), you have to position containerDiv on the map, assigning to it one of the positions shown in Figure 3-11. In this case, I chose the position TOP_RIGHT, the standard one for the MapType control. (I also disabled default MapType control since it will be replaced by the new control. The code to use to do this is: mapTypeControl:false). For every map, control positions are contained in an array contained in the property controls of the Map object – in this case, map.controls. This array includes all the available positions. Every position, as I showed you previously in this chapter, is of the type google.maps.ControlPosition.NAME_OF_THE_POSITION. To assign containerDiv to a position, you have to use the push() method:

```
map.controls[google.maps.ControlPosition.TOP_RIGHT].push(containerDiv);
```

As you can see, containerDiv has been assigned to the TOP_RIGHT position. Every position possesses an MVCArray of all the controls that have been assigned to it. It is possible to assign the same position to more than one control. In this case, first the standard Google control for that position is set (if one is enabled), and then the other controls are positioned according to the order determined by their index property. Controls with lower index values go first. Every control can have an index value. If you added another control to the position TOP_RIGHT and you wanted to position containerDiv before this one, you would have to assign the value 1 to the index property of containerDiv. Inside the initialize() function you would simply add containerDiv .index = 1.

Once that containerDiv is positioned onto the map, the three custom controls that it contains will be displayed along with the default Zoom and Street View controls automatically provided by the API (see Figure 3-14).

In this example app, I showed you how to build map controls by using only CSS and <div> elements. It is a very effective solution in that it permits one to design a light interface without needing to use images. Thanks to CSS 3, as we saw, it is possible to generate rounded corners for the controls, making them more appealing. In the example I completely rebuild the MapType control so as to unify its aspect to the Home control. I made the controls big enough to be properly used on touch devices but it is also possible, by using the detect.browser() function I introduced in the previous chapter, to ensure that control size is adjusted according to the device that accesses the map (computer or iOS devices, for example).

In the example case, the controls possess a kind of Google Maps look and feel. As I mentioned in the first chapter, when designing UIs it is better to be in tune with what users are already accustomed to. There are cases where one might need to realize more original interfaces, far removed from the traditional look and feel of Google Maps (for instance, to match a brand logo). In these cases, it might be necessary to use images. A simple way to use an image for a control is to put it inside the <div> of the control by exploiting the innerHTML property. When using images, I recommend you use CSS sprites so as to reduce the data that is downloaded and make the application quicker to load.

Methods (and Controls) to Set the MapOptions Object

In the previous paragraph I showed you how to create a set of controls to dynamically change some of the map options – that is, some of the values set in the MapOptions object. Custom controls can be used for any functionality we want to offer the user, for example, a control to open a help window or a control to start geolocation. One of the basic ways to use controls is to dynamically change or set some of the properties within the MapOptions object. You can find a list of all the options that can be set in the MapOptions object here in the official API documentation: https://developers.google.com/maps/documentation/javascript/reference#MapOptions. The JavaScript API makes available a series of methods to change or set values for the MapOptions object. There are two main avenues to set MapOptions properties: making use of the generic setOptions() method or resorting to specific methods for each of the properties.

The setOptions() Method

This method takes a MapOptions object as its sole attribute. One way to use it is to create an object literal in the same way I showed you in the Hello World example. This object will contain new values for the properties you want to set or change. For instance, if you want to change zoom, map type, and map center, you can write:

```
var newOptions = {
  center: newCoordinates,
  zoom: 4,
  mapTypeId: google.maps.MapTypeId.SATELLITE
}
map.setOptions(newOptions);
```

A quicker way to use setOptions() is to create the object literal directly inside the method:

```
map.setOptions({center: newCoordinates, zoom: 4, mapTypeId:↵
google.maps.MapTypeId.SATELLITE});
```

By using this approach, you can change almost all the properties of the MapOptions object. You can obviously trigger the setOptions() method from a custom map control to do things like change multiple properties of the map with just one touch.

Property-specific Methods

In the example of custom controls I showed you earlier in this chapter, I made use of methods to change (or get) values related to a specific property. I used the setCenter() method to set the map on a given set of coordinates; I also used the getMapTypeId() method to identify which map type was currently shown and the map and the setMapTypeId() method to change the map type according to the user's choice. In this section, I will present the most generally used methods to change specific properties of the map. To see the complete list of methods, please consult the official documentation at:
https://developers.google.com/maps/documentation/javascript/reference#Map.

getZoom() and setZoom()

The getZoom() method returns a number that indicates the current zoom level. If the current zoom level is 4, getZoom() will return "4". Similarly, the companion method, setZoom()takes a number as argument, indicating the zoom level to be set. Here are some examples:

```
//It assigns the variable "currentZoom" a number indicating current zoom value
var currentZoom = map.getZoom();
//It sets the map to a zoom level "10"
map.setZoom(10);
```

getCenter() and setCenter()

The method getCenter() returns an object of the type LatLng containing coordinates of the current center. A LatLng object specifies the latitude value in degrees within the range [–90, 90] and the longitude value in degrees within the range [–180, 180]. Similarly the setCenter() method takes as argument a LatLng object indicating the set of coordinates on which the map is to be set. Here are some examples:

```
//It assigns the variable "currentCenter" a LatLng object indicating coordinates of the current
center of the map
var currentCenter = map.getCenter();
//It creates a new set of coordinates
var newCoordinates = new google.maps.LatLng(41.901514, 12.460774);
//It centers the map on the new set of coordinates
map.setCenter(newCoordinates);
```

getMapTypeId() and setMapTypeId()

The method getMapTypeId() returns a string with the identifier of the current mapTypeId.(The identifiers are: google.maps.MapTypeId.HYBRID, google.maps.MapTypeId.ROADMAP, google.maps. MapTypeId.SATELLITE, google.maps.MapTypeId.TERRAIN.) Similarly, the method setMapTypeId() takes as argument a string indicating the desired map type to set. Examples:

```
//It assigns the variable "currentMapTypeId" the map type ID currently used
var currentMapTypeId = map.getMapTypeId();
//It sets the map to the SATELLITE map type ID
map.setMapTypeId(google.maps.MapTypeId.SATELLITE);
```

Using styles, the Google Maps JS API makes it possible to modify the presentation style of its maps. For instance, you can select the elements to show and set specific formatting for them. Thanks to styles, it is possible to create maps using colors that recall the colors and look and feel of a specific brand or theme. As an example, the Australian company Aquila uses styles to create maps of its shoe stores that match the branding and website color schemes, as you can see at the following link: http://www.aquila.com.au/aquila-store-locations-melbourne.php.

Styles can help communicate and generate emotions: The map of the Italian newspaper Corriere della Sera in Figure 3-15 showing the diffusion of organized crime in Northern Italy mainly uses strong colors to communicate a feeling of fear, drama, and violence.

Figure 3-15. The diffusion of organized crime in Northern Italy (map from
`http://www.corriere.it/cronache/speciali/2011/mafiopoli/`)

Customizations made available by the Google Maps JS API are basically of three types:

- Turning on/off specific elements
- Simplifying specific elements
- Coloring specific elements

There are two ways to apply styles to a map:

1. By setting the `.styles` property of the map's `MapOptions` object. Please note that it is possible to modify only the style of the standard map type (ROADMAP). If you set the `.styles` property using a TERRAIN or SATELLITE map type, basic imagery won't be affected but elements like roads and labels will respect styling rules.

2. By creating a styled map type and applying it to the map. In this way you create a new map type with a custom style, which can be selected from the MapType control.

Whether you follow the first or the second approach, you will make use of an array of `MapTypeStyles` (a JSON object), each of which is composed of selectors and stylers. Thus, before following either approach, you need to understand how selectors and stylers work, which you'll learn about in the following sections.

Understanding Selectors and Stylers

Selectors indicate which are the map elements (called "map features") you want to customize, while stylers specify the visual modifications to apply to selected map elements (an approach similar to CSS). The JSON object containing selectors and stylers has the following form, as shown in Listing 3-9.

Listing 3-9. The structure of the JSON object containing selectors and stylers

```
var stylesArray = [
  {
    featureType: '',
    elementType: '',
    stylers: [
      {hue: ''},
      {saturation: ''},
      {lightness: ''},
      // etc...
    ]
  },
  {
    featureType: '',
    // etc...
  }
]
```

Selectors

The elements of a map that you can customize, like roads, rivers, and parks, are called features and they are specified through a `MapTypeStyleFeatureType`. The feature types are organized in a category tree, with `all` as the root. Before applying a style rule, you need to select the feature to which to apply the style. The syntax to use is the following: `featureType: 'feature'`. The following example will select all features:

```
{
  featureType: "all"
}
```

In this other example only bodies of water are selected:

```
{
  featureType: "water"
}
```

Many features have subcategories, defined with a dotted notation. For instance, the category poi (points of interests) contains many subcategories among which government indicates government buildings. To apply a styling rule just to government buildings you would write: featureType: "poi.government". If you had written featureType: "poi", not only the government buildings but all the other subcategories of poi would have been selected. (If you select the parent features children features are automatically selected as well.) In the API documentation you can find the category tree of the currently available features: https://developers.google.com/maps/documentation/javascript/reference#MapTypeStyleFeatureType.

An important thing you need to know about features is that some of them can be composed of different elements: geometries (like the outline of a body of water) and text labels used to denote feature's name (like the name of a body of water). Elements within features can be selected by specifying the following categories:

- all (default): Selects all elements of that feature, geometry, and text labels
- geometry: Selects all geometric elements of that feature
  - geometry.fill selects only the fill of the feature's geometry
  - geometry.stroke selects only the stroke of the feature's geometry
- labels: Selects only textual labels associated with that feature
  - labels.icon selects only the icon displayed within the feature's label
  - labels.text selects only the text of the label
  - labels.text.fill selects only the fill of the label, which is usually rendered as a colored outline that surrounds the label text
  - labels.text.stroke selects only the stroke of the label's text

The following code selects the labels for all park features:

```
{
  featureType: "poi.park",
  elementType: "labels"
}
```

Stylers

Stylers are formatting options that you can apply to map features to define their presentation style. The following stylers are currently available:

- hue: Takes an RGB hex string that indicates the basic color. In this case, the color RGB hex string, unlike it happens in the styler color (see below), indicates only the basic color and not the final color of the feature that will result by a mix of hue, saturation, and lightness.
- saturation: Takes a floating point value between −100 and 100 and indicates the percentage change in intensity of the basic color

- ▨ lightness: Takes a floating point value between −100 and 100 and indicates the percentage change in brightness of the element. Use negative values to increase darkness (–100 specifies black) and positive values to increase brightness (+100 specifies white).

- ▨ gamma: Takes a floating point value between 0.01 and 10.0 and indicates the amount of gamma correction to apply to the element. Gamma modifies the lightness of hues and is generally used to modify the contrast of multiple elements. Low gamma values (< 1) increase contrast, high values (> 1) decrease contrast, and the value 1.0 means no correction.

- ▨ inverse_lightness: Takes true or false values; if true it inverts the current lightness.

- ▨ visibility: Can take the values on, off, or simplified and indicate whether and how the element is displayed on the map. The simplified value hides some style features from the affected features; for example, roads are drawn with thinner lines.

- ▨ color: Takes an RGB hex string and sets the color of the feature

- ▨ width: Takes an integer value greater than or equal to zero and sets the width of the feature, in pixels

You probably noticed that there are two way to indicate a color for a feature: by using a combination of hue, saturation, and lightness or by specifying an RGB hexadecimal string. The first method is a little bit more laborious because you need to specify three values: hue indicates the basic color, saturation indicates the intensity of that color, and lightness indicates the relative amount of white or black in the constituent color. The second method is easier as you only need to indicate the RGB hex value of the color. RGB hex values are commonly used in HTML language, so you can easily find color codes online. (A useful online color schemer tool is: http://www.colorschemer.com/online.html).

You need to know that style rules are applied in the order they appear within the stylers array. The API documentation recommends not to combine multiple operations into a single styler operation; it is better to define each operation as a separate entry in the styler array because "Order is important, as some operations are not commutative. Features and/or elements that are modified through styler operations (usually) already have existing styles; the operations act on those existing styles, if present."

Now that you have been introduced to stylers, here some examples. In the first example, a dark blue color is set for the feature by using the color styler.

```
stylers: [
{color: "#000099"}
]
```

In this next example, I use the HSL notation to express a color (dark green) for a feature.

```
stylers: [
{
  color: "#f00000"},
{
  hue: "#80ff00"},
```

```
{
  saturation: 70},
{
  lightness: -60}
]
```

Combining Selectors and Stylers

Now that we know how to select features and apply stylers, we can combine the two things to create JSON objects containing styling rules. If, for instance, we want to to color all road elements red, then we can simply write:

```
[
    {
        featureType:"road",
        stylers:[
            {color:"#ff0000"}
        ]
    }
]
```

As I previously told you, style rules have to be applied separately. If you want to apply a rule only to the labels of a feature (for example, to turn off the labels of the road feature) and another rule only to the geometry elements of the same feature (for example, to color the road geometries red), then you have to select two times road and apply the relative style rule every time, as I show in the following code (Listing 3-10).

Listing 3-10. How to turn off the labels of the road feature and color the road geometries red

```
[
    {
        featureType:"road",
        elementType:"labels",
        stylers:[
            {visibility:"off"}
        ]
    },
    {
        featureType:"road",
        stylers:[
            {color:"#ff0000"}
        ]
    }
]
```

Now that you know how selectors and stylers work, let's move on to examining the first approach to implementing a custom style in a map.

Approach 1: Set a `.styles` Property of the Map's `MapOptions` Object

Once you have created a JSON object containing styling rules, the easiest way to implement it is by modifying the `.styles` property of the `MapOptions` object. You can do this either at the time of the construction of the object or by calling the `setOptions()` method. First, you need to assign the JSON to a variable, and then you set the variable to the `.styles` property. In this case, to stick to the U2's Dublin study case, I created a JSON object to simplify the standard map type of a Dublin map, by removing all manmade features' labels from the landscape category (`landscape.man_made`). Manmade labels don't add any useful information to a map whose purpose will be to show U2 landmarks (that will have their custom markers). In Figure 3-16 you can see the two versions: on the left the standard map and on the right the map without manmade features. The second map is simpler and constitutes a better base on which to overlay U2 landmarks data.

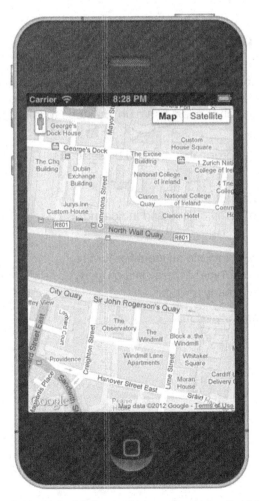
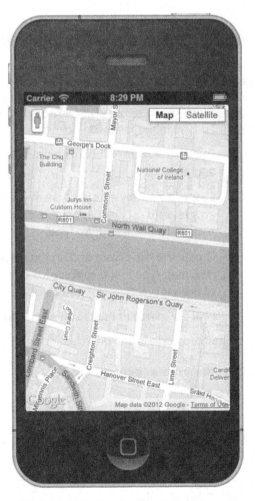

Figure 3-16. On the left the standard map type and on the right the modified map type without manmade features

The code is shown in Listing 3-11.

Listing 3-11. Removing all manmade features' labels from the landscape category

```
var customStyle = [
  {
    featureType:"landscape.man_made",
    elementType:"labels",
    stylers:[
      {visibility:"off"}
    ]
  }
]

//Set the custom style
map.setOptions({styles: customStyle});
```

Approach 2: Create a Styled Map Type

The second approach to using styles does not affect the standard map type since you create a new map type, besides the standard one, to which you apply some style rules. You can then add a new button to the MapType control to easily switch to the new styled map type. As in the first method, in this case you will need to use a JSON object containing style rules. I sum up the steps to implement a styled map type in the following points:

1. Build a JSON object containing style rules (appropriately defined by selectors and stylers).

2. Create a new styled map type (it is an object of the type google.maps.StyledMapType), passing it the JSON object, and indicating a name for the new map type.

3. Create the Map object and, in the map options, include an identifier for the new map type in the mapTypeIds array. (The mapTypeIds array is a property of the mapTypeControlOptions object we've already seen.)

4. Link the identifier in the last step with the new styled map.

The commented code is shown in Listing 3-12.

Listing 3-12. How to create a styled map type

```
function initialize()
{

  //Create 1. a JSON object containing styling rules.
  var customStyle = [
  {
    featureType: "landscape.man_made",
    elementType: "labels",
```

```
    stylers: [
    {
      visibility: "off"
    }]
  }]


  /* Create a new StyledMapType object passing it the previously created JSON object and indicating
a name for the new map type.*/
  var styledMap = new google.maps.StyledMapType(customStyle,
  {
    name: "No man made feat."
  });

  var myOptions = {
    center: new google.maps.LatLng(53.344104, - 6.267494),
    zoom: 14,

    //Include the new MapTypeId to add to the MapType control.
    mapTypeControlOptions: {
      mapTypeIds: [google.maps.MapTypeId.ROADMAP, 'map_style']
    }
  };

  var map = new google.maps.Map(document.getElementById("map_canvas"), myOptions);

  //Link the MapTypeId with the styled map type created
  map.mapTypes.set('map_style', styledMap);

  //Set the new map type ID so that is shown as default map type
  map.setMapTypeId('map_style');
}
```

The styled map type added to the MapType control is shown in Figure 3-17.

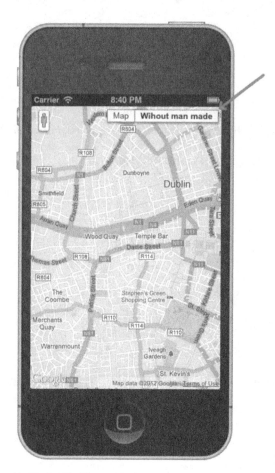

Figure 3-17. The styled map type added to the MapType control

You can have many styled map types in your app and let users select which they prefer by using the setMapTypeId() method. This way, a user could decide whether to show or hide roads or parks, for example.

Styled Maps Wizard

Manually composing JOSN objects with style rules can be a bit frustrating, particularly if you intend to apply many different customizations and you want to do many tries to find the best solution. Luckily, Google has created an online web app, the Styled Maps Wizard (Figure 3-18), that permits you to easily select and try different style combinations, set colors, and more, getting a real-time preview. Once you are satisfied with the result, you can copy the JSON object that is automatically generated and paste it in your code. The online wizard is at the following link: http://gmaps-samples-v3.googlecode.com/svn/trunk/styledmaps/wizard/index.html.

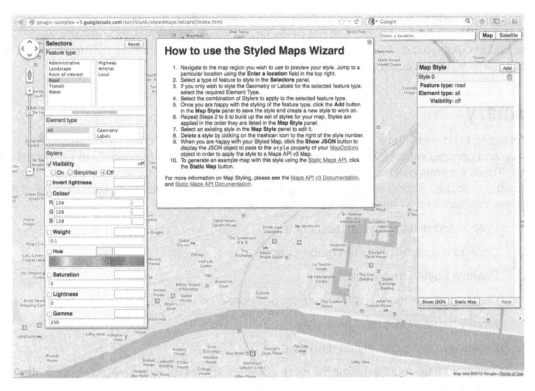

Figure 3-18. The Google Styled Map Wizard

Some Final Recommendations When Using Styles

Cartography is the art of synthesizing geographical information in a map. Styles, if properly used, are a valid way to your map goals. In the case of the Dublin map example, I showed you that it is possible to remove some useless information to make the map clearer and easier to use. Every time you produce a map you have got to think and decide which map features to show and which features are useless and therefore can be hidden without causing any problems. There is no universal rule; the choice depends on the purpose of the map. In a map that aims to show sports complexes in a city, you might want to hide some subcategories of poi – for instance, attraction, business, and government, but in another type of map you might need those subcategories. You could also present the user with a choice of different styled map types, so the user might select what he or she considers more appropriate. In this case, be aware that every time a styled map type is shown, all the map tiles are reloaded from the server and this can take a certain amount of time, depending on the bandwidth available.

To attract a users's attention, you may be tempted to use very bright or contrasting colors, but you should be aware of what you are doing: Bright colors may initially attract the user but they could make it very difficult for extended use of the map. You should also know that some colors are not recommended for accessibility reasons, as they may be difficult to perceive for some users.

Moreover, when using styles, you need to be aware of cartographic conventions: Even if you can change the color of a body of water and make it yellow, unless you have a very specific reason to do that, you should avoid it since people are used to specific colors schemes for map features and changing these schemes could confuse them.

Summary

In this chapter, I showed you how to manipulate standard built-in map controls by enabling, disabling, and configuring them. I then showed you how to build custom controls to be placed on the map. These controls can replace standard controls or implement new functionalities. I also introduced you to map styling either by altering standard map type style or by creating new styled map types. You should now know how to do the following:

- Enable and disable built-in map controls.
- Configure options of built-in map controls.
- Position built-in map controls.
- Create and configure custom controls positioned on the map.
- Modify the standard map type style.
- Create and set a new styled map type.

In the next chapter I'll talk about realizing a more complex app's GUI with custom controls positioned outside the map.

Chapter 4

Creating a GUI for the App with jQuery Mobile

So far, I have shown you how to build a simple UI for map-based web apps with controls directly positioned on the map, according to the positions allowed by the API. However, by using HTML, CSS, and JavaScript combined with a framework like jQuery Mobile, it is possible to create complete GUIs for our iOS geo apps easily and quickly. In this chapter I introduce you to the basics of jQuery Mobile. You will learn how to load the framework in a web app, how to design a UI composed of a header, a map in the middle, and a footer, and how to add controls to the UI. Then you will put everything in practice by learning to build a simple GUI for the U2's Dublin example app. Notice that is not necessary to know jQuery to proceed in the reading.

What is jQuery Mobile?

jQuery Mobile is a web framework (basically a JavaScript library) whose purpose is to make it simpler for developers to create user interfaces for their mobile web apps. jQuery Mobile is based on the jQuery framework and is currently being developed by the jQuery project team (Figure 4-1).

Figure 4-1. The home page of the jQuery Mobile website (`http://jquerymobile.com/`)

The main benefits of the framework, which make it particularly suitable for developing UIs for map-based apps, are:

- Free of charge: It is free to use this open-source framework with dual license: GPL or MIT. For more information, visit: `http://jquery.org/license/`.

- Portability: The framework embodies the "write less, do more" philosophy in that it permits developers to design a single web app interface that will work on all the popular devices (smartphones, tablets, laptops and desktops) and operating systems (iOS, Android, BlackBerry, Windows Phone, and others are currently supported). Thus, by using jQuery Mobile, our app will be accessible not only to iOS devices but also to many other operating systems and browsers. (You can view a complete list here: `http://jquerymobile.com/gbs`).

- Ease of use: jQuery Mobile does not require knowledge of JavaScript and the jQuery framework. If you know basic HTML, you can start building a mobile web app right away.

- Design and theming capabilities: jQuery Mobile permits you to design effective interfaces, with the look and feel of mobile apps by offering pre-themed pages, dialogs, toolbars, and ready-to-use icons . Developers can choose from five basic themes but it is also possible to create new ones by using specific tools (`http://jquerymobile.com/themeroller/`) or by manually writing them.

The jQuery Mobile framework provides compatibility with different mobile app frameworks including Worklight and PhoneGap. On its official website, `http://jquerymobile.com/`, you can find useful tutorials, documentation, and tools to make developing easier. To learn jQuery Mobile there are also many books available from the primary technology publishers.

Setting Up the Project

In this chapter I show you how to build a simple UI for the previously mentioned U2's Dublin case study app. The UI will be composed of a header bar, the map in the middle, and a footer bar (Figure 4-2). The header bar will include an Info button that, when touched, will open a dialog box with information regarding the app. The footer bar will include two controls (buttons), one called Set Home and the other called Reset. When touched, the first control will memorize the current center of the map and change the button's appearance, color, and text (the text will read "Go to home"). When touched again, the button that is in the state "Go to home" will recenter the map on the memorized set of coordinates. The Reset control will delete the memorized coordinates and center the map on its initial position. As you can see in this app, we make use of some new controls not positioned on the map (see the previous chapter) but outside of it, inside specific UI elements. Please note that the two controls in the footer I show you here will not be used in the final U2's Dublin app. I use them here just as an example to help you get more familiar with the controls and UI.

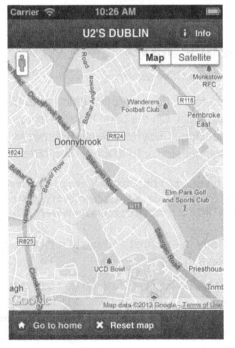

Figure 4-2. The resulting app: Notice how the appearance of the Set Home control changes

Before starting, I have to state that in this chapter I do not intend to give an exhaustive introduction to jQuery Mobile. This is not the purpose of this book and there are already lots of introductory tutorials online, beginning with the jQuery Mobile official site.

It is now time to start setting up the basic jQuery Mobile template. There's nothing to it – it is just a matter of adding the following files to the Hello World app we built in Chapter 2:

- The jQuery JavaScript library

- The jQuery Mobile JavaScript library

- The jQuery Mobile CSS

In addition to these files, jQuery Mobile will make use of a series of PNG files for some of the UI elements, but it is not necessary to explicitly link them. Please note that the files mentioned are required for every type of web app you want to build with jQuery Mobile.

There are two ways of adding these files to our web app:

- Using a CDN (a Content Delivery Network) – a public server that hosts the files for us. For instance, the official jQuery Mobile site acts as a CDN so that it is possible to access jQuery mobile files simply by using URLs like `http://code.jquery.com/mobile/1.1.1/jquery.mobile-1.1.1.js`.

- Hosting all the files within the project (in the same web server folder where the web app is hosted).

Using a CDN Server

If you are using a CDN server:

1. Go to the jQuery Mobile official site CDN where CDN links are made available: On the page `http://jquerymobile.com/download/` and, below the heading "Copy-and-Paste Snippet for CDN-hosted files," you will find a code snippet similar to the following (Xs below indicate the version number):

```
<link rel="stylesheet" href="http://code.jquery.com/mobile/X.X.X/jquery.mobile-X.X.X.min.css" />
<script src="http://code.jquery.com/jquery-X.X.X.min.js"></script>
<script src="http://code.jquery.com/mobile/X.X.X/jquery.mobile-X.X.X.min.js"></script>
```

2. Copy the snippet and paste it into the `<head>` element of your HTML page. Save the page.

CDN servers are usually very fast, so you can take advantage of their capabilities. One disadvantage of this approach is that your app will depend on the CDN server to work properly: If the server is down, your app will also be affected. (CDN servers are designed to be online 24/7 and they are very unlikely to be down.)

Hosting Files

If you are hosting the files within the project:

1. Go to the jQuery Mobile official site page http://jquerymobile.com/download/ and download the ZIP file containing the Query Mobile JavaScript library, CSS and images folder. Once you have downloaded the files decompress them and move them into your app's root folder.

2. Go to the jQuery official site http://jquery.com/ and download the jQuery JavaScript library. Once you have downloaded the file decompress it and move it into your app's root folder.

3. Now you should have inside your app's root folder the following files:

   ▪ jquery-X.X.X.min.js or jquery-X.X.X.js This is the core jQuery JavaScript library and it can be downloaded from http://jquery.com/ (production version is recommended).

   ▪ jquery.mobile-X.X.X.min.js or jquery.mobile-X.X.X.js This is the jQuery Mobile JavaScript library.

   ▪ jquery.mobile-1.1.1.min.css or jquery.mobile-1.1.1.css This is the jQuery Mobile CSS.

   ▪ Images folder. The folder contains icons and other images for the standard jQuery Mobile themes.

Note that the JavaScript and CSS files can also have the .min suffix, which indicates that this is a minimized version of the same code; it has been compressed and is recommended for production in that it is quicker to load. Non minimized versions are useful if you need to debug inside jQuery Mobile.

4. Configure <link> and <script> tags in your HTML document <head> so that they point the files in your app's root folder, for example:

```
<link rel="stylesheet" href="jquery.mobile-X.X.X.min.css" />
<script src="jquery-X.X.X.min.js"></script>
<script src="jquery.mobile-X.X.X.min.js"></script>
```

Save the HTML page.

Notice that when you download the files, you have to pay attention to which version of jQuery you are going to use. Some versions of jQuery Mobile could require a specific version of jQuery to work properly, so please consult the online documentation to be sure which jQuery version is needed.

Implementing jQuery Mobile in Our App

It is now time to get our hands dirty with the jQuery Mobile template by implementing the framework starting from the Hello World app we created in Chapter 2. Please note that at the end of the chapter I attach the complete code so you can get a global view of it every time you need. First, we have to add the references to the jQuery and jQuery Mobile JavaScript libraries and to the jQuery Mobile CSS. In the example I use jQuery 1.8.0 and jQuery Mobile 1.1.1. The code has to be put inside the <head> element of the page.

```
<link rel="stylesheet" href="http://code.jquery.com/mobile/latest/jquery.mobile.min.css" />
<script src="jquery-1.8.0.min.js"></script>
<script src="http://code.jquery.com/mobile/latest/jquery.mobile.min.js"></script>
```

Creating the Basic Structure of the Template

Let's now get to the `<body>` of the page and create inside it a `<div>` with a data-role attribute of the page as I show in the following code:

```
<div data-role="page"> </div>
```

This `<div>` is used to define a page and will wrap the content of our app. The concept of a page in jQuery Mobile is different from the standard HTML page concept: A page in jQuery Mobile is just a `<div>` element with a specific role; this way a single HTML file can host just one page or many pages. jQuery Mobile uses standard HTML markup, as you can see in the example where we used a `<div>` element. To define what the framework has to do with that `<div>`, we define roles using the data-role attribute. Note that data-role is not an HTML 5 attribute, it is just a sort of "internal agreement" understood by the framework. Typically, a jQuery Mobile page is divided into three sections: *header*, *content*, and *footer*. Only the content section is mandatory; the header and footer can be omitted. In our example, we will make use of all three parts.

Every section is declared by using `<div>` elements with the appropriate data-role attribute:

```
<div data-role="page">
  <div data-role="header"></div>
  <div data-role="content">
    <div id="map_canvas"></div>
  </div>
  <div data-role="footer"></div>
</div>
```

You may notice in the above code that map_canvas is contained inside the content section. The basic structure of the page is now defined. However, if we tried to visualize the page in a web browser, we would get a blank screen and the map would not be shown. The reason for this behavior is that we have to define the positioning of the elements better. Unfortunately, it is not so easy to use jQuery to correctly position a Google map in between the header and the footer, so we have to make use of absolute positioning of some elements and to define a fixed size for the header and footer bars. First, we have to set an id value for the header and footer: the id value it will be used for styling via CSS. It is also necessary to set a data-position attribute with the value fixed for each element. You can find more information about positioning in jQuery Mobile in the official online documentation. Here is the modified code:

```
<div data-role="header" id="divHeader" data-position="fixed"></div>

<div data-role="footer" id="divFooter" data-position="fixed"></div>
```

Then we need to set the styles for header and footer via CSS (Listing 4-1):

Listing 4-1. CSS rules for header and footer

```
#divHeader {
position:absolute;
top:0;
height:40px;
}

#divFooter {
position:absolute;
bottom:0;
height:40px;
}
```

In the CSS styling we have to absolutely position the header and footer and to define a specific height in pixels for them. In this case, I thought a height of 40 pixels was appropriate. After setting style rules for the header and footer, we also have to absolutely position map_canvas in this way (Listing 4-2):

Listing 4-2. CSS rules for map_canvas

```
#map_canvas {
width:100%;

position:absolute;
top:40px;
bottom:40px;
left:0;
right:0;
}
```

In Figure 4-3 you can see how the app's UI appears now: The header and footer are absolutely positioned with a height of 40 pixels and the map occupies the remaining space in the middle. By simply declaring the data-role attribute for the header and footer, we can get them automatically colored with a CSS 3 gradient. It is the jQuery Mobile framework that does this for us.

Figure 4-3. The header and the footer are correctly positioned both in portrait and landscape orientation

jQuery Mobile offers five default themes, called swatches. Every swatch is named with a letter (Figure 4-4). To create custom themes, you can use the online tool ThemeRoller at http://jquerymobile.com/themeroller.

★	data-theme="a"
★	data-theme="b"
○	data-theme="c"
○	data-theme="d"
★	data-theme="e"

Figure 4-4. The five default themes are indicated with their respective letters

If you do not specify a theme, jQuery Mobile applies swatch "a" by default; otherwise, you can indicate a specific theme. Themes can be applied to any of the widgets on a page (page, header, footer, list, button), and it is possible to apply different themes to different widgets. To apply a theme, just add a data-theme="X" attribute (substituting X with the desired swatch letter) inside the widget you want to apply the theme to. For instance, if you want to apply swatch "e" to the header, inside the header <div> you will add the appropriate value for the data-theme attribute:

```
<div data-role="header" id="divHeader" data-position="fixed" data-theme="e">
```

You can see the result in Figure 4-5.

Figure 4-5. *Theme swatch "e" has been applied to the header bar*

As you can see, it is possible to mix swatches. If you add the theme swatch directly to the page, you will see how all the widgets inside the page will automatically inherit the theme (except for headers and footers, which do not inherit as they are always set by default to swatch "a"). Now you know how to change themes for the elements of the UI. In our example, I think the default theme appears quite readable so I will keep it. Also, U2's brand colors are black, gray, and white, so the default theme fits rather well.

You can now include a title in the header. To do this, simply put a <h1> element containing the title of the app inside the footer:

```
<div data-role="header" id="divHeader" data-position="fixed">
   <h1>U2'S DUBLIN</h1>
</div>
```

As you can see in Figure 4-6, the title's font and color are automatically styled by the framework.

Figure 4-6. A title has been added to the header

Adding an Info Button

We now want to add a button to the header that, when clicked, opens an Info modal dialog, reporting basic information about the app. By using jQuery Mobile it is very simple to build this element. First, we have to create a new page – that is, a simple <div> element with the appropriate data-role. We also set an id attribute for the <div>. Here is the code: `<div data-role="page" id="infoPage"></div>`. Inside the new page we put a header and a content section (Listing 4-3):

Listing 4-3. The content of the Info modal dialog

```
<div data-role="header">
    <h1>U2'S DUBLIN</h1>
</div>
<div data-role="content">
  <p>This app shows on the Dublin map significant landmarks related to U2 rock
    band's story and also the places where some of their music videos were
    set.</p>
  <p><a data-rel="back" data-role="button" data-icon="back">Back to the map</a>
  </p>
</div>
```

Note that in the content section I also added a button to go back to the app's main screen. To create the button, I simply defined an anchor and put inside it the data-rel attribute set to back and the data-role set to button. This is sufficient to create a working back button; there is no need to write any more code thanks to the jQuery Mobile framework. To improve the appearance of the button, you can add the data-icon attribute set with the value back. The jQuery Mobile framework includes the most commonly needed icons for mobile apps. An icon can be added to a button by adding a data-icon attribute on the anchor specifying the icon to display. A list of the available values for the data-icon attribute is here:

http://jquerymobile.com/demos/1.1.1/docs/buttons/buttons-icons.html.

After setting the content of the dialog box, it is necessary to create the button that will trigger the dialog. To do this it is sufficient to create an anchor element, setting its href attribute with the id value of the page with the dialog's content. You also have to add a `data-rel` attribute set to `dialog` to the anchor. This way, when touched, the anchor will open inside a modal dialog the page. To make the button look better, you may set an icon for it (in this case I used the `info` icon). Here is the code:

```
<a href="#infoPage" data-rel="dialog" data-icon="info" class="ui-btn-right">Info</a>
```

Note also that to position the button to the right of the title we have to add the class `ui-btn-right` to the anchor. You can specify the button's position by using the classes `ui-btn-left` or `ui-btn-right`. The dialog's final appearance is shown in Figure 4-7.

Figure 4-7. The Info button we built and its relative dialog

It is now time to build the two footer buttons, Set Home and Reset Map, and the connected JavaScript functions. To include the two buttons inside the footer, we can simply build a `<div>` and add the data-role value `controlgroup`. This makes it possible to group the two buttons in a single navigation component. We want the buttons to line up horizontally, so we have to add to the `<div>`: `data-type="horizontal"`. We also have to set a `margin-top` and `margin-bottom` value to properly center the component inside the footer. Here is the code:

```
<div data-role="controlgroup" data-type="horizontal" style="margin-top:4px;margin-left:4px;"> </div>
```

Inside the component we can then design the two buttons:

```
<a data-role="button" data-icon="home"><span id="homeControl">Set Home</span></a>
<a data-role="button" data-icon="delete">Reset map</a>
```

Note that I set an id value for the Set Home button. Now we can design the JavaScript functions that have to be connected to the relative buttons. First, we declare three variables as global and attribute some values to them. We can do this by declaring them at the beginning of the script and attributing them the following values (the reason will be explained soon):

```
var coordinates = null;
var map = null;
var status = 0;
```

We can then write the first function named setHome(). Here is the code (Listing 4-4):

Listing 4-4. The setHome() function

```
function setHome() {
  if (status == 0) {
    coordinates = map.getCenter();
    status = 1;
    document.getElementById('homeControl').innerHTML = "Go to home";
    document.getElementById('homeControl').style.color = "yellow";
  } else {
    map.setCenter(coordinates);
  }
}
```

This function checks the value of status, which by default is set to 0. If it is 0, then the current center of the map is obtained by using the API method getCenter(), which we saw in the previous chapter. Once you have the current center coordinates, they are attributed to the variable coordinates. Next, the status value is changed to 1, the text of the button is changed to "Go to home," and the text color is changed to show the changed status of the button. If the status value is already 1, when the function is triggered it simply centers the map on the value of coordinates. Now let's see the other function that has to be connected to the Reset button (Listing 4-5):

Listing 4-5. The Reset() function

```
function reset() {
  map.setCenter(new google.maps.LatLng(53.344104, - 6.267494));
  status = 0;
  document.getElementById('homeControl').innerHTML = "Set Home";
  document.getElementById('homeControl').style.color = "white";
}
```

The function centers the map on the initial set of coordinates, sets status to its default value, and changes the button style to its initial appearance. Here is the complete JavaScript code (Listing 4-6):

Listing 4-6. The complete code of the script

```
<script type="text/javascript">
  var coordinates = null;
  var map = null;
  var status = 0;

  function initialize() {
  var myOptions = {
      center: new google.maps.LatLng(53.344104, - 6.267494),
      zoom: 14,
      mapTypeId: google.maps.MapTypeId.ROADMAP
    }
    map = new google.maps.Map(document.getElementById("map_canvas"), myOptions);
  }

  function setHome() {
    if (status == 0) {
      coordinates = map.getCenter();
      status = 1;
      document.getElementById('homeControl').innerHTML = "Go to home";
      document.getElementById('homeControl').style.color = "yellow";
    } else {
      map.setCenter(coordinates);
    }
  }

  function reset() {
    map.setCenter(new google.maps.LatLng(53.344104, - 6.267494));
status = 0;
    document.getElementById('homeControl').innerHTML = "Set Home";
    document.getElementById('homeControl').style.color = "white";
  }
</script>
```

Now we just need to connect the buttons to their relative functions and we can do this by setting the href attribute of the buttons' anchors with the call to the relative JavaScript functions: href="javascript:setHome()" and href="javascript:reset()". Here is the code for the two buttons:

```
<a href="javascript:setHome()" data-role="button" data-icon="home"><span id="homeControl">Set
Home</span></a>
<a href="javascript:reset()" data-role="button" data-icon="delete">Reset map</a>
```

Showing a Splash Screen While Tiles Are Loading

To further improve the user's experience, we can add a "loading" splash screen to our app's UI, thus showing the user a message until the map tiles are loaded. Actually, when you launch the app, you can see that there is a moment (sometimes it can be several seconds, depending on your current Internet connection) when the map tiles are loading and you are presented with a blank screen (Figure 4-8).

Figure 4-8. *The user is presented with a blank screen while the tiles are loading*

Looking at an empty screen can be annoying for the user. It would be better to show the user a message. Building a splash screen that appears when tiles are loading is very easy because we can take advantage of a specific event of the Google Maps JS API called `tilesloaded`. You can use the event in a listener in this way:

```
google.maps.event.addListener(map, 'tilesloaded', function () {
});
```

There are many ways to build a splash screen. Here I suggest you build a simple `<div>` with the following content (the image I use here is available on the book website):

```
<div id="tilesSplashScreen">
  <table>
    <tr>
      <td>
```

```
        <img src="loading.gif" />
        <br />Please wait, the map is loading</td>
    </tr>
  </table>
</div>
```

Here is also a bit of CSS code to style the <div>. Note that I leave room for the header and the footer (Listing 4-7):

Listing 4-7. The CSS code for the splash screen

```
#tilesSplashScreen {
width:100%;
z-index:100;
position:absolute;
top:40px;
bottom:40px;
background-color:#000;
}

#tilesSplashScreen table {
 width:100%;
height:100%;
}

#tilesSplashScreen tr {
vertical-align:middle;
text-align:center;
font-weight:700;
color:#FFF;
font-family:Helvetica,Arial,sans-serif;
font-size:16pt;
padding:5px;
}
```

Once we have built the <div> and its CSS code, we can add the listener to the `initialize()` function based on the `tilesloaded` event:

```
google.maps.event.addListener(map, 'tilesloaded', function () {
  document.getElementById("tilesSplashScreen").style.display = 'none';
});
```

The splash screen is shown in Figure 4-9.

Figure 4-9. The splash screen to be displayed until the tiles are completely loaded

Specifying a Launch Image

In addition to the splash screen, which may be displayed when the tiles are being loaded, another useful addition to our web app is a launch image to be displayed when the app is launched from the Home screen (before the splash screen is displayed). Adding a launch image to an iOS web app is really easy. We can just add the following <link> element to the HTML page:

```
<link href="/images/u2splash320-460.png" media="(device-width: 320px)" rel="apple-touch-startup-image" />
```

You can substitute the PNG file with the image you want to use. Note that you must use a 320 x 460 pixel image for the standard iPhone and iPod. Launch images for high-resolution iPhone, for iPad, and for high-res iPad require different sizes. Consult the Apple documentation for the correct size for your projects: http://developer.apple.com/library/ios/#documentation/userexperience/conceptual/mobilehig/IconsImages/IconsImages.html.

Figure 4-10 shows a simple startup image I added to the app. Please note that you must use the correct size for your startup image in relation to the device it is to be shown on, otherwise it will not be displayed.

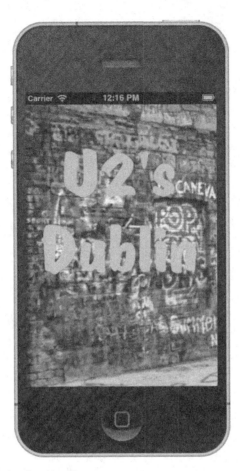

Figure 4-10. The startup image I added to the example app

Complete Code

The complete code of the jQuery Mobile UI is available at www.apress.com.

Summary

In this chapter I provided you with the jQuery Mobile basics necessary to rapidly build an elegant and usable interface for map-based web apps. I also showed you how to realize map controls positioned outside the map, inside specific UI elements. Finally, I showed some optimizations that may be applied to the app to make it more usable, like a splash screen to be shown when the app is loading. Before moving on to the next chapter, you should know how to do the following:

- Set up a jQuery Mobile template for your map-based web app.

- Implement map controls connected to elements of the UI created with jQuery Mobile.

- Add a splash screen to the app to be shown until the map tiles are loaded.

- Add a startup image to the app to be shown when the app is launched from the Home screen.

Chapter 5

Overlays

In the previous chapters I talked about integrating a map into a web app, building controls to manipulate it, and styling a map's existing content. It is now time to show you how to build your own geographic content and put it on the map. Content may include markers, lines, polygons, and other kinds of layers. These objects, unlike the on-map controls, are tied to one or more sets of geographical coordinates, so they move when you zoom or drag the map. In the Google Maps JavaScript API jargon these objects are called overlays.

In this chapter I illustrate the general methods you can implement to draw, remove, and delete overlays on your maps. Later I will show you three methods to plot points of interest (POIs) on a map by using different types of overlays: using the Marker constructor, importing POIs data from KML files with the KmlLayer constructor, and importing POIs data from the Google Fusion Tables service with the FusionTablesLayer constructor. I will give an overview of each method's pros and cons so that you know when it is better to use one method over another.

Types of overlays include different kinds of objects, as you can see in the following list:

- Markers are used to indicate single locations on the map. Markers display a default icon that can be substituted with a custom image. Markers are objects of type Marker.

- Lines are displayed on the map by indicating an ordered series of sets of coordinates. Lines are objects of type Polyline.

- Polygons are used to display areas of arbitrary shape on the map. Polygons are similar to polylines since they are built from an ordered sequence of points on the map. Unlike polylines, however, polygons define the region that they enclose. Polygons are objects of type Polygon. Some geometrical shapes, like circles and rectangles, can be easily built using specific classes as well (for example, Circle and Rectangle).

- Info windows are used to display content (usually text, images, or video) inside a pop-up balloon that appears on top of the map. Info windows are usually associated with markers so that when a user clicks on a marker an info window is displayed. They are objects of type InfoWindow.

- Ground overlays allow the developer to place an image on the map constraining it to a set of given bounds (defined by geographical coordinates). For instance, it is possible to overlay historical cartography layers on the map. These are objects of type `GroundOverlay`.

- Custom overlays implement the `OverlayView` interface. For more information see `https://developers.google.com/maps/documentation/javascript/overlays#CustomOverlays`.

- Layers are a sub-category of overlays. A layer may contain several items but it is manipulated as a single object. For instance, the `kmlLayer` layer makes it possible to import KML files (a collection of markers) onto the map but it does not make it possible to access and manipulate a single marker inside the collection. The entire collection will be treated as a single unit. Below is a list of the currently available layers (from `https://developers.google.com/maps/documentation/javascript/layers`). You can see an example in Figure 5-1 (`BicyclingLayer` overlay).

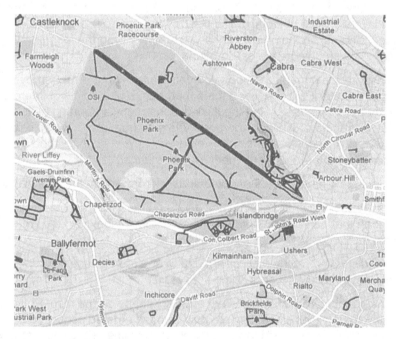

Figure 5-1. *A portion of a Google Map centered on Dublin with the `BicyclingLayer` activated (dark green routes represent bicycle routes)*

- The `KmlLayer` object renders KML (and GeoRSS) elements in a Maps API V3 tile overlay.

- The `HeatmapLayer` object renders geographic data using a heatmap visualization.

- The `FusionTablesLayer` object renders data contained in Google Fusion Tables.

- The `TrafficLayer` objects renders a layer depicting traffic conditions and overlays representing traffic.

- The TransitLayer objects displays the public transport network of a city on the map.

- The WeatherLayer and CloudLayer objects allow you to add weather forecasts and cloud imagery to your map.

- The BicyclingLayer object renders a layer of bike paths and/or bicycle-specific overlays in a common layer.

- The PanoramioLayer object adds photos from Panoramio as a layer.

- The DemographicsLayer object renders United States demographic information as a layer but is available to Google Maps API for Business customers only.

In this chapter I am not going to examine all the types of overlays I just listed (and that you can find more information about in the API official documentation). Instead, I am going to focus on the constructors Marker, InfoWindow, KmlLayer, and FusionTablesLayer, which I will use to illustrate the three aforementioned methods to plot POIs on a map.

General Methods For Manipulating Overlays

The Google Maps JavaScript API makes available some general methods for manipulating overlays. To properly understand the three specific methods to plot POIs I will illustrate later in this chapter, first you need to understand the general methods I am going to explain here. To display an overlay you have to use the setMap() method, which receives as argument the map to which the overlay has to be applied. In this section, I show you how to use this method by applying it to the Hello World example presented in Chapter 2. (Refer back to that chapter if you need a refresher.) You can simply take the Hello World file and save it with another name since you are going to work on that code. Let's begin by adding an overlay to the map.

Adding Overlays to the Map

I would like to display a marker in the center of the map (so this marker will have the same set of coordinates used to center the map). First, you need to create the marker by using the Marker constructor: it takes as argument an object literal containing certain properties, a required one being position. Here is the example code that you can put inside the initialize() function of the map:

```
var sampleMarker = new google.maps.Marker({
  position: coordinates,
  title: "This is a marker"
});
```

The title option is not required. It shows the title of the marker when the map is displayed on computers and the mouse cursor hovers over the marker. Once the marker is created, you have to use the setMap() method to display the overlay on the map. Here is the code:

```
sampleMarker.setMap(map);
```

The code could also be written in this way, adding a map property inside the marker's object literal:

```
var sampleMarker = new google.maps.Marker({
  position: coordinates,
  title: "This is a marker",
  map: map
});
```

In Figure 5-2 I show you the resulting screen with the marker overlay displayed on the map.

Figure 5-2. The marker overlay is displayed on a map on an iPhone (on the left) and on a computer (on the right)

Removing and Deleting Overlays From the Map

To remove an overlay that you previously added to the map, you need to use the same method setMap() but this time pass it null as argument. This way, the overlay is removed from the map but it is not deleted. To delete an overlay, you have to remove it from the map and then set the overlay itself to null. Now I am going to show you another example so that you can put this concept into practice. In the new example I also introduce the use of arrays to manage many markers at the same time. This sample app will allow the user the create a marker in the point where he touches the map (that is, where the click event happens on the map). Additionally, by using specific controls, the user will be able to remove all the created markers, display them all, or completely delete them.

Setting the Example's GUI

To create this example I use the jQuery Mobile-based app discussed in the previous chapter. You can simply take the app's files and save them with another name so that you can work on them here. You will have to change the app's title and modify buttons to get a UI like the one shown in Figure 5-3. I would like to point out a simple workaround that allows you to show the full-length title in the header. In this case, the title of the app ("Add, remove, and delete markers") is quite long, and   jQuery mobile UI would automatically abbreviate it. To override this default behavior, you have to add a short CSS integration. To do this, the jQuery Mobile documentation (http://jquerymobile.com/demos/1.0rc2/docs/api/themes.html) explains that you should add an external stylesheet to the <head>. This stylesheet should be placed after the structure and theme stylesheet references, which contain all your style overrides. To add a longer title in the CSS override, you can simply write:

```
.ui-header .ui-title {
margin-left: 1em; margin-right: 1em;
}
```

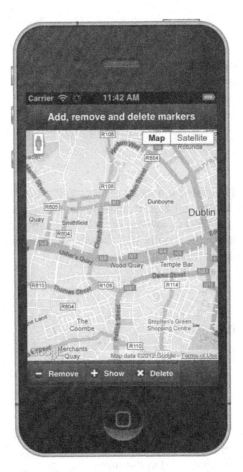

Figure 5-3. The template prepared for the example

Once the jQuery Mobile template for this example is created, it should look like the one I show in Figure 5-3. (Note that there are no functions connected to the buttons yet.)

Coding the JavaScript Functions

First, you need to add a listener to the map so that a click event on the map triggers the addition of a marker at the point where the click event occurred. Inside the initialize() function you can put the following code:

```
google.maps.event.addListener(map, 'click', function (event) {
  addMarker(event.latLng);
});
```

In the above code, notice that the addMarker() function receives as argument the LatLng property of event, containing the coordinates of the point where the user clicked on the map. Now I will show you the content of the function addMarker(). To make it work properly, we must first declare the array that we are going to use as a global variable:

```
var markersArray = [];
```

Then we add the function:

```
function addMarker(eventCoordinates) {
  var newMarker = new google.maps.Marker({

    position: eventCoordinates,
    map: map
  });
  markersArray.push(newMarker);
}
```

The addMarker() function simply creates a marker assigning the event's coordinates to its position property and finally adds the created marker to markersArray[]. Then we move on to the construction of another function, called removeMarkers(), that, when called, will remove markers from the map by using the setMap(null) method. This way, markers will not be removed from the array but only from the map. Here is the code:

```
function removeMarkers() {
  if (markersArray.length != 0) {
    for (i in markersArray) {
      markersArray[i].setMap(null);
    }
  } else {
    alert("There are no markers to remove");
  }
}
```

To make clear the concept that by using the setMap(null) method markers are only removed from the map and not deleted, we also create the showMarkers() function, which uses the setMap(map) method to display all the markers contained in the array.

```
function showMarkers() {
  if (markersArray.length != 0) {
    for (i in markersArray) {
      markersArray[i].setMap(map);
    }
  } else {
    alert("There are no markers to show");
  }
}
```

To definitively delete markers, first we need to remove them from the map using the setMap(null) method, and then we have to set the array's length property to 0 so that every element of the array is deleted. Here is the code for the function deleteMarkers().

```
function deleteMarkers() {
  if (markersArray.length != 0) {
    for (i in markersArray) {
      markersArray[i].setMap(null);
    }
    markersArray.length = 0;
  } else {
    alert("There are no markers to delete");
  }
}
```

Once the functions are ready, you can connect them to the jQuery Mobile buttons in the footer and the app is complete. In Figure 5-4 I show you how the working application appears.

1) Some markers are created   **2) Previously created markers are now removed**

3) New markers are created   **4) By clicking on Show, all of the array's elements are shown including those that have been removed**

Figure 5-4. The application at work

Note that the same methods and procedures shown in this section can be used to manipulate not just markers but every type of overlay – for instance, lines and polygons. Now that you know the general methods for adding, removing, and deleting map overlays of every type, in the next section I am going to describe three methods for displaying points of interest on a map using different types of overlays.

Three Methods to Display POIs On a Map

It is possible to display points of interest on the map using different types of overlays. For the remainder of the chapter I want to show you how to use three different types of overlays to plot POIs by applying them to our main case study, the U2's Dublin app. I will show the pros and cons of each technique.

The first method, which I partially showed you in the previous section, consists of using markers created with the API's Marker constructor. With this method, markers are drawn by means of the browser's JavaScript interpreter, and the rendering is performed by the client (computer or mobile device). This can be very slow when hundreds or thousands of markers have to be displayed.

The second method is a more high-performance technique, especially if you have to deal with a large number of points or other geometric elements. It consists of importing geometry data onto the map in the form of KML data by using overlays of type KmlLayer.

The third method I want to talk about involves of making use of an overlay of type FusionTablesLayer. This type of overlay makes it possible to retrieve data from the tables of the Google cloud database called Fusion Tables. This data can then be rendered on the map. In this case (similar to what happens when we use KmlLayer), points and other geometric elements are not drawn by the client device. Instead, the overlay elements are drawn directly on the tiles by the Google servers. This way the client device may receive the tiles with the elements already drawn on them. We will have to deal with point elements defined by pairs of coordinates. Additionally, we will connect balloons to the points with the relative content, so that when clicking on a POI, the user is shown a balloon containing the appropriate content.

Method 1: Using the Marker Constructor

Before proceeding with how to use the Marker constructor, you should review the pros and cons of this method, as listed in Table 5-1. Note that these considerations also apply to other constructors that work as Marker like Polyline and Polygon.

Table 5-1. Marker Constructor Pros and Cons

PROS	CONS
Easy implementation – you do not need existing KML data, Fusion Tables, or other kind of data.	It does not allow you to directly show KML data or Fusion Tables data on the map.
Wide control of the marker's aspect and behavior.	Client-side JavaScript rendering, which means slow performance when a large number of markers is displayed.

Now that you know something about the `Marker` constructor, you should be able to create a new marker, remove it from the map, or completely delete it. Methods, properties, and events related to the `Marker` constructor are all well explained in the official API documentation here: https://developers.google.com/maps/documentation/javascript/reference?hl=it-It#Marker.

In addition to the previously seen `map` and `position` properties , I would like to explain another useful property named `icon` that allows you to set a custom icon for the marker. Then I will show you how to add an info window object (that is, a balloon) to the marker.

Setting Custom Marker Icons

A particularly useful property is `icon`, which allows you to define a custom image to be used instead of the default marker's icon. In the following code, I show you how to set the icon property by assigning it a custom image called `customicon.png` (Figure 5-5).

```
var sampleMarker = new google.maps.Marker({
  position: coordinates,
  title: "This is a marker",
  icon: 'customicon.png'
});
```

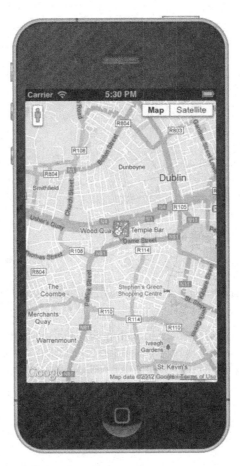

Figure 5-5. A marker with a custom icon is displayed on the map

It is also possible to define properties for the icons in more detail (for instance, their size, shadow, and animation) using the appropriate methods and properties from the API, as illustrated here:

`https://developers.google.com/maps/documentation/javascript/overlays#Icons`.

Finding the appropriate icons for markers is not a task to neglect or underestimate. There are many occasions when Google default icons are not the best solutions for displaying specific content, so we have to decide which alternative icons best suit our purposes. You should always keep in mind this rule when choosing icons: the icon's relation to the content it refers to should always be clear and you should avoid using overly complex images that the user can not understand immediately. It is also important to make sure that the colors are visible on the app's default map background. For instance, blue icons displayed on the sea would not be visible to the user. If you do not want to use Google icons but you also do not want to draw new ones from scratch, you can find ready-to-use icons in some online free galleries. An important collection of free icons is available here: `http://code.google.com/p/google-maps-icons/`. On this website you can find more than 700 free icons organized into categories (Figure 5-6).

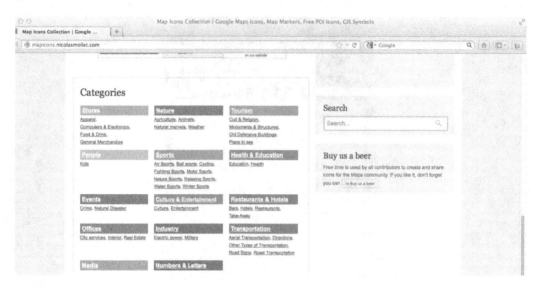

Figure 5-6. *The Google Maps icon collection hosted at* `http://mapicons.nicolasmollet.com/`

Once you select a category, you are presented with a set of icons that can be rendered in different styles – including an iOS style, which is recommended for our kind of app (Figure 5-7). To use an icon, you have to download it and host it on your webserver, so that it can be retrieved by the Google Maps JavaScript API.

Culture map markers

The website is under testing, please read the post about it.

Note : Hotlinking is not allowed on this site. Please download and host the icons on your own server or Dropbox.

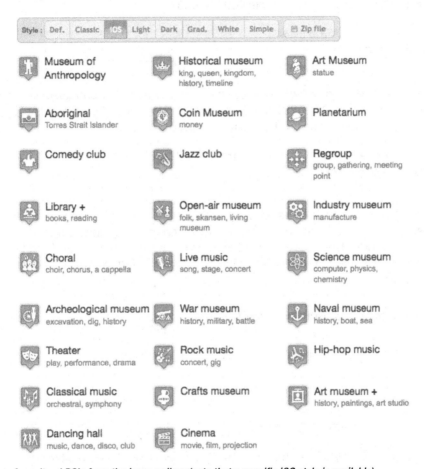

Figure 5-7. *Icons for cultural POIs from the icons gallery (note that a specific iOS style is available)*

Adding Balloons to Markers: the InfoWindow Constructor

An info window is an object separated from the marker but belonging to the same category of overlays. An info window can be attached to a marker using the addListener() method, so that when a specific event happens on the marker, for instance the click event, the connected info window's balloon is displayed. The constructor to create an info window is InfoWindow, which takes as argument an object literal whose content property is used to host the balloon's content.

In the following code, I show you how to build an info window, put content in it, and attach it to a marker. First, you need to declare a variable that will host the content of the ballon as a text string:

```
var balloonContent = "Sample content for the balloon";
```

Then you have to create an info window object with the InfoWindow constructor and assign to its content property the balloonContent variable you created:

```
var balloon = new google.maps.InfoWindow({
  content: balloonContent
});
```

Once the info window is created and content has been added to it, you can associate it to the marker using the addListener() method. In the following code, when the marker is clicked or touched, the balloon is displayed using the open() method.

```
google.maps.event.addListener(sampleMarker, 'click', function () {
  balloon.open(map, sampleMarker);
});
```

Note that the open() method receives as arguments the name of the map on which you want the marker to be displayed and the name of the marker to which the info window has to be attached. This way, the info window obtains the coordinates to position itself on the map from the marker's position property. Here is the complete code (Listing 5-1) and in Figure 5-8 you can see a screenshot of the app.

Listing 5-1. The complete code used to add an info window to a marker

```
function initialize() {
  var coordinates = new google.maps.LatLng(53.344104, - 6.267494);

  var myOptions = {
    center: coordinates,
    zoom: 14,
    mapTypeId: google.maps.MapTypeId.ROADMAP
  }
  var map = new google.maps.Map(document.getElementById("map_canvas"),↵ myOptions);

  //Create a new marker
  var sampleMarker = new google.maps.Marker({
    position: coordinates
  });
  sampleMarker.setMap(map);

  //Create the content to be shown in the balloon
  var balloonContent = "Sample content for the balloon";

  //Create the balloon and assign it the previously created content
  var balloon = new google.maps.InfoWindow({
    content: balloonContent
  });
```

```
    //Attach the balloon to the marker using a listener
    google.maps.event.addListener(sampleMarker, 'click', function () {
        balloon.open(map, sampleMarker);
    });
}
```

Figure 5-8. The balloon attached to the marker is open, showing its content

The info window's `content` property also makes it possible to insert HTML code so that you can apply formatting to the text, add hyperlinks and images, and so on, as content for the balloon. In the following example, I show you how to insert a hyperlink in the info window's content. (The outcome is shown in Figure 5-9.)

```
var balloonContent = "To open the Google Maps JS API's documentation home page click <a
href='https://developers.google.com/maps/documentation/javascript/'>here</a>";
```

Figure 5-9. A hyperlink has been added to the balloon's content

Beyond content there are other useful properties, well illustrated in the documentation (https://developers.google.com/maps/documentation/javascript/overlays#InfoWindows). Among those, it is important to mention position and maxWidth.

The position Property

The position property allows you to indicate a set of coordinates (an object of type LatLng) on which to center the info window. If the info window is attached to a marker, it is not necessary to indicate a value for the position property because the info window will use the marker's coordinates. You can set this property when you want to display an info window not attached to a marker. For instance, you can set the info window so that when a user clicks on a point on the map, a balloon opens, positioned on a given set of coordinates. The following code is an example of this (Figure 5-10):

```
//Define a set of coordinates to position the balloon
var balloonCoordinates = new google.maps.LatLng(53.352889, - 6.271667);

//Create the balloon and assign previously created content to it
var balloon = new google.maps.InfoWindow({
  content: balloonContent,
  position: balloonCoordinates
});

//Attach the balloon to the map using a listener
google.maps.event.addListener(map, 'click', function () {
  balloon.open(map);
})
```

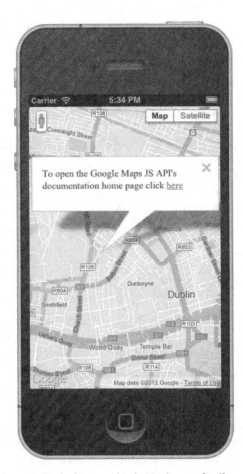

Figure 5-10. Example of an info window not attached to a marker but to the map itself

The maxWidth Property

You can use the maxWidth property to indicate the maximum width in pixels that the info window must have. By default, an info window expands to fit its content and auto-wraps text if the info window expands to fill the map. This can sometimes create excessively wide balloons. Consider, for instance, Figure 5-11, where a balloon with a lot of text is displayed on an iPad 2 device. The balloon appears excessively long and cumbersome, occupying almost two thirds of the map's width.

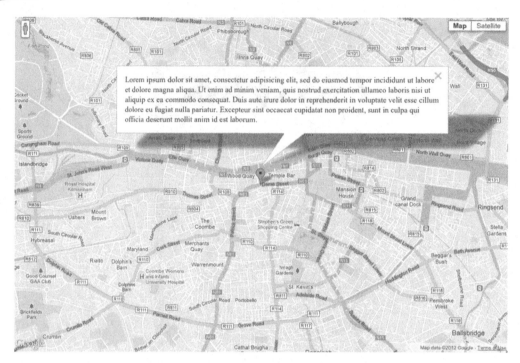

Figure 5-11. *An info window's balloon with a lot of text appears cumbersome on an iPad screen*

Luckily by using the maxWidth property it is easy to set a different size for its width. You just need to specify a value, in pixels, for maxWidth. Note that when the balloon reaches the maximum width, the info window may still expand vertically if screen space is available. A good size for an info window's balloon to be displayed both on iPad and on iPhone devices is 250 pixels, so, within the InfoWindow constructor, you can write:

```
var balloon = new google.maps.InfoWindow({
  content: balloonContent,
  maxWidth: 250
});
```

After applying a maxWidth value of 250 pixels the balloon now displays more nicely on an iPad map (Figure 5-12).

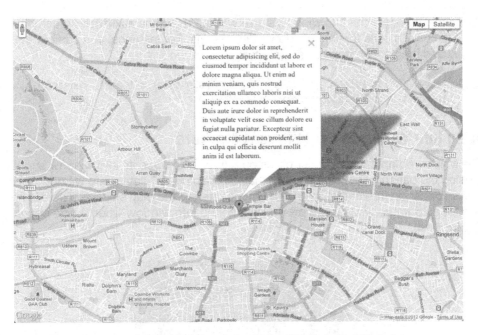

Figure 5-12. Now the info window's balloon displays more nicely with its width limited to 250 pixels

When the info window's content cannot be displayed in its entirety, even if scrollbars are not explicitly shown it can be easily scrolled up and down, both on iPad and iPhone devices (Figure 5-13).

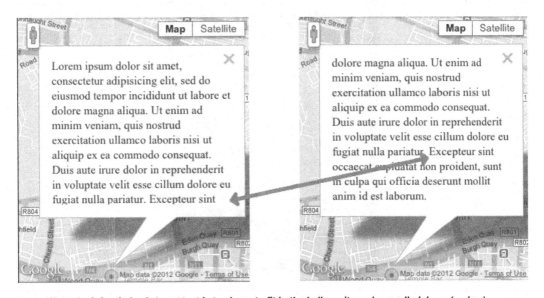

Figure 5-13. When the info window's 's content is too large to fit in the balloon, it can be scrolled down (and up)

It is also possible to control the info window's size without using the maxWidth property but simply by using HTML code to style the info window's dimensions. For instance, you can put the content inside a <div> and then set an appropriate width for the <div>:

```
var balloonContent = "<div style='width:250px;'>Lorem ipsum dolor sit amet, consectetur adipisicing
elit, sed do eiusmod tempor incididunt</div>";
```

Separating Info Windows For Different Markers

In a Google Maps web app, when a user clicks on a marker to open its info window and then, without closing the balloon, clicks on another marker opening its relative info window, the two info windows appear on the map at the same time, cluttering the map's space. There is no default mechanism for automatically closing a previously opened info window when a user clicks on a new marker (Figure 5-14).

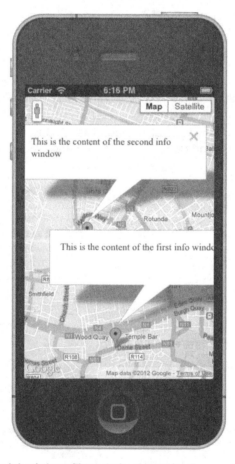

Figure 5-14. When a user opens a new info window without closing the previously opened one, all the info windows remain displayed on the map

This API behavior might raise a usability problem in many situations, since users might expect that when clicking on a new marker the previously opened info window would automatically close in order to make room for the new one. This is indeed the standard behavior of the default iOS Maps app, Google Maps, and Google Earth apps, and of many other map-based iOS apps. Luckily, it is possible to reproduce this behavior even when using Google Maps JavaScript API V3 with the following workaround: create a single info window object to which different content is assigned every time. The API makes available the setContent() method, which allows you to set an info window's content on the fly. In the following example, I show you how, given two markers, marker1 and marker2, it is possible to create a single info window object so that when a user clicks on a new marker the previously opened info window is automatically closed before the new one is displayed. This way, two or more info windows cannot be displayed at the same time. Here is the code (Listing 5-2):

Listing 5-2. How to create a single info window for multiple markers

```
//Create the content to be shown in the balloons
var balloonContent1 = "This is the content of the first info window";
var balloonContent2 = "This is the content of the second info window";

//Create the balloon without assigning any content to it
var balloon = new google.maps.InfoWindow();

//Attach the balloon to the markers using a listener
google.maps.event.addListener(marker1, 'click', function () {
  balloon.setContent(balloonContent1);
  balloon.open(map, marker1);
});

google.maps.event.addListener(marker2, 'click', function () {
  balloon.setContent(balloonContent2);
  balloon.open(map, marker2);
});
```

To further improve the usability of the map, I also suggest adding a listener so that, when clicking on or touching the map, every open info window is closed. IOS Maps and many other apps behave in this way, so the user expects this kind of behavior. In this case, you can simply use the API's close() method, applying it to the info window object:

```
google.maps.event.addListener(map, 'click', function () {
  balloon.close();
});
```

Creating Custom Balloons

Using objects of type InfoWindow is not the only available way to build balloons attached to a marker. You can also create a custom overlay to be used as a balloon. The procedure in this case is more complex than using a standard info window object but the possibilities of customization are far greater. The page http://gmaps-samples-v3.googlecode.com/svn/trunk/infowindow_custom/ infowindow-custom.html shows an example of a custom overlay used as a balloon. (The comments present in the code explain all the steps in detail.) In Figure 5-15 I show the custom balloon for this example.

Figure 5-15. Example of a custom overlay used to create a custom balloon

Using the Marker Constructor in the Case Study

Now that you have a general idea of how to create and manipulate marker objects created with the constructor Marker(), we can move on to realizing the POIs for the U2 's Dublin app. To build this sample app, you should use the basic jQuery Mobile template composed of header, map, and footer. We used this template in the "Removing and deleting overlays from the map" section earlier in this chapter. We are going to show a number of markers and the best way to do this is by creating a data structure based on arrays. The structure will contain the coordinates to position the POIs and the information that will be shown in the balloons. I decided to split the app's code into three files: poismethod1.html (the HTML page), poismethod1.css (the CSS file containing style rules), and poismethod1.js, which contains all the JavaScript code for the app. This last file includes the array containing the data necessary to build the POIs.

The Structure of the Array

The array containing all the data necessary to generate the balloons of the POIs will have the following fields: latitude, longitude, name, URL of the image, address, status, and description.

The fourth field will contain the URL of an image to be shown in the balloon, if available. Here is the model of the array. Please note that it actually is an array of arrays (the data of each POI is contained in a subarray). For this example, I filled the array with three subarrays:

```
[
  ["latitude", "longitude", "name", "image URL", "address", "status", "description"],
  ["latitude", "longitude", "name", "image URL", "address", "status", "description"],
  ["latitude", "longitude", "name", "image URL", "address", "status", "description"]
    ]
```

Once you have set up the three files that compose the app, defined the interface, and written the initialize() function centering the map, you can move on to build and populate the array with data. (You can put the array outside the initialize() function but be sure to assign it to a global variable as in the example below.) In the following code example, I populated the array with three sample subarrays to create three POIs pointing to U2's places in Dublin (Listing 5-3).

Listing 5-3. The array containing three sample subarrays

```
pois = [
  ["53.3457", "-6.2274", "East Link Bridge",↵
"/apress/code/u2images/eastlinkbridge.jpg", "not available",↵
"existing", "The bridge, in a raised state, features as the entry point↵
to Dublin in the music video for the song <a↵
href='http://www.youtube.com/watch?v=LHcP4MWABGY' target='blank'>Pride↵
(In The Name Of Love)</a>."],

  ["53.345914", "-6.245921", "Windmill Lane Studios/U2 Wall",↵
"/apress/code/u2images/windmillstd.jpg", "4 Windmill Lane", "not↵
existing anymore", "In Windmill Lane Studios, also known as the 'U2↵
studio', U2 recorded their first albums. Here Boy, October, the single↵
A Celebration, and War came to life as well as U2 first EP U2Three. In↵
1989 the Windmill Lane Recording Studios moved to Ringsend Road but the ↵
legendary U2 Wall is still located here, covered with tributes from U2↵
fans from all the world."],

  ["53.343371", " -6.230446", "Lock by Grand Canal Docks",↵
"/apress/code/u2images/grandcanaldocks.jpg", "not available",↵
"existing", "The cover picture of October was shot by the eastern lock↵
of Gran Canal Docks."]
    ]
```

The JavaScript Functions

If data is not available for some fields, you can obviously leave them empty, but the coordinates fields must always be filled, otherwise the markers will not be displayed on the map. Once you have created the array, you can move on to writing the JavaScript functions necessary to create and display markers and their connected balloons. I suggest that you work with just one info window object following the procedure I explained in the previous section so that only one ballon is shown at a time. First, you need to create an object of type InfoWindow inside initialize() so that it is immediately available to the function that will make use of it. The content of the info window initially will be an empty string. While creating the object I suggest that you also set its maxWidth property:

```
var balloon = new google.maps.InfoWindow({
  content: "",
  maxWidth: 250
});
```

Inside initialize() you also have to recall the addMarkers() function (I will explain this later) whose purpose is to create the markers, display them on the map, and link each of them to its related balloon. The addMarkers() function receives as argument the current map and the info window object:

```
addMarkers(map, balloon);
```

Inside initialize() I suggest you always create a listener, associated to the current map, whose purpose is to close every open balloon when the user clicks on or touches the map:

```
google.maps.event.addListener(map, 'click', function () {
  balloon.close();
});
```

It is now time to examine the addMarkers() function. It uses a *for* loop to loop through all the elements contained in the POIs array. At every cycle, the createMarker() function is triggered. Here is the code:

```
function addMarkers(map, balloon) {
  for (i in pois) {
    createMarker();
  }
```

Inside addMarkers() you then have to write the createMarker() function. In the following code (Listing 5-4) I show the first part of createMarker():

Listing 5-4. The first part of the createMarker() function

```
function createMarker() {

  //Create the LatLng object to be used to position the marker
  var poiLatitude = pois[i][0];
  var poiLongitude = pois[i][1];
  var poiPosition = new google.maps.LatLng(poiLatitude, poiLongitude);

  //Create the marker
  var poiMarker = new google.maps.Marker({
    position: poiPosition,
    map: map
  });
```

In the above code, latitude and longitude values are extracted from the array and passed to their respective variables. In the code line var poiLatitude = pois[i][0];, the part pois[i] indicates the element (that is, the subarray) being considered in the current loop, while [0] indicates the position, inside the subarray, of the field that contains the latitude value. It is necessary to sort the set of coordinates into two distinct variables since the LatLng constructor takes two variables, one for latitude and one for longitude. Then the marker is created by setting the position property inside the Marker constructor with the LatLng object and also setting the map property.

Now let us move on to the second part of the createMarker() function (Listing 5-5). Here is the code that I will then comment on:

Listing 5-5. The second part of the createMarker() function

```
//Create the blocks of content to be displayed in the balloon
  var poiName = pois[i][2];
  var poiImage = pois[i][3];
  var poiAddress = pois[i][4];
  var poiStatus = pois[i][5];
  var poiDescription = pois[i][6];

  //Put the content all together

  var balloonContent = "<strong>" + poiName + "</strong>" + "<br />" + "<img src='" + poiImage + "'
/>" + "<br />" + "<strong>Address: </strong>" + poiAddress + "<br />" + "<strong>Status: </strong>"
+ poiStatus + "<br />" + "<strong>Description: </strong>" + poiDescription;

  //Add a listener to the marker so that when this is touched its relative balloon is displayed
  new google.maps.event.addListener(poiMarker, 'click', function↵
  openBallon() {
    balloon.setContent(balloonContent);
    balloon.open(map, poiMarker);
  });
}
```

The code can be divided into three parts. In the first one, the elements that will be used to form the content of the balloon are extracted from the array and passed to specific variables. In the second part, the various elements are put together to form the content along with some snippet of HTML code to give them a basic formatting. The content is then assigned to the variable balloonContent. In the third part, a listener is added to the marker so that, when touched, its connected balloon and appropriate content are displayed. With this, the createMarker() function and the parent addMarkers() function are complete. In Figure 5-16 you can see a screenshot of the app running on an iPhone while in Figure 5-17 the same app is shown running on an iPad device (obviously the web app can also run on a desktop computer). For the example, I created three markers for the U2's Dublin app, but with the same method and structure you can add all the markers you need.

Figure 5-16. *The app running on an iPhone. Notice that not all of the content of the balloon can be shown so the user will have to scroll down*

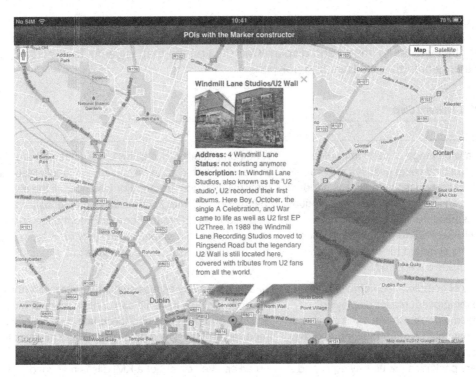

Figure 5-17. The same app running on an iPad. In this case, the content of the balloon is fully displayed

Method 2: Using the KmlLayer Constructor

The second method to represent and manage POIs on a map consists of importing data onto the map in Keyhole Markup Language (KML) format by creating overlays of type KmlLayer.

KML is a markup language (like HTML) based on XML. Technically speaking, you can say that KML is a grammar of XML. KML is focused on geographic visualization, including annotation of maps and images. In virtual globes like Google Earth, KML permits not only the presentation of graphic data on the globe but also the control of the user's navigation in terms of where to go and where to look.

Keyhole is the name of the company that initially developed Google Earth and the first versions of the language before being acquired by Google in 2004. After the acquisition of Keyhole, Google continued developing KML and proposed to the Open Geospatial Consortium that it become a standard geodata interchange format for geobrowsers. KML became an international standard in April 2008. The current version of the language is KML 2.2 and is maintained by the Open Geospatial Consortium (OGC). The complete specification for OGC KML can be found at http://www.opengeospatial.org/standards/kml/. Currently, KML is supported (although there are some differences in its implementations) by many geobrowsers including Google Earth, Google Maps, Microsoft Bing Maps, ESRI ArcGIS Explorer, and NASA WorldWind. Google, by exploiting the mechanism for extensions present in the OGC KML standard, has provided some extensions to KML to support a number of new features. The Google KML Reference Version 2.2, including the elements in the Google extension namespace, is available here: https://developers.google.com/kml/documentation/kmlreference.

Let's now examine the pros and cons of using KML data to display map POIs on a mobile iOS web app, according also to the official API documentation (Table 5-2). Please note that the `KmlLayer` constructor that we use to import and display KML data on the map is useful to import not just POIs but also other geometries like lines and polygons.

Table 5-2. KML Pros and Cons

PROS	CONS
Access to a wide range of data: Importing KML data onto a map by using overlays of type KmlLayer makes it possible to access geodata expressed in an international standard language that is widespread. KmlLayer permits access to geodata in GeoRSS format as well, which is an emerging standard for encoding location information inside a web feed.	KML compatibility: Not all KML elements that are available in Google Earth can be displayed on Google Maps using the KmlLayer constructor. For instance, all the elements that have to do with 3D visualization obviously cannot be visualized on a 2D map. For more information about the KML support in Google Maps, see https://developers.google.com/kml/documentation/mapsSupport.
Easy display of complex geometries: KmlLayer speeds up the procedures for displaying complex geometric structures, such as lines or polygons, that could end up too long to draw using direct API constructors. In fact, the main GIS software packages are usually equipped with plugins and exporting tools that allow you to export data directly into KML format. This way of exporting data from GIS software and importing it into Google Maps is a very quick procedure. If we want to remain in the Google family, Google Earth Pro has GIS data importing capabilities and, obviously, KML exporting.	Inability to directly access single features inside the KML. Although a single KML file can contain many different features like lines and polygons and these features can be correctly imported and displayed on a map using KmlLayer, it is not possible to access a single feature via the API, for instance, a marker. The content of a KML file is managed by the API's KmlLayer class as a single object that can be shown or hidden, but the elements that compose the object cannot be singularly accessed. If, for example, you import a single KML file containing points, lines, and polygons, you cannot choose to display only points or only lines. You can only show or hide it all together. If you wanted to manage points, lines, or polygons separately, you would have to create three different KML files, one for the points, one for the lines, and one for the polygons, and then import them by means of three different instances of KmlLayer.
Light CPU/memory charge on client devices. KML data imported using KmlLayer is not directly rendered via the JavaScript interpreter of the iOS browser. KML data is sent to Google servers where they are rendered, and then the rendered data are sent back to the device in the form of tiles with transparency. The device then only has to overlay the new tiles with transparency to the active map type. This way it is possible to make the device show thousands of markers with a very light CPU and memory load, avoiding annoying delays in displaying the data.	

Let's see how to use KmlLayer to import and display data for our case study app. For the example, I chose to display just three POIs, the same as in the previous example. The steps to follow are:

1. Create KML data to import (if not already existing).

2. Create an overlay using KmlLayer.

3. Display the overlay on the map.

Creating KML Data

If you do not have any previously existing KML data at your disposal, you can create it in various ways: starting from GIS data and exporting it in KML format, coding it manually in KML language using an editor, or using a geobrowser like Google Earth. For the example, I chose this last way since it is very simple, although it is not the best way when you have to create thousands of KML elements. For this kind of activity, you can use the free version of Google Earth, available both for Mac OS X and Windows here: http://www.google.com/earth/index.html. Once you have launched Google Earth, creating a POI is a very simple task.

In the toolbar, click on the "Add a placemark" button. A dialog window will be displayed like the one in Figure 5-18.

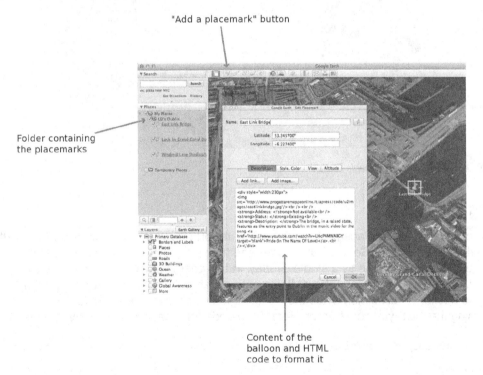

Figure 5-18. The dialog window to fill in order to create a placemark. In the Description field, you can add HTML code to format the content of the balloon

You have to fill the available fields, that is, Name, Latitude, Longitude, and then in the Description field add the content of the balloon (image and other information) using HTML code, as shown in Figure 5-18. Please note in the code that by wrapping the Description's content into a <div> element and then setting the <div> width , it is possible to control the width of the balloon itself. Once you have filled in all the fields, click on OK to save the placemark. In Figure 5-19 you can see how the example appears when the placemark has been clicked.

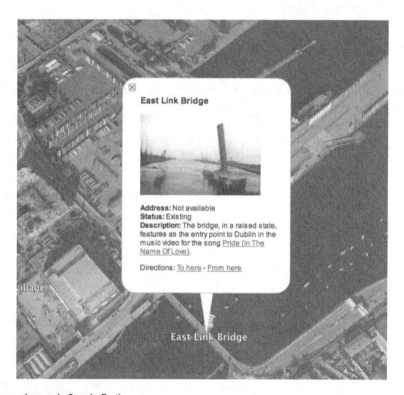

Figure 5-19. *A placemark open in Google Earth*

Creating an Overlay

Once you have created the placemarks you want to import into your web app in Google Earth, you need to gather them up in a Google Earth folder and then save that folder as a KML file if you want to import all of the placemarks as a single overlay. In this case, I saved the folder with the name u2pois.kml. Then you have to load the KML file onto a web server. (Note that the KML, or GeoRSS file, must be publicly accessible.) Once the file is loaded on the web server, you can import it onto the map using the KmlLayer constructor. Here is the code for creating the overlay of type KmlLayer:

```
var poisKml = new google.maps.KmlLayer('http://www.progettaremappeonline.it/apress/code/u2pois.kml');
```

Displaying the Overlay

Once the overlay is created, you need to use the setMap() method to display it on the map:

```
poisKml.setMap(map);
```

When you import a KML file, the map gets centered and zoomed by default on the KML data displayed, overriding the initial center and zoom settings. To avoid this behavior, which sometimes can be annoying, you need to pass to the KmlLayer constructor a set of options that allow you to set a value for the property preserveViewport. If the property is set to true, initial zoom and center map settings will be maintained. Here is an example:

```
var poisKml = new google.maps.KmlLayer('http://www.progettaremappeonline.it/apress/code/u2pois.kml', {
  preserveViewport: true
});
```

In Figure 5-20 you can see on the left the imported KML with no preserveViewport property set and on the right the KML imported with preserveViewport set to true.

Figure 5-20. *Imported KML with no preserveViewport property set (left); KML imported with preserveViewport set to true (right)*

In the second example, you can see that the placemarks are not shown as they lie on a part of the map that is not visible with the current centering.

Method 3: Using the `FusionTableslayer` Constructor

The last method I suggest you consider for displaying POIs (and other elements) on the map is based on the use of the Google Fusion Tables service. Fusion Tables is a web service provided by Google for data management. Data is stored in multiple tables that can be accessed and modified online by anyone who possess a Google account. Tables data can be also made publicly available on the Internet, so that users who are not registered can view it. The service was born in 2009 and then, after an experimental period, Fusion Tables was integrated in Google Docs and is now a feature of Google Drive since this last supplanted Google Docs, inheriting its functionality and adding improved storage capabilities. The Google Maps API features the `FusionTablesLayer` constructor, which allows you to display data coming from Fusion Tables on the map, in the form of points and other geometries. By combining Google Maps JavaScript API and Fusion Tables data, it is possible to have at your disposal a sort of GIS. You can indeed modify data on the tables, perform different types of queries, and see the results displayed on the map. Official documentation on the API's `FusionTablesLayer` constructor is available here: `https://developers.google.com/maps/documentation/javascript/layers#FusionTables`.

There is also a specific API available, called Fusion Tables API, that, among other things, makes it possible to connect Fusion Tables with external databases. More information is on the API's official page: `https://developers.google.com/fusiontables/`. We will not use the Fusion tables API here – only of the object `FusionTablesLayer` offered by the Google Maps JavaScript API.

When you display a data set on the map using FusionTablesLayer, similar to what happened with `KmlLayer`, points and other geometric elements are not drawn by the client device but are rendered on the server that then sends the drawn tiles to the client device. This way, the CPU and memory load on the device is very limited and it is possible to fluently display large amounts of POIs and complex geometries, aspects that make FusionTablesLayer particularly indicated when developing for mobile devices. Table 5-3 gives you an overview of the pros and cons of this method. Note that these considerations apply also to other constructors that work as `Marker` like `Polyline`, `Polygon`, etc.

Table 5-3. FusionTablesLayer Constructor Pros and Cons

PROS	CONS
Server-side tiles elaboration allows the app to display large numbers of markers on the map without slowing the performances.	You need to store your data in publicly accessible tables (unless you use the Google Maps API For Business).
Data stored in tables allows data queries (also spatial queries) and very easy updating procedures.	You have less control over the POIs aspect (for example, icons image and size).

In the following pages I show you how to use Google Fusion Tables to display on the map the U2-related POIs I have already dealt with in the previous paragraphs. The steps to follow are the following:

1. Create a table in Fusion Tables containing the data necessary to generate the POIs.

2. Prepare the data so that it is properly displayed on the map.

3. Import Fusion Tables data on the map using the `FusionTablesLayer` constructor.

4. Once the data is imported on the map, you can perform queries on it, as I will show you later.

Creating a Table with Fusion Tables

To create a table with Fusion Tables, you need a Google Account. If you do not have one, you can easily register one here: `https://accounts.google.com/SignUp`. Once you are registered, open the page `http://www.google.com/fusiontables/`. Click on the button See my tables that is located on the top-right corner of the page. You will be presented a page from the Google Drive service like the one shown in Figure 5-21. (You could also directly access the Google Drive page: `drive.google.com`.)

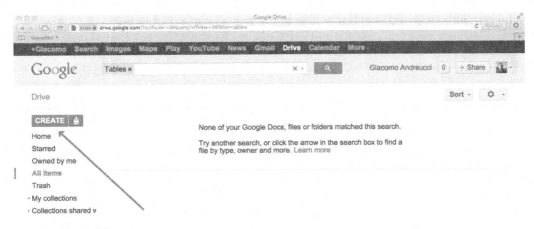

Figure 5-21. The Google Drive page

Adding a New Table

Click on the Create button on the left side of the page (Figure 5-21), then click on More, and finally click on Fusion Table (experimental), as shown in Figure 5-22.

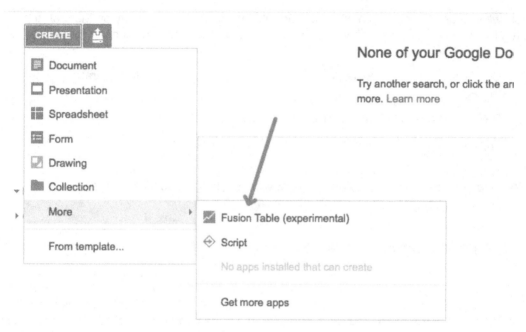

Figure 5-22. The Google Drive page

You will be presented with a dialog box similar to the one shown in Figure 5-23.

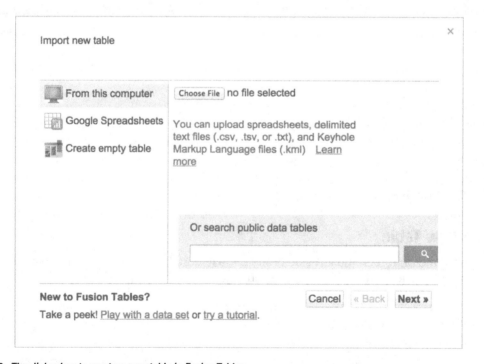

Figure 5-23. The dialog box to create a new table in Fusion Tables

As you can see in the available options, you can create a table by importing data from your computer (data can be spreadsheets, delimited text files like CSV, TSV, TXT, and also KML files), by importing data from Google Spreadsheets or by creating a table from scratch. When importing data, you have to pay attention to the file size. There are some limits – for instance the maximum size permitted for a single file is generally 100 MB; there is also a quota of up to 250 MB per user. When someone shares a table with you or if a table is in your trash, it does not count against your quota. For more information about permitted types and sizes to import, consult the page http://support.google.com/fusiontables/bin/answer.py?hl=en&answer=171181.

To show data on the map, no matter what method is used to create a table, the data must have a field that contains geographic information to allow for positioning on the map. The geographic information needed can be sets of coordinatesor even addresses that can be geocoded by Fusion Tables and then shown on the map.

Importing KML Data

For our example, we are going to import KML data rather than build the table from scratch. This way, we can reuse KML data from the previous example (method 2). I select the KML file u2pois.kml containing the three sample POIs we saw in the previous sections, and then I click on the Next button. As you can see in Figure 5-24, Fusion Tables recognizes the different elements of the KML file and sorts them into different columns, one containing the Description field, one containing the Name field, and a third one containing the geometric and geographic data (in this case, points and their coordinates). Fusion Tables is also able to identify a row containing the column names.

Figure 5-24. Fusion Tables KML importation dialog box

In Figure 5-25 I show you the correspondence between the Fusion Tables columns of the imported KML file and the corresponding fields of KML file's properties in Google Earth.

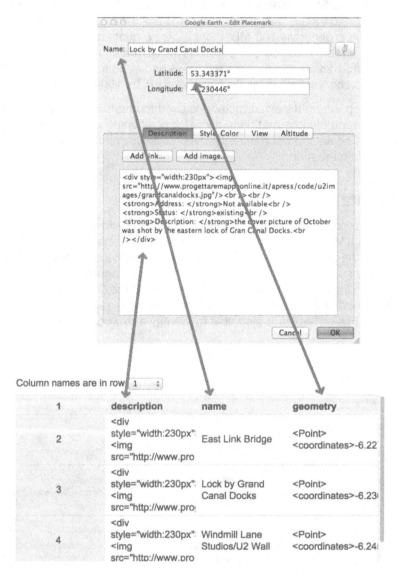

Figure 5-25. *Correspondence between the Fusion Tables columns of the imported KML file and the corresponding fields of KML file's properties in Google Earth*

Click on the Next button to proceed to the next step. (A dialog box is shown where you can define the name of the table and other fields.) You can also leave the default values, as shown in Figure 5-26.

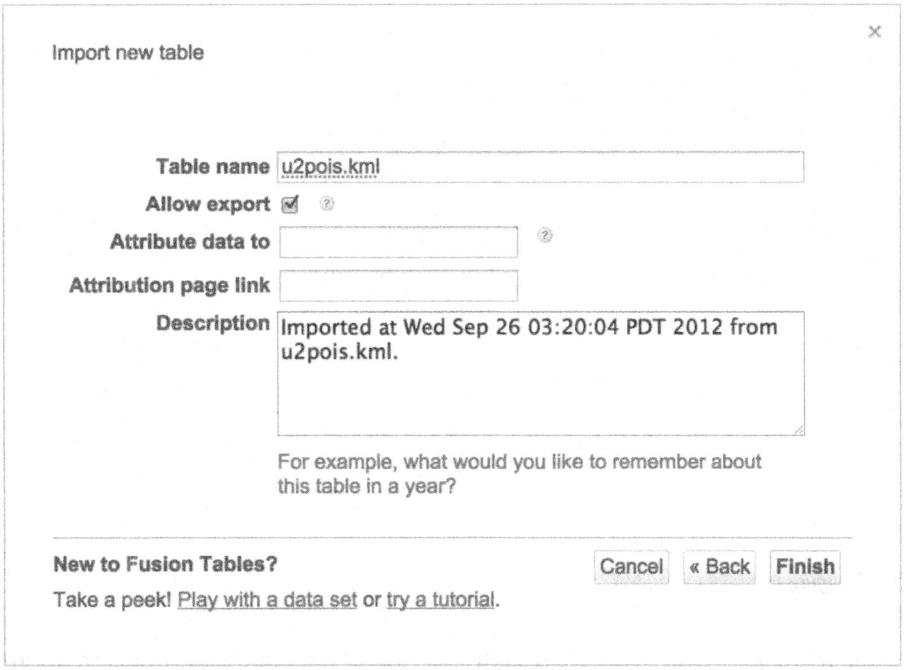

Figure 5-26. Name and other table properties

By clicking on the Finish button, the table is then created. In Figure 5-27, I show you how the table appears in the standard Fusion Tables visualization.

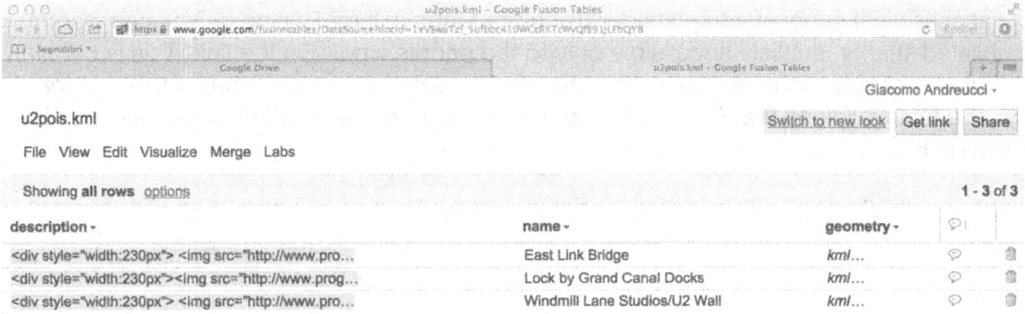

Figure 5-27. The table created

Preparing the Data to Be Displayed on the Map

Similar to a spreadsheet, every column of the table can be set for different data types (Text, Number, Location, Date/Time). In the example, the *description* and *name* columns should be of type Text while the *geometry* column must be of type Location, since this type indicates a column that will be used to georeference the data on the map. To change the type of column, click on Edit in the File menu, then Modify columns. In the Configure columns dialog box (Figure 5-28), you can then set the appropriate type for every column and also change its name and the format.

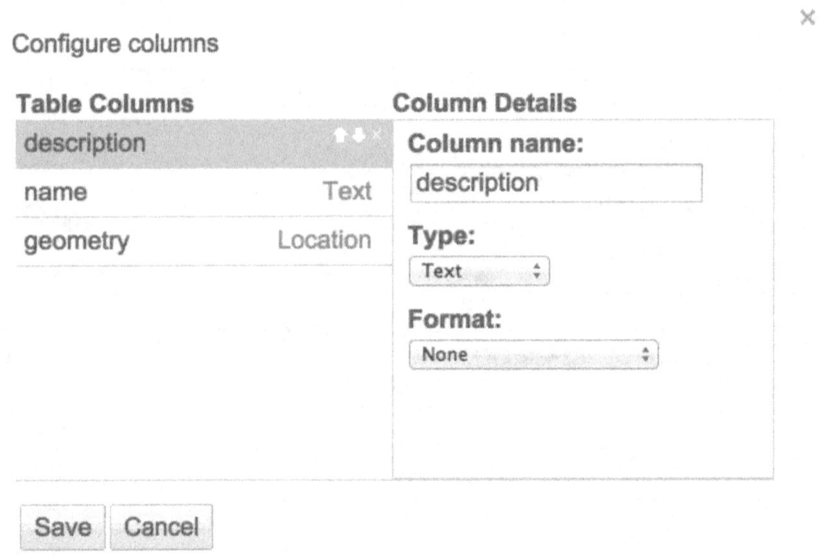

Configure columns

Table Columns		Column Details

Table Columns

description	⬆⬇✕
name	Text
geometry	Location

Column Details

Column name:

description

Type:

Text ⬍

Format:

None ⬍

Save   Cancel

Figure 5-28. The Configure columns dialog box

If you don't have a column containing coordinates or geometries but you know the addresses of some points you want to show on the map, you can write the addresses in one column and then use the column as the Location column. In this case, you need to geocode the addresses in the column by clicking on the File menu and then Geocode. To show Fusion Tables data on a map using the Google Maps JavaScript API, the table must be public (unless you use the Maps API Premier, which is not free).

This could be a problem for those cases where you need the table data to be protected and not publicly accessible. I suggest you consider using the Maps API for Business. You can also make the tables unlisted–that is, publicly accessible only to the people who own the link. This is certainly not a method for completely protecting them, but at least the data is kept more private. To set the sharing settings of a table, click on the Share button at the top-right corner. A dialog box will open like the one shown in Figure 5-29.

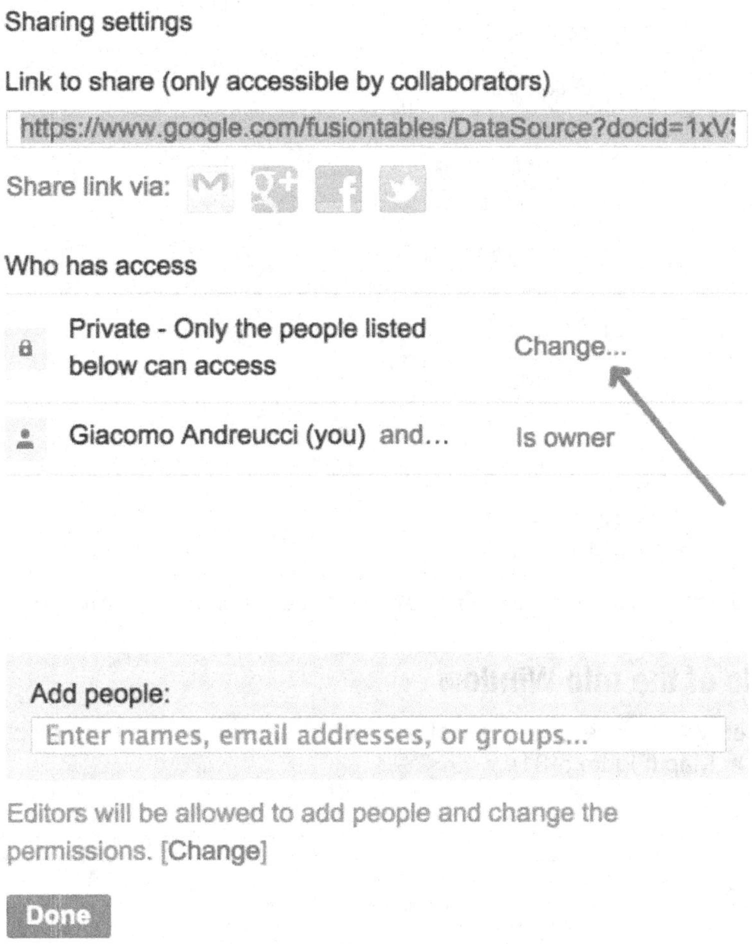

Sharing settings

Link to share (only accessible by collaborators)

https://www.google.com/fusiontables/DataSource?docid=1xV!

Share link via: M 🔲 f 🔲

Who has access

🔒   Private - Only the people listed   Change...
      below can access

👤   Giacomo Andreucci (you) and...   Is owner

Add people:

Enter names, email addresses, or groups...

Editors will be allowed to add people and change the
permissions. [Change]

Done

Figure 5-29. *The Sharing settings dialog box*

Next you click on the Change button (Figure 5-29). In the following dialog box, you need to select
Anyone with the link or Public for using the table data inside Google Maps (Figure 5-30). I suggest
you select Anyone with the link (that would be unlisted), unless you have a specific reason to make
your data completely public (that is, searchable inside the public database of Fusion Tables here
http://www.google.com/fusiontables/search). After you have selected the desired settings, click
Save and then Done.

Sharing settings

Visibility options:

○ **Public on the web**
   Anyone on the Internet can find and access. No
   sign-in required.

◉ **Anyone with the link**
   Anyone who has the link can access. No sign-in
   required.

○ **Private**
   Only people explicitly granted permission can
   access. Sign-in required.

[**Save**]   [Cancel]

Figure 5-30. To show the data through the Google Maps JS API, it is necessary to make it Public or unlisted

Define the Style of the Info Window

Once the table is set, you can get a preview of the data displayed on the map by clicking in the File menu on Visualize ➤ Map (Figure 5-31).

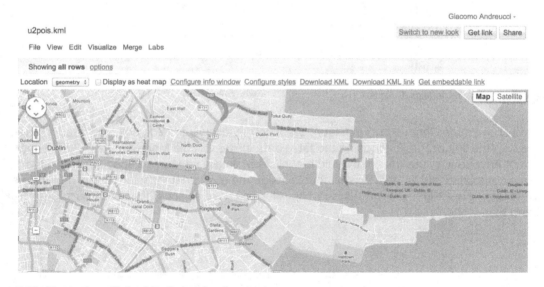

Figure 5-31. The preview with the data displayed on the map

Now you can customize some of the map elements. First, it is important to define the aspect of the info window that opens when a POI is clicked. Fusion Tables offers a set of default settings for the info window but generally they need some customization. To proceed, click on the Configure info window link among the links just above the map. In the dialog box that appears, select the Custom panel (Figure 5-32).

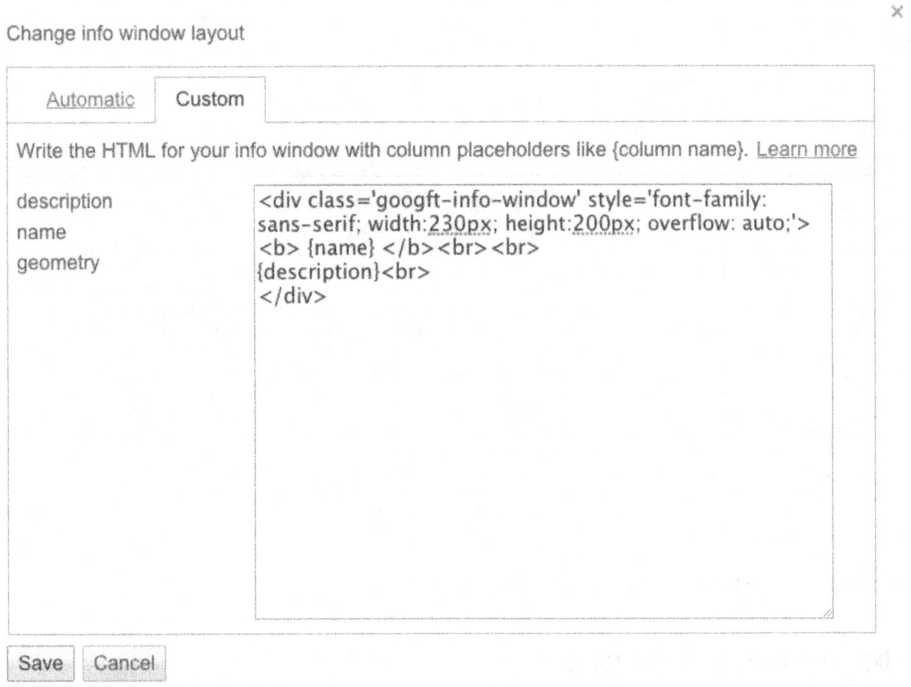

Figure 5-32. How to customize the info window content

Here you can create an HTML template that specifies the layout of the info windows. To pull in data from each row of a table, use the column's name inside curly braces: `{Column Name}`. For example, I have a column named "Name" in the table, so I put {name} into the HTML template. Note that in the example, all the content of the info window, except name and coordinates, was included inside the field description of the original KML, so here I simply put `{description}` below `{name}`. To adapt the info window to iOS devices, it is also necessary to enable scrolling so that the content inside the info window can be scrolled down if it is too long to be shown immediately. Scrolling is not activated by default; you have to wrap the template inside a `<div>` element. You can use the default `<div>` provided in the template and then, inside the `style` attribute of the `<div>` you have to specify the info window's size, like in the example: `width:230px; height:200px;overflow: auto;`.

Once you have defined the HTML template, press Save and then check it out in the map preview (Figure 5-33). If you are not satisfied with it, you can click again on Configure info window, modify the template, and then click again on Save it. The template is now applied to all the info windows and changes will be shown immediately in the map preview. To learn more about how to customize info window's content in Fusion tables, see also `http://support.google.com/fusiontables/bin/answer.py?hl=en&answer=171216`.

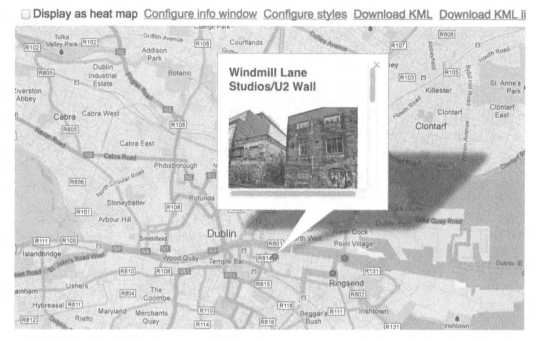

Figure 5-33. The info window with the custom template we defined

Defining the Style of the Markers

It is now possible to customize styles for the marker icon by clicking on the link Configure styles. The Change map styles dialog box opens. If you want to change the default marker icon, click on the Marker icon on the left side of the dialog box (Figure 5-34).

Figure 5-34. How to change the default marker icon

Unfortunately it is not possible to use a custom image as an icon; you can select an icon only among the ones in the list. Note that there are two types of icons: "small" and "large." Since we are going to use Fusion Tables for iOS devices, I suggest you select icons of the "large" type, because they are easier to spot and to touch on the map. (Users can get somewhat frustrated when they have to spot and touch the icons of type "small.") There are cases, especially when you have to display thousands of markers, when it might be better to use the "small" type to improve visibility in areas crowded with markers. Once you have selected the icon, click on Save.

Importing Fusion Tables Data on the Map Using the `FusionTablesLayer` Constructor

Once the table is ready, you can connect it with the Google Maps JavaScript API using the `FusionTablesLayer` constructor. It creates a layer from a public Fusion Table using the table's Encrypted ID, which can be found by clicking on File > About in the Fusion Tables File menu. Once the dialog box has opened, you can easily copy the Encrypted ID (Figure 5-35).

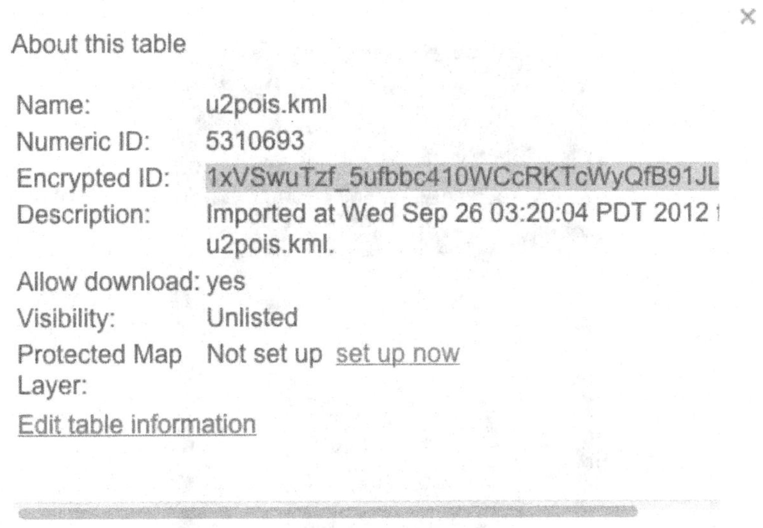

About this table

Name: u2pois.kml
Numeric ID: 5310693
Encrypted ID: 1xVSwuTzf_5ufbbc410WCcRKTcWyQfB91JL
Description: Imported at Wed Sep 26 03:20:04 PDT 2012
                  u2pois.kml.
Allow download: yes
Visibility: Unlisted
Protected Map   Not set up set up now
Layer:
Edit table information

Figure 5-35. The Encrypted ID of the table

To add a Fusion Tables layer to your map, you have to create the layer, passing a query object with the following elements:

- A `select` property set with the column name containing the location information. You must use quotes around any column name that contains spaces, reserved words, or that does not begin with a letter.

- A `from` property whose value is the Encrypted ID.

In the following code, I show you how to use FusionTablesLayer to display data on the map from the previously created table (the code is placed inside initialize():

```
var layer = new google.maps.FusionTablesLayer({

query: {
    select: 'geometry',
    from: '1xVSwuTzf_5ufbbc41OWCcRKTcWyQfB91JLEbQY8'
  },
});
```

After creating the layer, to display it on the map you need to use the setMap() method, as with any other overlay.

```
layer.setMap(map);
```

In Figure 5-36 you can see the table's data displayed on the sample app. Note that users can easily scroll down the data inside the info window thanks to the HTML customization applied.

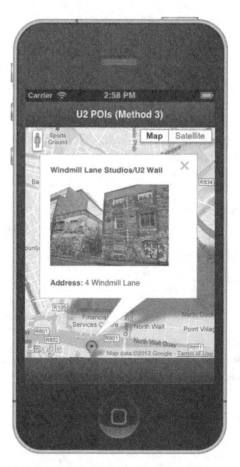

Figure 5-36. The table's data is now displayed on the sample app

If you want to try Fusion Tables without having to prepare your data, you can train yourself by using public tables that you can search here: `http://www.google.com/fusiontables/search`. Note that to show a table's data on a map, the table must always have a column containing location information.

Performing Queries

The FusionTablesLayer constructor allows you to query the table's data and show the results on the map. Queries are specified inside the already seen query object by setting a `where` field. The following example will make things clearer. This time I use another data set, the public table "Crime Stats London 2011-10", available here (Figure 5-37):
`https://www.google.com/fusiontables/DataSource?docid=1tYve4qCvwqKmAAB2LgnkkQOp5akPxTZHuaGHaeI`

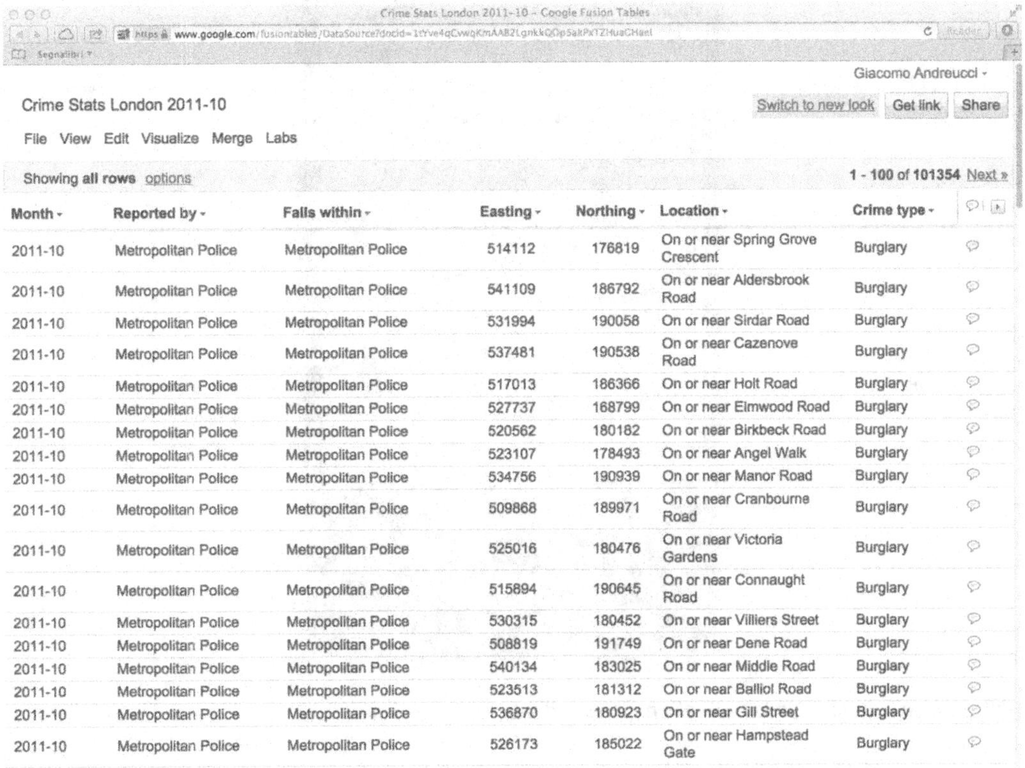

Crime Stats London 2011-10

File View Edit Visualize Merge Labs

Showing all rows options — 1 - 100 of 101354 Next »

Month	Reported by	Falls within	Easting	Northing	Location	Crime type
2011-10	Metropolitan Police	Metropolitan Police	514112	176819	On or near Spring Grove Crescent	Burglary
2011-10	Metropolitan Police	Metropolitan Police	541109	186792	On or near Aldersbrook Road	Burglary
2011-10	Metropolitan Police	Metropolitan Police	531994	190058	On or near Sirdar Road	Burglary
2011-10	Metropolitan Police	Metropolitan Police	537481	190538	On or near Cazenove Road	Burglary
2011-10	Metropolitan Police	Metropolitan Police	517013	186366	On or near Holt Road	Burglary
2011-10	Metropolitan Police	Metropolitan Police	527737	168799	On or near Elmwood Road	Burglary
2011-10	Metropolitan Police	Metropolitan Police	520562	180182	On or near Birkbeck Road	Burglary
2011-10	Metropolitan Police	Metropolitan Police	523107	178493	On or near Angel Walk	Burglary
2011-10	Metropolitan Police	Metropolitan Police	534756	190939	On or near Manor Road	Burglary
2011-10	Metropolitan Police	Metropolitan Police	509868	189971	On or near Cranbourne Road	Burglary
2011-10	Metropolitan Police	Metropolitan Police	525016	180476	On or near Victoria Gardens	Burglary
2011-10	Metropolitan Police	Metropolitan Police	515894	190645	On or near Connaught Road	Burglary
2011-10	Metropolitan Police	Metropolitan Police	530315	180452	On or near Villiers Street	Burglary
2011-10	Metropolitan Police	Metropolitan Police	508819	191749	On or near Dene Road	Burglary
2011-10	Metropolitan Police	Metropolitan Police	540134	183025	On or near Middle Road	Burglary
2011-10	Metropolitan Police	Metropolitan Police	523513	181312	On or near Balliol Road	Burglary
2011-10	Metropolitan Police	Metropolitan Police	536870	180923	On or near Gill Street	Burglary
2011-10	Metropolitan Police	Metropolitan Police	526173	185022	On or near Hampstead Gate	Burglary

Figure 5-37. The table "Crime Stats London 2011-10"

In Figure 5-37 you can see that the table contains a Crime type column that indicates the type of crime committed. I want to perform a query that shows on the map only the crimes of type Burglary. First, let us have a view of the map showing all the crime types (Figure 5-38). Here is the code to show the above map using the `FusionTablesLayer` constructor.

```
var layer = new google.maps.FusionTablesLayer({
  query: {
    select: 'Location',
```

```
    from: '1tYve4qCvwqKmAAB2LgnkkQOp5akPxTZHuaGHaeI'
  },
});

layer.setMap(map);
```

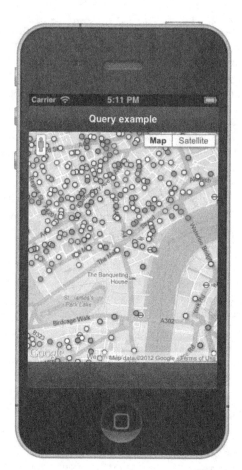

Figure 5-38. *An area of central London with all crime types displayed on the map*

Now let us add a query to the previous code:

```
var layer = new google.maps.FusionTablesLayer({
  query: {
    select: 'Location',
    from: '1tYve4qCvwqKmAAB2LgnkkQOp5akPxTZHuaGHaeI',
    where: "'Crime type' = 'Burglary'"
  },
});

layer.setMap(map);
```

As you can see, inside the where property I indicated the name of the column ('Crime type') and the value it has to be equal to ('Burglary'). Note that I had to put the name of the column and the type of crime inside quotes. In Figure 5-39 you can see the result of the query.

Figure 5-39. The result of the query showing on the map only the crime type Burglary

You can view the many search operators available to perform queries in the comprehensive specifications: https://developers.google.com/fusiontables/docs/developers_reference#Select.

I suggest you also consult this page, where many examples are made available (for instance, queries based on drop-down menu choices and checkboxes): https://developers.google.com/fusiontables/docs/sample_code#FTLayers.

Among the available types of queries with Fusion Tables, there are spatial queries, which I will discuss in the next section.

Spatial Queries

Spatial queries are one of the most interesting functions of Fusion Tables. They basically consist of queries made according to spatial criteria. You can use spatial queries to perform three types of tasks:

1. Find all features that are located within (or overlap with) a given distance from a location.

2. Find all features that are located within (or overlap with) a given bounding box.

3. Find a given number of features closest to a location.

To perform spatial queries, you to need to use specific Fusion Tables operators. In the following example, I show you how to perform a spatial query of the third type, that finds and displays on the map a given number of features closest to a location. For this example, I use the previous London data, setting St. James's Square (51.507244, -0.135299) as the center for the spatial query. I chose to display the two crimes closest to the location. In the map the location is indicated by a marker. Here is the code:

```
var layer = new google.maps.FusionTablesLayer({
  query: {
    select: 'Location',
    from: '1tYve4qCvwqKmAAB2LgnkkQOp5akPxTZHuaGHaeI',
    orderBy: "ST_DISTANCE('Location', LATLNG(51.507244, -0.135299))",
    limit: 2
  }
});


layer.setMap(map);
```

As you can see, the syntax I used is pretty self-explanatory. You have to set the values for the query's orderBy and limit properties (pay attention to the use of quotes). In Figure 5-40 I show on the left a screenshot of the St. James's Square area in London without the query activated and on the right the result of the query.

Figure 5-40. The result of the spatial query

As I mentioned, different types of spatial queries can be performed. You can view examples at https://developers.google.com/fusiontables/docs/sample_code#FTLayers, in the Spatial queries section. I suggest you also read an introductory article from the Google Geo Developers blog: http://googlegeodevelopers.blogspot.ie/2010/11/search-your-geo-data-using-spatial.html.

The syntax to perform spatial queries used in the article is old, but the concepts are still valid.

Summary

The goal of this chapter was to introduce you to creating and displaying geographic content on the map using overlays. I showed you the types of overlays currently made available by the Google Maps JavaScript API and the general methods necessary to manipulate them. I then explained three major methods to display POIs on a map: using the Marker API constructor, using the KmlLayer constructor, and using the FusionTablesLayer constructor. I illustrated the pros and cons of these methods. Before moving on to the next chapter, you should know how to do the following:

- Add, remove, and delete overlays from a map.

- Use the Marker constructor to display POIs on a map and configure a marker's options and related info window.

- Use the KmlLayer constructor to import and display KML data on the map (for example, POIs and geometric elements).

- Create and configure a table with Google Fusion Tables.

- Use the FusionTablesLayer constructor to show Fusion Tables data on a map.

- Perform queries and spatial queries using the FusionTablesLayer constructor.

Chapter 6

Implementing Geolocation

Geolocation is undoubtedly one the the most relevant functions that a geo app may implement, so in this chapter I present the procedures for handling geolocation in an app. I will consider geolocation capabilities offered by HTML5 with the W3C Geolocation API. Since this is the last chapter dedicated to realizing map-based web apps, I will conclude it by gathering some of the functions I showed you in previous chapters to form a simple, yet complete, U2's Dublin web app.

Understanding Geolocation

Using specific sensors and methods, geolocation can identify the position of a device – in our case, an iOS device – within a geographic reference system (that is using geographical coordinates, latitude and longitude). You can approach geolocation in a number of ways, including analysizing an IP address (IP geolocation), a cell phone network, the Wi-Fi networks present in the area, and the use of a GPS chip. However, when it comes to accuracy, the methods do not produce the same results. For instance, Global Positioning System (GPS) location data is generally more accurate than Wi-Fi location data. It is important to know that some of the methods, like IP address geolocation, are available both on computer and mobile devices. This can be useful if you want to create map-based apps across multiple platforms.

In their latest versions, iOS devices like iPhone and iPad integrate different sensors and techniques to get location data, like Assisted GPS and GLONASS, cellular networks, Wi-Fi data, and IP geolocation. By integrating different data sources, the process of locating a device's position with good accuracy (a margin of error of a few meters) is now very efficient. This has made it possible to create navigation apps and augmented reality apps that show information related to POIs that are located around the user.

The W3C Geolocation API

In the first part of this chapter I will show you how to exploit geolocation capabilities of iOS devices integrating location data with Google Maps. To get location data, we will use a set of APIs proposed by the World Wide Web Consortium (W3C) and called the W3C Geolocation API. With this API, the

W3C hopes to standardize on an interface that retrieves the geographical location information for a client-side device. The API defines a set of objects, ECMAScript (that is, JavaScript) standard compliant, that can be used in an app to get a client's device location by consulting Location Information Servers, which are transparent for the API. The most common sources of location information are IP address, Wi-Fi and Bluetooth MAC address, radio-frequency identification (RFID), Wi-Fi geolocation, GSM/CDMA cell networks, and device GPS.

W3C Geolocation API Current Support

The current status of the W3C Geolocation API is "Proposed Recommendation," not yet a W3C Recommendation (which means an official standard). The W3C Geolocation Specification is available here: `http://dev.w3.org/geo/api/spec-source.html`.

Almost all major browsers support the W3C Geolocation API, as listed here:

- Apple Safari: version 5.0 and higher

- Apple Mobile Safari: iOS 3.0 and higher

- Google Android: version 2.0 and higher

- Google Chrome: version 5.0 and higher

- Microsoft Internet Explorer: version 9.0 and higher

- Mozilla Firefox: version 3.5 and higher

- Opera: version 10.6 and higher

Using W3C Geolocation API allows you to make the app geolocation work not only on iOS devices but on Android mobile devices and desktop computers as well.

Implementing the W3C Geolocation API

W3C API geolocation is implemented through the `Geolocation` object, which is an instance variable of the `Navigator` object: `navigator.geolocation`. The W3C API makes available these three geolocation methods:

- `getCurrentPosition(successCallback, errorCallback, options)` – used to obtain a one-shot position. I will show you how to use the method to get current device position and then center the map and a marker on the obtained position.

- `watchPosition(successCallback, errorCallback, options)` – used to obtain updates every time device position changes. I will show you how to use the method to update the center of the map and the position of a marker every time the position of the device changes.

- `clearWatch(watchTimerID)` – used to stop watchPosition() when it is running. I will show you how to apply it.

In the next sections I will show you how to implement these three methods. But before you can implement the methods, you must first receive user permission for geolocation (see the sidebar). Without user permission you cannot collect location data.

ALWAYS ASK FOR PERMISSION

In Section 4, Security and privacy considerations, The WC Geolocation Specification states that: "A conforming implementation of this specification must provide a mechanism that protects the user's privacy and this mechanism should ensure that no location information is made available through this API without the user's express permission."

Thus, when using W3C API location methods, you need to know that users will be asked for permission for geolocation. Every browser has its own way of asking for user permission, but the basic mechanism is the same: users cannot avoid answering the request; a negative or positive answer is required. Usually, browsers also ask users if they want to save permission data so that the browser can remember it without asking for it every time the geolocation function is triggered. In iOS devices the request for permission is implemented as shown in Figure 6-1.

Figure 6-1. Example of a web app requesting user permission for geolocation on an iPhone device

The getCurrentPosition() Method

The getCurrentPosition() method allows the app to get a one-shot position. For example, this would be used to center a map or display a marker whose position does not need to be continuously updated. In the next paragraphs I describe how the method works and which are its constituent parts. Then I will show you some JavaScript code to implement the method. In the code example the method will be used to get current device position and then set the center of the map on the obtained position. A marker will be centered on the obtained position as well. I will then comment the example and illustrate in detail the properties of the objects used in the method (Position, PositionError, PositionOptions).

How the getCurrentPosition() Method Works

When called, getCurrentPosition() immediately returns and then asynchronously attempts to get the current location of the device by using available Location Information Servers, which, as I mentioned earlier, are transparent for the API. If the attempt is successful, the successCallback function is invoked with a Position object, indicating the current location of the device. The successCallback function is required; you may also specify an errorCallback function that will be invoked in case the location attempt fails.

This function will handle a PositionError object, indicating the reason for the failure. It is possible (although not required) to specify a set of options as a third argument.

getCurrentPosition() Example

This example shows the code for a simple app that makes use of the W3C Geolocation API to get current device position, and then creates the map and centers it on the obtained position. The app also displays a marker centered on the current position. This function includes a callback function, which is triggered in case of an error. It returns an appropriate error message by reading the PositionError object. Here is the code of the initialize() function (Listing 6-1).

Listing 6-1. Implementation of the getCurrentPosition() method

```
function initialize() {

  navigator.geolocation.getCurrentPosition(function (position) {
    positionCoordinates = new google.maps.LatLng(position.coords.latitude,
position.coords.longitude);

  var myOptions = {
      center: positionCoordinates,
      zoom: 14,
      mapTypeId: google.maps.MapTypeId.ROADMAP

  }
```

```
      var map = new google.maps.Map(document.getElementById("map_canvas"), myOptions);

      var marker = new google.maps.Marker({
        position: positionCoordinates,
        map: map
      });
    },
    function (error) {
      var typeOfError = error.code;
      switch (typeOfError) {

      case(1):
        alert("Permission denied");
        break;

      case (2):
        alert("Position unavailable");
        break;

      case (3):
        alert("Timeout error");
        break;
      }
    },
    {
      enableHighAccuracy: true

  });

}
```

Let us now take a closer look at the above code. As you can see, the object of type `Position` possesses a coords attribute that contains latitude and longitude coordinates, which can be accessed this way: `position.coords.latitude` and `position.coords.longitude`.

The coords Attribute

The coords attribute has a complete set of properties to define the coordinates's interface, as shown in Table 6-1.

Table 6-1. coords Properties

Property	Notes
coords.latitude	The geographic coordinate reference system used by the attributes is the World Geodetic System (2d) [WGS84]. The latitude and longitude attributes are specified in decimal degrees.
coords.longitude	The geographic coordinate reference system used by the attributes is the World Geodetic System (2d) [WGS84]. The latitude and longitude attributes are specified in decimal degrees.
coords.altitude	Denotes the height of the position, specified in meters above the [WGS84] ellipsoid.
coords.accuracy	Denotes the accuracy level of the latitude and longitude coordinates. It is specified in meters and the value of the attribute must be a non-negative real number.
coords.altitudeAccuracy	Specified in meters and the value must be a non-negative real number.
coords.heading	Denotes the direction of travel of the hosting device and is specified in degrees, where $0° \leq$ heading $< 360°$, counting clockwise relative to true north.
coords.speed	Denotes the magnitude of the horizontal component of the hosting device's current velocity and is specified in meters per second. The value of this attribute must be a non-negative real number.

Only three of the properties are guaranteed to be there (coords.latitude, coords.longitude, and coords.accuracy). The rest might come back null, depending on the capabilities of your device and the Location Information Server that it talks to. Heading and speed properties are calculated based on the user's previous position, if available.

The timestamp Attribute

In addition to the coords attribute, the Position object possesses the timestamp attribute, which represents the time when the Position object was acquired; timestamp is represented as a DOMTimeStamp and it works similarly to the Date JavaScript object.

Returning to commenting the previous sample code (in the section called "getCurrentPosition() Example"), if the geolocation attempt is positive, the Position object is updated with the current location coordinates on which the map gets centered and the marker positioned, as you can see in Figure 6-2.

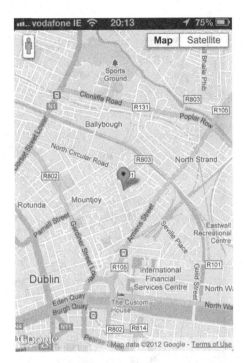

Figure 6-2. *The map is centered on the current device's location and a marker is added and positioned in the center*

Handling Errors

If the geolocation attempt fails, the second argument of getCurrentPosition() is triggered (the errorCallback function). The callback function will handle a PositionError object indicating the error code. The code attribute of the PositionError object returns one of the following code errors:

- PERMISSION_DENIED (numeric value 1). The location acquisition process failed because the user did not give permission to use the Geolocation API.

- POSITION_UNAVAILABLE (numeric value 2). The position of the device could not be determined. For instance, one or more of the location providers used in the location acquisition process reported an internal error that caused the process to fail entirely.

- TIMEOUT (numeric value 3). The length of time specified by the timeout property has elapsed before the implementation could successfully acquire a new Position object (later I will explain you how to set a timeout value).

By using the code attribute of the PositionError, it is then possible to display an appropriate error message, as is done in the last part of the sample code presented above. (The result is shown in Figure 6-3.)

Figure 6-3. *Example of an error message generated by analyzing the* `code` *property of the* `PositionError` *object. In this case, the error code was POSITION_UNAVAILABLE (numeric value 2)*

Position Options

The `getCurrentPosition()` method may also take as a third argument (not required) a set of options, which is an object literal of type `PositionOptions`. This object has three optional properties named `enableHighAccuracy`, `timeout`, and `maximumAge`.

Let's review these now.

enableHighAccuracy

This property takes a boolean value. If the `PositionOptions` parameter in `getCurrentPosition()` or `watchPosition()` is omitted, the default value used for the `enableHighAccuracy` property is `false`. The same default value is used when the `enableHighAccuracy` property is omitted. This property, if set to `true`, indicates that the application would like to receive the best possible location results. This may result in slower response times or increased power consumption. The user might also deny this capability, or the device might not be able to provide more accurate results than if the flag was not specified. The intended purpose of this attribute is to allow applications to inform the implementation that they do not require high accuracy geolocation fixes so as to avoid using geolocation providers that consume a significant amount of power (for example, GPS). In the previous code example, the enableHighAccuracy property was enabled:

```
{
enableHighAccuracy: true
}
```

timeout

This property indicates the maximum length of time (expressed in milliseconds) that is allowed to pass from the call to getCurrentPosition() or watchPosition() until the corresponding successCallback function is invoked. If it is not possible to successfully acquire a new Position before the given timeout elapses, and no other errors have occurred in this interval, then the corresponding errorCallback must be invoked with a PositionError object whose error code is set toTIMEOUT (numeric value 3). The time that is spent obtaining the user permission is not included in the period covered by the timeout attribute. The timeout attribute applies only to the location acquisition operation. If the PositionOptions parameter to getCurrentPosition() or watchPosition() is omitted, the default value used for the timeout attribute is Infinity. If a negative value is supplied, the timeout value is considered to be 0. The same default value is used when the timeout property is omitted.

maximumAge

This property indicates that the application will accept a cached position whose age is no greater than the specified time in milliseconds. If maximumAge is set to 0, the implementation must immediately attempt to acquire a new Position object. If you set the maximumAge to Infinity, the implementation will return a cached position regardless of its age. If an implementation does not have a cached position available whose age is less or equal to the specified maximumAge, then it must acquire a new Position object. In the case of watchPosition(), the maximumAge refers to the first Position object returned by the implementation. If the PositionOptions parameter in getCurrentPosition() or watchPosition() is omitted, the default value used for the maximumAge attribute is 0. The same default value is used if a negative value is supplied or when the maximumAge property is omitted. The maximumAge property is useful for avoiding an excessive waste of resources spent getting fresh position data when that information is not necessary. Here is a simple example:

```
navigator.geolocation.getCurrentPosition(
successCallback, errorCallback, {
  maximumAge: 80000
}); but you had be
```

It is a geolocation simulation based on the previous code. The implementation invokes getCurrentPosition() and obtains a position taken at 08.00 a.m. At 08.01 a.m., getCurrentPosition() is called again. The position that will be sent this time will not be actually obtained at 08.01 a.m. but it will the one obtained at 08.00 a.m. since maximumAge is set to

80,000 milliseconds, which is 80 seconds. This way, the device will not waste time and resources on calculating a new position since it will reuse the one cached. Thus, you may set maximumAge according to the level of freshness of position data required by the app, avoiding wasted resources. Now that you know how to implement a function to retrieve a one-shot position, it is time to move on to examining the watchPosition() method, which the W3C Geolocation API makes available to get position updates.

The watchPosition() method

As I have just shown, the getCurrentPosition() method allows you to obtain a one-shot position. However, if you want the app to use continuously updated position data, use the watchPosition() method, which is specifically meant for this kind of application. In the next pages I will describe how the method works and which are its constituent parts. Then I will show you some JavaScript code to implement the method. In the code example, a map gets centered on a set of coordinates obtained by using watchPosition(). Also, a marker is added to the map and its coordinates are the same used to center the map. Once the map and marker are created, the app, always using the watchPosition() method, takes care of updating the center of the map and the position of the marker every time the position of the device changes. After the sample code, I will illustrate the clearWatch() method that you need to use when you want to stop watchPosition().

How the watchPosition() Method Works

The watchPosition() method can take up to three arguments – the same as the getCurrentPosition() method. When called, it immediately returns a long value that uniquely identifies a watch operation and then asynchronously starts the watch operation. This operation first attempts to obtain the current location of the device. If the attempt is successful, the successCallback function is called with a new Position object, indicating the current location of the device. If the attempt fails, the errorCallback function is invoked with a new PositionError object, indicating the relative error code. The watch operation then continues to monitor the position of the device and call the appropriate callback function every time the position changes. The watch operation will continue until the clearWatch method is called with the corresponding identifier. Note that is not possible to set the polling interval; it is up to the device itself to determine the best interval.

watchPosition() Example

Here I show you a simple example using watchPosition(). The app will generate a map centered on a set of coordinates obtained using watchPosition(). Also, a marker will be added to the map, and its coordinates will be the same used to center the map. Once the map and marker are created, the app, always using the watchPosition() method, will take care of updating the center of the map and the position of the marker every time the position of the device changes. To update the position of the map and the marker, map.setCenter() and marker.setPosition() methods will be used. A set of options will be passed, setting enableHighAccuracy property to true. Note that even if enableHighAccuracy is set to true, the initial position might not be accurate since while waiting for accurate GPS position data, other less accurate sources can be used for initial geolocating – for instance, IP address or Wi-Fi networks. Here is the code for the script (Listing 6-2)

Listing 6-2. Example of the watchPosition() method

```
var positionCoordinates = null;
var map = null;
var marker = null;
function initialize() {

   navigator.geolocation.watchPosition(function (position) {
      if (positionCoordinates == null) {
         positionCoordinates = new google.maps.LatLng(position.coords.latitude,
position.coords.longitude);
         var myOptions = {
            center: positionCoordinates,
            zoom: 19,
            mapTypeId: google.maps.MapTypeId.ROADMAP
         }
         map = new google.maps.Map(document.getElementById("map_canvas"), myOptions);
         marker = new google.maps.Marker({
            position: positionCoordinates,
            map: map
         });
      }

      else

      {

positionCoordinates = new google.maps.LatLng(position.coords.latitude, position.coords.longitude);
         marker.setPosition(positionCoordinates);
         map.setCenter(positionCoordinates);
      }
   },

   function (error) {
      var typeOfError = error.code;
      switch (typeOfError) {
      case(1):
         alert("Permission denied");
         break;

      case (2):
         alert("Position unavailable");
         break;
```

```
    case (3):
      alert("Timeout error");
      break;
    }
  },

  {
    enableHighAccuracy: true

  });

}
```

Figure 6-4 shows an app running the previous code. The map is re-centered every time the position of the device changes, and a marker is positioned on the coordinates of the current position.

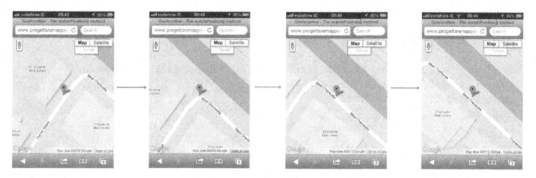

Figure 6-4. The app, running on an iPhone, re-centers the map and repositions the marker every time the position changes

Unfortunately, at the time of writing this chapter, a bug affects iOS 6 devices using `watchPosition()`. The method does not work if the app is added to the Home Screen to be executed full screen. To work around the problem, it is currently necessary to remove from the HTML page the line: `<meta name="apple-mobile-web-app-capable" content="yes">`. This obviously prevents the app from running full screen when launched from the Home Screen, so it is not such a good solution. Hopefully, Apple will fix the bug soon.

The clearWatch Method

You can also stop `watchPosition()` to avoid wasting resources when position data is no longer necessary. To do this it is necessary to use the `clearWatch()` method, which works in a way that is similar to the JavaScript `setInterval()` method. When called, `watchPosition()` returns a long value that uniquely identifies a watch operation and that we can name `watchId`. The `clearWatch()` method takes this value as argument. When `clearWatch()` is called, it first checks the value of the given `watchId` argument. If this value does not correspond to any previously started watch process, then the method returns immediately without taking any further action. Otherwise, the watch process identified by the `watchId` argument is immediately stopped and no further callbacks are invoked.

In the following code, I declare a `watchId` variable, assigning it the value returned by `watchPosition()`, and then I use the `clearWatch()` method, passing the `watchId` variable to it:

```
watchId = navigator.geolocation.watchPosition(omissis);
navigator.geolocation.clearWatch(watchId);
```

By using this code, it is possible to create a button that allows the user to stop position updates.

Putting Things Together

It is now time to put together all the functions and procedures discussed in previous chapters, to churn out a complete U2's Dublin web app. As previously mentioned, the purpose of this app is to show U2's story-related spots in Dublin through an online map. Users access the app from an iOS device (iPhone, iPad, or iPod touch). They will be able to show all the POIs at once, select them using a menu or showing the ones nearest to their current position. By clicking on a POI, users will open its relative info window and scroll through the content (text and images). To assemble this app, you will make use of the following elements:

- Map initialization procedures examined in Chapter 2.
- Controls handling and map styles explained in Chapter 3.
- The jQuery Mobile Interface developed in Chapter 4.
- Fusion Tables layers to display POIs, as explained in Chapter 5.
- Geolocation functions as seen earlier in this chapter.

The app will be composed of three files: u2sdublin.html (it contains the structure of the app web page), u2sdublin.css (it contains the style rules that define some elements of the UI), and u2sdublin.js (it contains the JavaScript code of the functions implemented in the app). Figure 6-5 shows a screenshot of the final U2's Dublin web app.

Figure 6-5. The U2's Dublin web app running on an iPhone

The HTML File

In the HTML file you will have to set the tags necessary to optimize the page for iOS devices and link all the necessary files. Then you will define the structure of the UI interface (header, content area, footer, and buttons). You will also add the content to be displayed in the Info window of the app.

The <head> Element

In the <head> element you set the tags necessary to optimize the web page for iOS and link all the necessary files (CSS, scripts, for example).

Following is the commented code of <head> (Listing 6-3).

Listing 6-3. The commented code of <head>

```
<head>
        <title>
            U2'S DUBLIN
        </title>
        <meta name="viewport" content="width=device-width, initial-scale=1.0,minimum-scale=1.0,
maximum-scale=1.0" />
        <meta name="apple-mobile-web-app-capable" content="yes" />

        <!-- Home Screen icon for iPhone and iPod touch -->
        <link rel="apple-touch-icon" sizes="57x57"
href="http://www.progettaremappeonline.it/apress/code/images/logo114.png" />
        <!-- Home Screen icon for iPhone 5 and iPod touch (5th generation) -->

    <link rel="apple-touch-icon" sizes="114x114"
href="http://www.progettaremappeonline.it/apress/code/images/logo57.png" />
        <!-- Home Screen icon for iPad -->
        <link rel="apple-touch-icon" sizes="72x72"
href="http://www.progettaremappeonline.it/apress/code/images/logo72.png" />
        <!-- Launch image for iPhone and iPod touch -->

<link href="http://www.progettaremappeonline.it/apress/code/images/u2splash320-460.png"
media="(device-width: 320px)" rel="apple-touch-startup-image" />
        <!-- Launch image for iPhone 5 and iPod touch (5th generation) -->

        <link href="http://www.progettaremappeonline.it/apress/code/images/u2splash640-920.png"
media="(device-width: 320px) and (-webkit-device-pixel-ratio: 2)" rel="apple-touch-startup-image" />
        <!-- Launch image for iPad -->

        <link rel="apple-touch-startup-image" sizes="768x1004"
href="http://www.progettaremappeonline.it/apress/code/images/u2splash768-1004.png" media="screen
and (min-device-width: 321px) and (max-device-width: 1024px) and (orientation:portrait)" />
        <meta name="apple-mobile-web-app-status-bar-style" content="translucent" />
        <link rel="stylesheet" href="http://code.jquery.com/mobile/latest/jquery.mobile.min.css" />

  <script src="jquery-1.8.0.min.js"></script>
        <script src="http://code.jquery.com/mobile/latest/jquery.mobile.min.js"></script>
        <script type="text/javascript"
src="http://maps.google.com/maps/api/js?key=AIzaSyBa6jRCpFGLh691Ve_Srm5a7KPqi-
HlrWO&amp;sensor=true"></script>

        <link rel="stylesheet" href="u2sdublin.css" />

        <script type="text/javascript" src="u2sdublin.js"></script>

    </head>
```

As you can see, you have to indicate specific Home Screen icons and launch images for different models of iOS devices. Home Screen icons and launch screen might seem like meaningless elements, but they are very important for giving the app an attractive look and feel. The Home Screen icon especially needs to be carefully chosen to entice the user to click on it when saved on the Home Screen. In Figure 6-6 you can see the Home Screen icon and launch image I used.

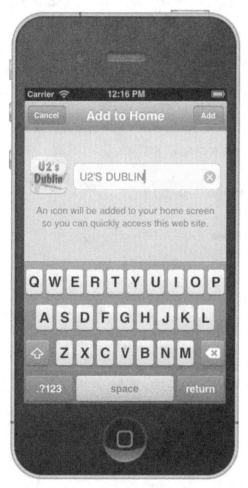

Figure 6-6. The Home Screen icon (left) and launch image (right)

The <body> Element

Inside the <body> element you then define header, content, and footer sections, filling them with the appropriate content and buttons. Later in this chapter I will explain the functions that are called. You can see that a select menu is implemented (I show only some menu options to keep the code short) and an Info dialog box and a message to be shown while tiles are loading are defined (Listing 6-4).

Listing 6-4. The commented code of <body>

```
<body onload="initialize()">

<div data-role="page">

    <!--Define the header and the elements inside of it -->

    <div data-role="header" id="divHeader" data-position="fixed">
        <a href="#infoBox" data-rel="dialog" data-icon="info" class="ui-btn-left">Info</a>
        <h2>U2'S DUBLIN</h2>
        <a href="javascript:showAll()" data-role="button" data-icon="plus" class="ui-
btn-right"><span>All</span></a>
        </div>
        <!--Define the section that contains the map-->
        <div data-role="content">
            <div id="map_canvas"></div>
</div>

        <!--Define the footer and the elements inside of it -->
        <div data-role="footer" id="divFooter" data-position="fixed">

<div data-role="controlgroup" data-type="horizontal" style="margin-top:4px;margin-left:4px;">

        <!-- Structure of the select menu -->
        <select onchange="selectPlace()" name="select-choice-min" id="select-choice-min" data-
mini="true">
            <option selected="selected" value="">
            Choose
            </option>
            <option value="Dockers">
                Dockers Pub
            </option>
            <option value="Bridge">
                East Link Bridge
            </option>
            <option value="Grand Canal Docks">

    Grand Canal Docks
            </option>
            <option value="Hanover">
                Hanover Quay Studios
            </option>
            <option value="O2">
```

```
                    The O2
            </option>
            <option value="Windmill">
                Windmill Lane Studios
            </option>
        </select>
        <!--The button launches the function that shows the nearest spots-->
                <a href="javascript:nearestSpots()" data-role="button" data-icon="star"><span
id="nearestSpotsText">Nearest Spots</span></a>

</div>
        </div>

    </div>

        <!--Content of the Info box-->
        <div data-role="page" id="infoBox">
            <div data-role="header">
                <h1>U2'S DUBLIN</h1>
            </div>
            <div data-role="content">
              <p>This app shows on the Dublin map significant landmarks related to U2 rock band's story.
                <ul>
                    <li>Use the Choose menu to select a specific place.</li>
                    <li>Click on a marker to open its balloon.</li>

<li>Scroll through the balloon content.</li>

            <li>Click on the Nearest spots button to activate your location tracking and show the 2
nearest spots. Click again to stop the process.</li>
                </ul>
                </p>
                <p><a data-rel="back" data-role="button" data-icon="back">Back to the map</a></p>
            </div>
        </div>

        <!--Content to be shown while map tiles are loading -->
        <div id="tilesSplashScreen">
            <table>
                <tr>
                    <td>
                        <img src="loading.gif" />
                        <br />Please wait while the map is loading
</td>
 </tr>
            </table>
        </div>

    </body>
```

Now that we have written the HTML code, let us move on to the CSS part, where aspects of some elements of the UI are defined.

The CSS File

The CSS file is basically the same as the one we examined in Chapter 4 for the jQuery Mobile UI. It defines the positioning of the header, content area, and footer and also the appearance of the splash screen that is displayed while tiles are loading (Listing 6-5).

Listing 6-5. The CSS code

```css
html {
    height:100%;
}

body {
    height:100%;

    margin:0px;
    padding:0px;
}

#divHeader {
    position:absolute;
    top:0px;

    height:40px;
}

#divFooter {
    position:absolute;
    bottom:0px;
    height:40px;
}

#map_canvas {
    width:100%;
    position: absolute;
    top:40px;
    bottom:40px;
    left:0px;
    right:0px;
}

#tilesSplashScreen {
    width:100%;

 z-index: 100;
    position:absolute;
    top:40px;
    bottom:40px;
    background-color:#000000;
}
```

```css
#tilesSplashScreen table {
    width:100%;

 height:100%;
}

#tilesSplashScreen tr {
    vertical-align:middle;
    padding:5px;
    text-align:center;
    font-weight: bold;
    color:#FFF;
    font-family: Helvetica,Arial,sans-serif;
    font-size: 16pt
}
```

The JavaScript File

In the JavaScript file first some global variables are declared so that they can be used in the following functions. Then the initialize() function is defined. Inside initialize() a custom style is defined to be used as a custom map type. A custom style makes the map look more original and attractive, particularly since it is a map about a rock band. As I explained in Chapter 3, when defining a custom style, it is important to avoid making the map unintelligible, so be sure to keep custom styles under control! In this case, applying inverted lightness and a specific hue to all elements is more than sufficient to give the map a "cool" night effect. To improve readability of the map, some elements have also been simplified (see Listing 6-6 and Figure 6-7).

Listing 6-6. The custom style used for the map

```javascript
var customStyle = [ {
    "elementType" : "geometry",
    "stylers" : [ {
    "visibility" : "simplified" }
    ] }
, {
    "stylers" : [ {
        "invert_lightness" : true }

, {
        "hue" : "#00bbff" }
    ] }
, {
    "featureType" : "landscape.man_made",
    "elementType" : "labels",

"stylers" : [ {
        "visibility" : "simplified" }
    ] }
, {
    "featureType" : "water",
```

```
    "stylers" : [ {
        "invert_lightness" : true }
    ] }
]
```

Figure 6-7. *The custom style chosen for the map*

Within `initialize()`, the map is then created and its options are set. The custom style is assigned to a custom map type, and then it is set as the current map type. Always within `initialize()` a `fusionTablesLayer` object is created and set on the map to show all the POIs. When loaded, the app will welcome users, showing all the POIs at once. Now let us move on to the other functions that are found outside `initialize()`.

selectPlace()

The `selectPlace()` function (Listing 6-7) is connected to the select menu and starts a Fusion Tables query according to the user's selection (Figure 6-8).

Listing 6-7. The selectPlace() function

```
function selectPlace() {
    var optionsList = document.getElementById("select-choice-min");
    var requestedPlace = optionsList.options[optionsList.selectedIndex].value;
    var where = "name CONTAINS IGNORING CASE '" + requestedPlace + "'";
    layer.setOptions( {
        query : {
            select : 'geometry',
            from : '1xVSwuTzf_5ufbbc410WCcRKTcWyQfB91JLEbQY8',
            where : where }
        }
    );
    map.setZoom(12);
    map.setCenter(initialCenter);
    }
```

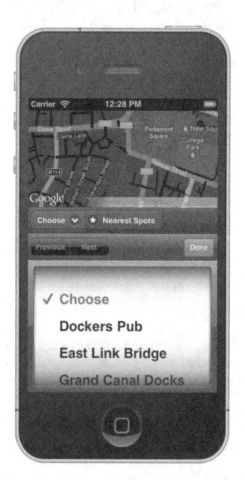

Figure 6-8. The select menu

showAll()

The showAll() function shows all the POIs on the map and sets the map to the initial zoom level and centering. This function is triggered when users click on the relative button in the top-right corner of the app (Listing 6-8).

Listing 6-8. The showAll() function

```
function showAll() {

  layer.setOptions( {
      query : {
          select : 'geometry',


          from : '1xVSwuTzf_5ufbbc41OWCcRKTcWyQfB91JLEbQY8' }
      }
  );
  map.setZoom(12);
  map.setCenter(initialCenter);
  }
```

nearestSpots()

The last function of the JavaScript page is called nearestSpots(). When the related button is pressed for the first time, the function launches the WatchPosition() geolocation method, discussed earlier in this chapter. The method individuates the user's current position (it shows an error message if geolocation fails), draws a marker indicating current position, and launches a spatial Fusion Tables query to show the two POIs nearest to the user's current position. If the user presses the button again, geolocation is stopped by the clearWatch() method to avoid consuming device resources. The map is then set to the initial zoom level and centering (Listing 6-9).

Listing 6-9. The nearestSpots() function

```
//Show the two POis nearest to the user's current position
function nearestSpots() {
   if (statusGeolocation == 0) {
      watchId = navigator.geolocation.watchPosition(function (position) {
         if (positionCoordinates == null) {
             positionCoordinates = new google.maps.LatLng(position.coords.latitude,
position.coords.longitude);
             marker = new google.maps.Marker( {
                 position : positionCoordinates,
                 icon : "blue_dot_circle.png",
                 map : map }
             );
             map.setCenter(positionCoordinates);
             map.setZoom(13);
             layer.setOptions( {
   query : {
                 select : 'geometry',
```

```
                from : '1xVSwuTzf_5ufbbc41OWCcRKTcWyQfB91JLEbQY8',
                orderBy : "ST_DISTANCE('geometry', LATLNG(" + position.coords.latitude + ',' +
position.coords.longitude + "))",
                limit : 2 }
            }
        );
        document.getElementById('nearestSpotsText').style.color = "yellow";
        }
    else {
        positionCoordinates = new google.maps.LatLng(position.coords.latitude,
        position.coords.longitude);
        layer.setOptions( {
            query : {
                select : 'geometry',
                from : '1xVSwuTzf_5ufbbc41OWCcRKTcWyQfB91JLEbQY8',

 orderBy : "ST_DISTANCE('geometry', LATLNG(" + position.coords.latitude + ',' +
position.coords.longitude + "))",
                limit : 2 }
            }
        );
        map.setCenter(positionCoordinates);
        marker.setPosition(positionCoordinates);
        }
    }
    ,
    function (error) {
        var typeOfError = error.code;
        switch (typeOfError) {

   case (1) : alert("Permission denied");
            break;
            case (2) : alert("Position unavailable");
            break;
            case (3) : alert("Timeout error");
            break;
            }
        }
    ,
    {
        enableHighAccuracy : true }
    );
    statusGeolocation = 1;
}
 else //Stop the gelocation process and reset the map to the initial view
 {
    alert("Geolocation stopped");
    navigator.geolocation.clearWatch(watchId);
    positionCoordinates = null;
    marker.setMap(null);
    marker = null;
    showAll();
```

```
        document.getElementById('nearestSpotsText').style.color = "white";
        statusGeolocation = 0;
    }
}
```

In Figure 6-9 is a screenshot showing the result of the nearestSpots() function.

Figure 6-9. The nearestSpots() function has just been executed

Promoting and Maintaining Your App

The web app is now complete and can be distributed online. What are the ways to distribute a web app? As I told you in Chapter 1, a web app cannot be directly uploaded to the Apple App Store, so you need to promote it using other channels. Apple had started a repository for iOS web apps (http://www.apple.com/webapps/index.html), but unfortunately it is no longer maintained and the latest entries date back to 2010. Even if web apps are increasingly used, Apple seems to have focused only on the App Store. So to promote your web apps, you need to rely on websites, forums, Facebook and other channels, more or less the same resources you would use to promote a website.

In the case of the sample U2's Dublin web app, it could be promoted as a free gadget on U2's fan websites, and revenue could be generated by including ads (also maps ads, argument we will see in the last chapter). Thanks to its structure, this web app could also be made available to non-iOS devices – for instance, Android devices, with their enormous user base, almost without changing a line of code. Also, computer users can enjoy the web app, even they are unable to use its geolocation functions (or at least they could enjoy a one-shot geolocation). Just a simple note: When you promote your web app, always invite the user to add it the Home Screen. This is a very simple thing, but it can actually make a big difference. When the app is saved on the Home Screen, its visibility is far greater than if it is saved only in the bookmarks. For instance, when you access its Google Maps web app (m.google.com/maps), see how Google recommends the user add the web app to the Home Screen (Figure 6-10).

Figure 6-10. *Google recommends users of its Google Maps web app add it to the Home Screen*

As for maintaining the web app, as I explained in Chapter 1, the process is far easier than maintaining native iOS apps. You just need to upload the updated code to the web server, overwriting previous files. In the sample U2's Dublin web app, the update process of the geodata (POIs) is made very easy thanks to Fusion Tables. To add new U2's spots or to change the existing ones, you just need to modify the relative rows on the relative Fusion Tables data table and the new updates will be immediately available (Figure 6-11).

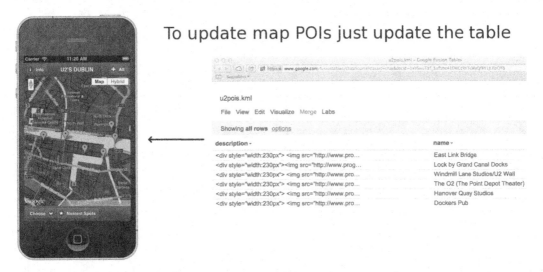

Figure 6-11. *The process of updating geodata is very easy and quick thanks to Fusion Tables*

Submitting the App to the App Store

If the web app cannot be distributed via the App Store, with a little effort it can be transformed into a hybrid app (that is, a web app inside a native app shell) and therefore uploaded in the store as I will explain in detail in the next chapter. I will show you how to create a hybrid app using Xcode, starting from the U2's Dublin web app that we put together here. I will also cover the PhoneGap framework that allows you to create hybrid apps compatible with iOS but also with Android and many other operating systems.

Summary

In this chapter you learned how to implement geolocation functions in a web app using the standard W3C Geolocation API. I illustrated how the getCurrentPosition(), watchPosition(), and clearWatch() methods are used to get location data, their peculiarities, and their configuration options. In the second part of the chapter I showed you how to put together the many functions illustrated in the previous chapters to assemble a complete U2's Dublin web app. You should be able to build a geo web app from scratch. In particular you should now be able to:

- Move through the Google Maps JavaScript API documentation.

- Implement a Google map in a web page optimized for iOS devices.

- Design a jQuery Mobile-based UI for your map-based web app.

- Manage map controls.

- Set custom styles for the map.

- Display overlays on the map with different methods.

- Implement geolocation functions in a web app.

Part 3

Hybrid Apps

Chapter 7 looks at hybrid apps, which are web apps accessed through a browser window embedded in a native app. But unlike web apps, hybrid apps can be uploaded and distributed through the App Store and thus provide more visibility. To develop hybrid apps you only need a basic knowledge of the Xcode environment.

7

Creating Hybrid Apps

In chapters 2–6 I showed you how to build geo web apps using HTML and JavaScript. Apps created this way can be accessed by a web browser via their URLs. As I explained in Chapter 1, one significant disadvantage of web apps is that they cannot be uploaded to the Apple App Store, and therefore have less visibility than a native app. In addition, it is much harder to sell a web app without access to App Store sales platform tools. However, by using a few lines of code, it is possible to embed a web app in a native app, thus creating a hybrid app.

The function of the native app will simply be to launch an embedded browser pointing to the web app home page. To create an app of this kind, you do not have to know Objective-C. You just have to follow one of two primary development options available for building hybrid apps:

- Realizing hybrid apps by directly using Xcode.

- Realizing hybrid apps using the PhoneGap (Apache Cordova) framework. With this option, you might need Xcode as well to compile the app or you can compile it through the cloud service (`https://build.phonegap.com`) without using Xcode. (You will need a Mac computer as I will explain).

In the following pages I will show you all the steps to create a hybrid app using Xcode and just a few lines of Objective-C that you can copy without actually knowing the language. Then I will give you an overview of PhoneGap showing its main functionalities.

In both cases, note that if you want to test the app on real devices and also distribute it in the App Store, you must be enrolled in the iOS Developer Program ($99/year, `https://developer.apple.com/programs/ios/`).

Creating a Hybrid App With Xcode

Before we begin the tutorial, make sure you have all the necessary tools. First, it is necessary to have Xcode installed on your computer. Xcode is an IDE containing a suite of software development tools created by Apple for developing software for OS X and iOS. The current version of Xcode, which I am going to use in this book, is Xcode 4.5. This version includes added support for iOS 6 and the 4-inch Retina display found on iPhone 5 and iPod touch 5th generation.

Please note that Xcode 4.5 runs only on OS X Mountain Lion (10.8). You can download the current version of Xcode for free from the Mac App Store. It includes the Instruments analysis tool, the iOS Simulator, and the latest Mac OS X and iOS SDKs. For more information, see the page `https://developer.apple.com/xcode/` and its many tutorials.

As I mentioned, if you want to distribute your apps on the App Store, you also need to enroll in the iOS Developer Program. Since this book is not a guide to Xcode and the iOS SDK, I assume that you have correctly installed and configured Xcode before proceeding to the next chapters. If you have a previous version of Xcode and the iOS SDK, the procedures will be a little different but on the Internet you can find sufficient tutorials and guides to adapt them.

In the next sections I will illustrate how to create a web view (the window–inside the native app, that will display your web app content). I will then talk about improving the hybrid app, showing you how to check the availability of the Internet connection, how to set links so that they open in an external app, and how to add an app icon and a launch image.

Creating a Web View (`UIWebView`)

To embed a web browser pointing to a web page in a native app, you need to use a so-called web view. In iOS development, you can build a web view by using the `UIWebView` class that displays web content through a WebKit engine. To implement a web view, you first create a `UIWebView` object, attach it to a window, and then send it a request to load web content. You can also use this class to move back and forth in the web page history, and you can even set some web content properties. In the following example, I show you how to create a simple web view that loads the web app we produced in Chapter 6.

Setting Up the Project

First, you need to start Xcode (by default it is in /Applications). Then, in the Welcome to Xcode window, click Create a new Xcode project (or choose File ➤ New ➤ New project). Within the iOS category, select Single View Application (Figure 7-1). Using a built-in template allows you to save time, thus avoiding manually writing all the app's structure.

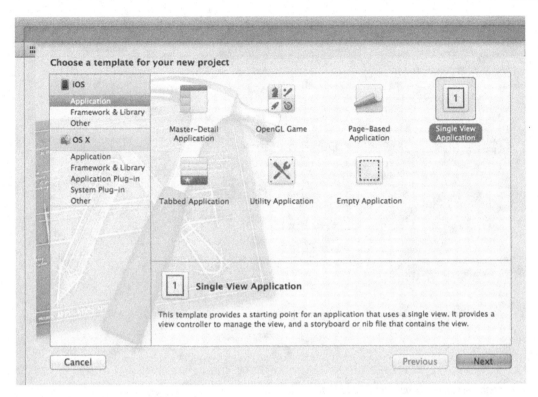

Figure 7-1. Select the Single View Application template

A new dialog appears that prompts you to name your app and choose additional options for your project (Figure 7-2). Fill the Product name field (it should have no spaces). It is usually given a shortened version of the app name (such as "myapp"). In the Organization Name field, you can put your name, and in the Company Identifier field, you can provide a unique string for the company name. (Reverse DNS notation works well, such as com.mycompanyname.) If you do not have a company identifier, you can use edu.self. In Devices, select Universal so that your app can work both on iPhone and iPad. Additionally, make sure that the Use Storyboard and Use Automatic Reference Counting options are selected and that the Include Unit Tests option is unselected, and then click on Next to proceed.

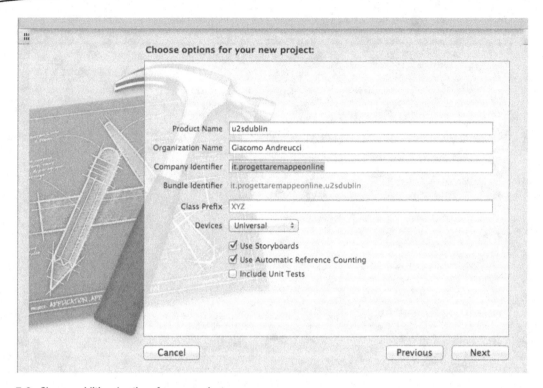

Figure 7-2. Choose additional options for your project

In the following window you must indicate a location for your project (leave the Source Control option unselected), and then click Create. Xcode opens your new project in a window (named the workspace window), which should look similar to the one shown in Figure 7-3.

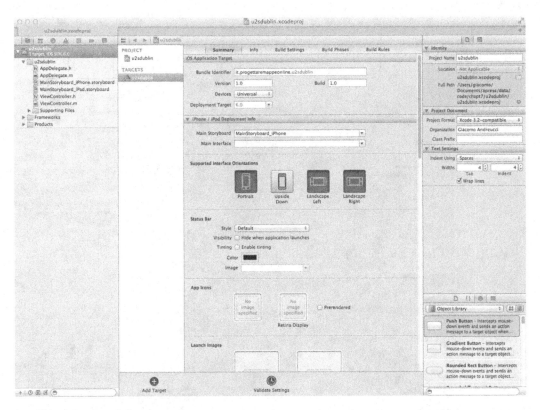

Figure 7-3. *The workspace window*

Note   Since the workspace window contains many different elements that I am going to use in the next pages, I suggest you familiarize yourself with the terminology by reviewing Figure 7-4, which was taken from the Apple official documentation: (https://developer.apple.com/library/ios/#referencelibrary/GettingStarted/RoadMapiOS/chapters/RM_YourFirstApp_iOS/Articles/01_CreatingProject.html).

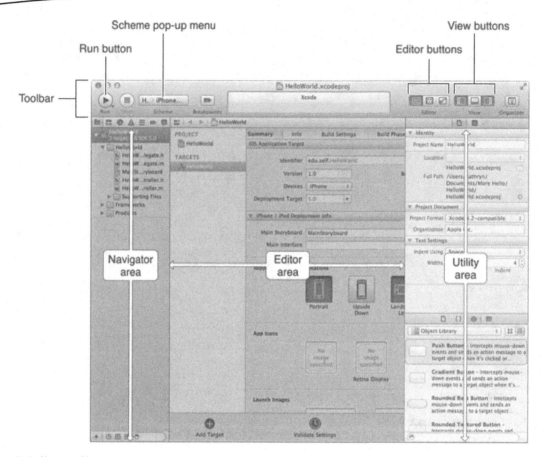

Figure 7-4. *Names of buttons and areas of the workspace window*

Now that the project is set up and you have an idea of the work environment, I will show you how to create the web view using the storyboard tool.

Using the Storyboard Tool to Create the Web View

If you look back at Figure 7-3, you notice on the left a list of files inside the u2sdublin folder. Without going into detail, just focus your attention on the two files called ViewController, each of which has a different extension: ViewController.h and ViewController.m. The .h file is the header file (the file that tells the app what we are going to do), while the .m file is the implementation file that implements the methods and properties we declared in the header file. You can also see two .storyboard files: one called MainStoryboard_iPhone.storyboard that will be used for laying out the iPhone view, and another called MainStoryboard_iPad.storyboard, for laying out the iPad view. Click on the MainStoryboard_iPhone.storyboard file. The aspect of the workspace window will change. In order to work properly, make sure the toolbar is displayed (View ➤ Show toolbar) and the Editor and View buttons at the right-top corner look like those in Figure 7-5.

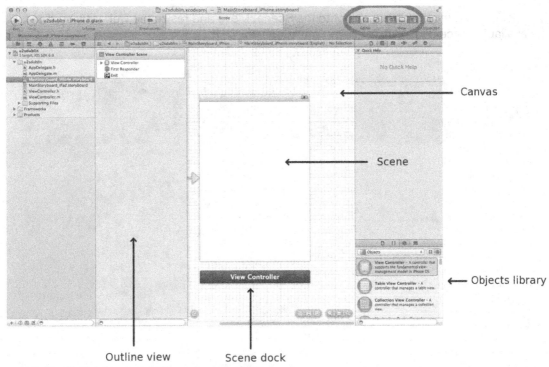

Figure 7-5. The file MainStoryboard_iPhone.storyboard is displayed

Make sure the Object library is displayed in the Utility area and scroll down until you find the Web View object (Figure 7-6).

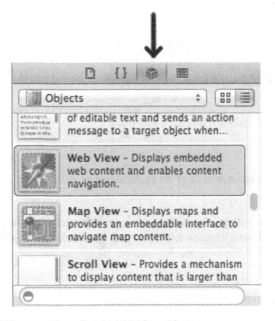

Figure 7-6. Scroll down the Object library until you find the Web View object

Now click and drag the Web View object to the Scene. Move and resize the web view so that it fills all the available space (Figure 7-7).

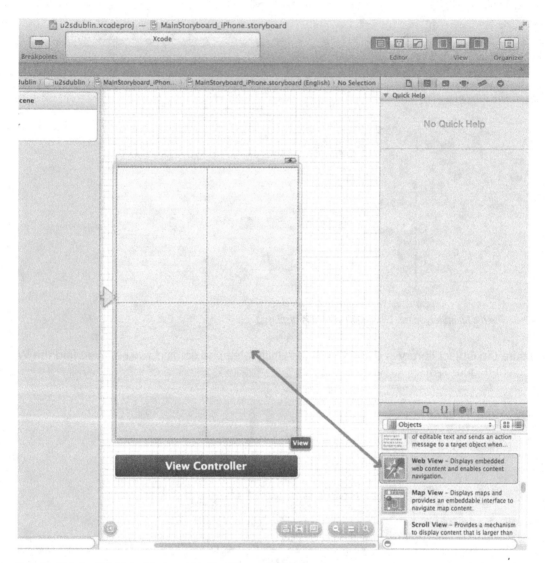

Figure 7-7. Position the Web View object so as to fill all the available space

When you release the mouse button, the web view is positioned. However, you can move and resize it. In the Outline section of the workspace window, you can now see the web view added to the View (Figure 7-8).

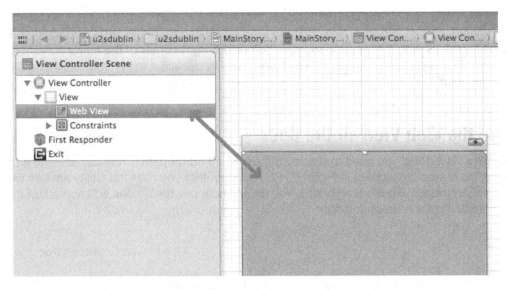

Figure 7-8. The web view has been added to the view

Make sure that Web View is selected in the Outline view (Figure 7-8) and then, in the Utility area, open the Attributes Inspector where you can set some attributes of the web view (Figure 7-9). It is not necessary to select Scale Page To Fit since that is already set in our web app code. In the Detection section, select Links (recognizes URLs and opens them in a new page), Addresses (opens the Maps app), and Phone Numbers (calls the number). It is not necessary to select Events (adds to Calendar) since events are not included in the sample web app.

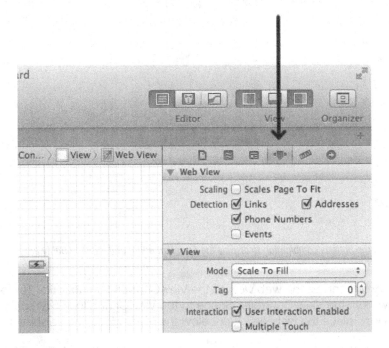

Figure 7-9. Attributes of the web view

Repeat all the steps you did for MainStoryboard_iPhone.storyboard for the companion file MainStoryboard_iPad.storyboard. Note that the iPad editor can be rather large. I suggest you use the magnifying glass with the minus symbol jn the bottom-right corner of the editor screen. Now that the web view is created in the storyboard, you need to declare it in the code so that it can be properly managed.

Declare the Web View in the Code

To proceed in the tutorial you need to display the Assistant editor panel. You can activate it by clicking on the button highlighted in Figure 7-10. I suggest that you hide the Utility area as well. Click on the MainStoryboard_iPhone.storyboard. You should now see the iPhone edit screen on the left and the ViewController.h file on the right.

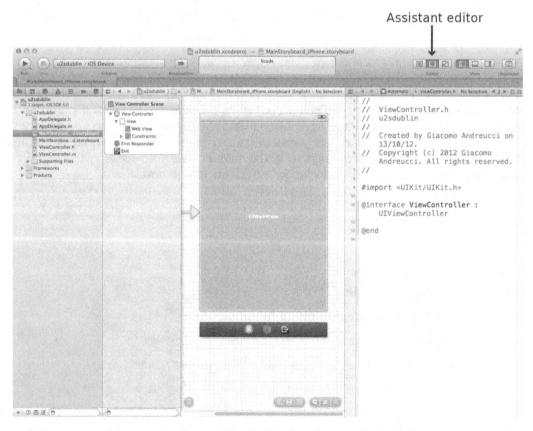

Figure 7-10. Reproduce the buttons combination to display the Assistant editor and hide the Utility area

Now it is necessary to connect the web view to the ViewController header file. To do this, click and drag the web view from the View Controller Scene to the ViewController.h edit screen while holding down the Control key: place the web view just below the @interface line as shown in Figure 7-11.

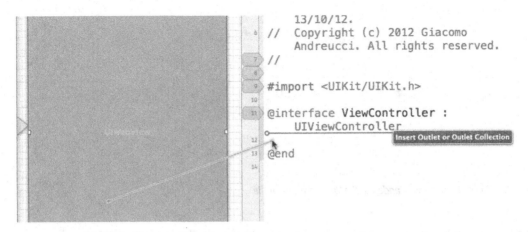

```
                                          13/10/12.
                                 6  //  Copyright (c) 2012 Giacomo
                                        Andreucci. All rights reserved.
                                 7  //

                                 9  #import <UIKit/UIKit.h>
                                10
                                11  @interface ViewController :
                                        UIViewController
                                12
                                13  @end
                                14
```

Figure 7-11. *While holding down the Control key, click and drag the web view from the View Controller Scene to the ViewController.h edit screen*

When you release Control-drag, Xcode displays a pop-over in which you can configure the connection you just made (Figure 7-12). In the Name section, type in webView, check that the other fields are like those in Figure 7-12, and then click Connect.

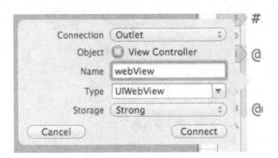

Figure 7-12. *How to configure the connection popover*

Some lines of code will automatically be added to the ViewController.h file (see the highlighted code in Figure 7-13). Xcode indicates that the connection has been made by displaying a filled-in circle to the left of the added code. Several other lines are automatically added to the ViewController.m file as well.

Figure 7-13. The code that Xcode added to the ViewController.h file

Now you need to link the web view in the iPad storyboard. On the left bar, click on MainStoryboard_iPad.storyboard. Also, while holding down the Control key, click and drag the web view from the View Controller Scene to the ViewController.h edit screen, but instead of creating a new line, drag it to the existing line, as shown in Figure 7-14.

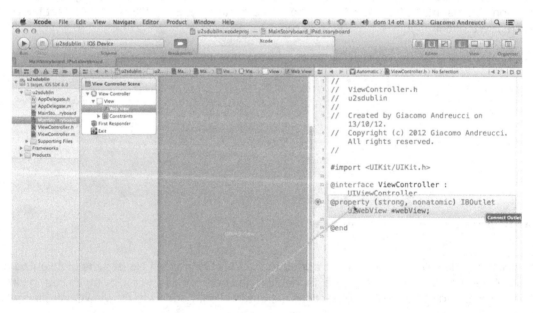

Figure 7-14. While holding down the Control key, click and drag the web view from the View Controller Scene to the existing line in the ViewController.h edit screen

The web view is connected to the View Controller in the iPad storyboard as well. Now that the web view created with the storyboard is declared in the code, you can implement it with a few lines of code, which I will illustrate in the next paragraph.

Implementing the Web View

To properly work, set the workspace window as shown in Figure 7-15 (reproduce the highlighted combination of buttons) and open the file ViewController.m.

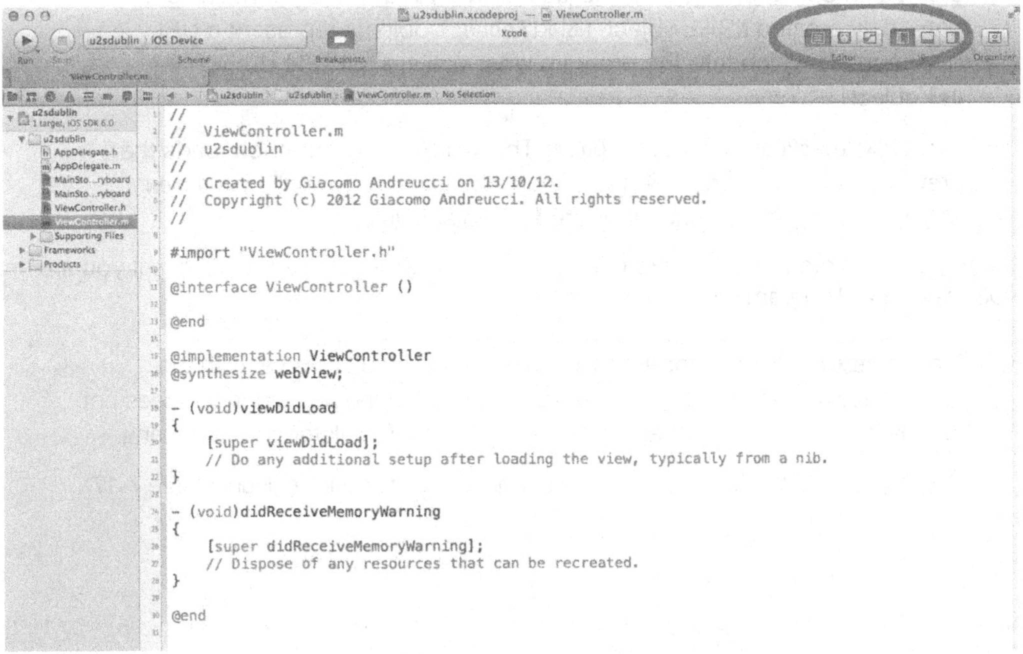

Figure 7-15. Arrange the workspace window so as to properly work on the ViewController.m file

Once you have opened the ViewController.m file within the `viewDidLoad` method, add the code I highlighted in Figure 7-16.

```
- (void)viewDidLoad
{
    [super viewDidLoad];
    NSString *webappURL = @"http://www.progettaremappeonline.it/apress/code/u2sdublin.html";
    NSURL *url = [NSURL URLWithString:webappURL];
    NSURLRequest *requestObj = [NSURLRequest requestWithURL:url];
    [webView loadRequest:requestObj];
}
```

Figure 7-16. Add the highlighted code to the `viewDidLoad` method

Let us now have a look at the code added to get a basic idea of what it does:

1. `NSString *webappURL = @"http://www.…";` First, you declared a variable called `webappURL` of type `NSString` (a text string) containing the URL of the web app you want to embed in the native app you are building. In this case, it is the URL pointing to the U2's Dublin HTML file but it could be any URL you want to use.

2. `NSURL *url = [NSURL URLWithString:webappURL];` You created a url object of type `NSURL` using the previously created string. This tells the program that the text string is actually a web address.

3. `NSURLRequest *requestObj = [NSURLRequest requestWithURL:url];` You created an object of type `NSURLRequest` named `requestObj` containing the previously created `NSURL` object. `NSURLRequest` objects represent a URL load request, which tells the program what you are going to do with the url object.

4. `[webView loadRequest:requestObj];` The `loadRequest:` method loads the previously created `requestObj` into the web view that we called `webView` earlier so that the web page is loaded and displayed.

Now the app is completed and you can test it on the simulator or on a real device if you are enrolled in the iOS Developer Program. To run the app:

1. Make sure the Scheme pop-up menu in the Xcode toolbar is set with the desired device (in this case, iPhone 6.0 Simulator). If the pop-up menu does not display that choice, open it and choose iPhone 6.0 Simulator from the menu.

2. Click the Run button in the Xcode toolbar or choose Product ➤ Run (Figure 7-17).

Figure 7-17. *How to run the code*

Xcode updates you on the build process. After Xcode finishes building your project, Simulator should start automatically. Because you specified an iPhone product (rather than an iPad product), iOS Simulator displays a window that looks like an iPhone and launches your app. It should look like Figure 7-18.

Figure 7-18. The app running on the iPhone simulator

You can also try the app on the iPad simulator, since you chose the Universal template and also set the view for the iPad. To do this, stop your current simulation by clicking on the Stop button in the Xcode toolbar, choose iPad 6.0 Simulator instead of iPhone 6.0 Simulator, and run the app again. iOS Simulator will display a window looking like an iPad and launch your application. Now the web view is complete but to make it fully functional, you had better add to it the improvements I will illustrate in the next sections.

Checking for an Internet Connection

Even if the hybrid app we created in the previous paragraph is still working, it needs some improvements if you want to upload it to the App Store. By the way, before uploading anything you created to the App Store, I suggest that you carefully read the App Review Guidelines specified here: https://developer.apple.com/appstore/guidelines.html. The App Review Board might refuse your app if it does not meet the guidelines criteria. In order for an iOS app that uses an Internet connection to be approved in the App Store, it must include a function that checks if the device is connected to the Internet when the app is launched. Since a hybrid app is based on online data it should not be launched if no Internet connection is available: if you try to execute the app realized in the previous paragraph on a device with no Internet connection available the app would show a blank screen, without displaying any error message to the user.

This app behavior is to be avoided since the user is not shown any error message and does not know what to to. The App Store is likely to refuse hybrid apps that show no error messages when the Internet connection is not available. So, before submitting your app I suggest that you implement a function that checks for an Internet connection when the app is launched and, in case it is not available, shows an appropriate error message to the user. I will now show you how to accomplish this. First, you need to implement a protocol called UIWebViewDelegate. Without getting into the details, you just need to open the ViewController.h file in the Navigator area on the left and implement the UIWebViewDelegate, adding: <UIWebViewDelegate>. The complete code of your ViewController.h file should now be the following:

```
#import <UIKit/UIKit.h>

@interface ViewController : UIViewController <UIWebViewDelegate>
@property (strong, nonatomic) IBOutlet UIWebView *webView;

@end
```

Now open the ViewController.m file and, inside the viewDidLoad method, add the following line:

```
webView.delegate = self;
```

Then, in the ViewController.m file, before the @end directive, add the following code, which will display an alert message in case the web view fails to load the web page. You can insert any title and text you want to be displayed in the alert box.

```
-(void)webView:(UIWebView *)webView didFailLoadWithError:(NSError *)error {
    UIAlertView *alert = [[UIAlertView alloc] initWithTitle:@"Error!" message:@"Internet
connection not available. Please connect to the Internet to use this app" delegate:self
cancelButtonTitle:@"Close" otherButtonTitles:nil, nil];
    [alert show];
}
```

Also, add the following method in the ViewController.m file so that the user can close the app when pressing the Close button shown in the alert message.

```
//Close app from AlertView
- (void)alertView:(UIAlertView *)alertView didDismissWithButtonIndex:(NSInteger)buttonIndex {
    exit(0);
}
```

Now run the code on the Simulator or on a real device. (First disconnect the computer or the device from the Internet.) A message like the one shown in Figure 7-19 will be displayed. If you then touch the Close button, the app will close.

Figure 7-19. The appropriate error message

Now that you have added a function to check the availability of the Internet connection, I will show you another improvement you could apply that allows the app to open links present in the balloon content in an external app.

Open Links in an External App

In the U2's Dublin web app, inside the content of info windows there might be links to external websites and to some of U2's videos. If you click on an external link inside the hybrid app we created, it opens by default inside the web view on the same page, hiding the app view. Since a navigation bar is not implemented in the hybrid app (it would take up excessive room), the user loses the app and has to restart it in order to get to the app view.

A simple way to bypass this problem is to implement a method so that when a link is clicked inside the web view, it opens in Safari or in its respective app if available (for instance the YouTube app), instead of opening inside the web view itself. To do this, you need to use the shouldStartLoadWithRequest: method. This method is defined by the UIWebViewDelegate protocol which we have seen how to add in the previous paragraph. If you are going to use the previous code, you do not need to add anything to the ViewController.h file. Now, open the ViewController.m file, check that within the viewDidLoad method the line webView.delegate = self; is present, and then add the following code outside viewDidLoad; this implements the shouldStartLoadWithRequest: method:

```
-(BOOL) webView:(UIWebView *)webView shouldStartLoadWithRequest:(NSURLRequest *)request
navigationType:(UIWebViewNavigationType)inType {
    if ( inType == UIWebViewNavigationTypeLinkClicked ) {
        [[UIApplication sharedApplication] openURL:[request URL]];
        return NO;
    }

    return YES;
}
```

Without getting into the details (for more information, see: http://developer.apple.com/library/ ios/#documentation/uikit/reference/UIWebViewDelegate_Protocol/Reference/Reference.html), when a user clicks on the link, this method intercepts the action. Instead of opening the content the link is pointing to inside the web view, it opens it in the appropriate external app (for example, Mobile Safari for web pages, YouTube app for videos). In Figure 7-20, you can see that after clicking on a link to a YouTube video inside the info window of a POI, the external YouTube app is being loaded to display the video.

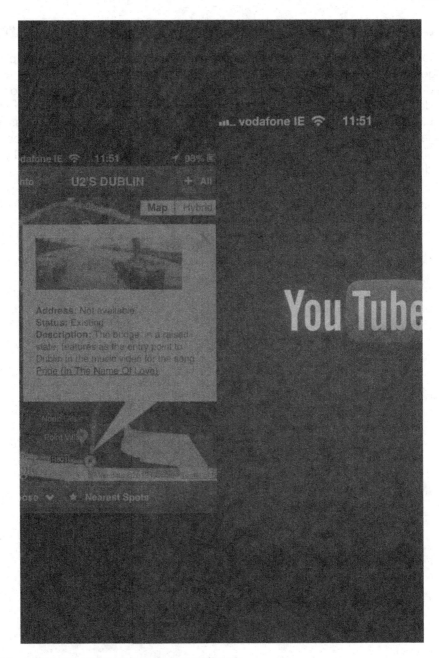

Figure 7-20. Links are now opened externally by the appropriate app

Now the app is almost ready to be submitted to the App Store. You just need to set up an app icon and a launch image. In the next section you will discover how to do this in few simple steps.

Adding App Icon and Launch Image for the App Store

If you intend to upload your hybrid app to the App Store, you must also provide an app icon and a launch image. The icon and launch image you set inside the web app are not visible; they are only displayed for web apps saved to the Home Screen and are not available when the web app is launched inside a hybrid app. Thus, you need to set these images again in Xcode. I suggest that you look at the table that Apple provides with the size in pixels of custom icons and images. Once you have the images ready (you can reuse the ones from the web app), you need to click on the project within the Navigator area in Xcode (Figure 7-21) and then scroll down the window until you see the App Icons and Launch Images sections for the iPhone layout (Figure 7-22).

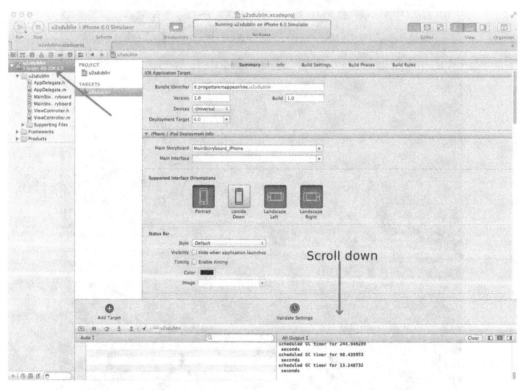

Figure 7-21. Click on the project on the left in the Navigator area

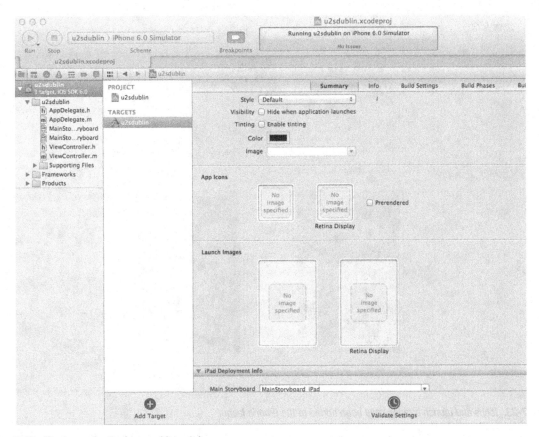

Figure 7-22. The boxes for the icon and launch image

You can now drag and drop the image you want to use for the icon and the relative box and then do the same for the launch image. You can also specify (recommended) the icon and launch image for Retina Display (Figure 7-23). If you want to change the image, simply drag and drop the new one onto the existing. Note that the icon's corners are rounded automatically by Xcode and also a gloss effect is applied. If you want the gloss effect removed from your icon, just select Prerendered, as shown in Figure 7-23.

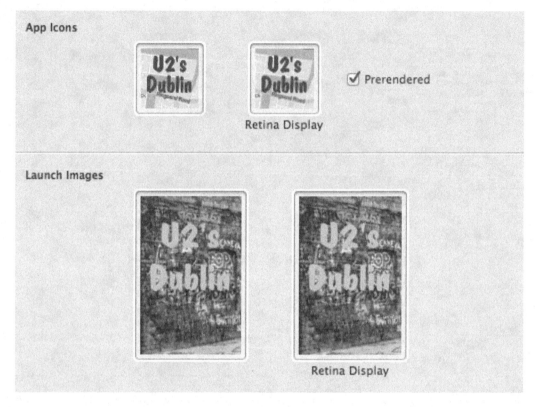

Figure 7-23. Icons and launch images have been added to the iPhone layout

Now you have to add the icon and launch image for the iPad layout. To do so, scroll further down the window and you will find a similar section where you can drag and drop icons and launch images for iPad. Now you have completed settings for this simple hybrid app so that it can meet the basic requirements to be uploaded to the App Store. By the way, I submitted to the App Store the U2's Dublin sample app that we built in the previous chapters and that I used here to demonstrate how to create a hybrid app. It got approved and now is available for free on the App Store here (Figure 7-24):

```
https://itunes.apple.com/us/app/u2s-dublin/id577629771?l=it&ls=1&mt=8
```

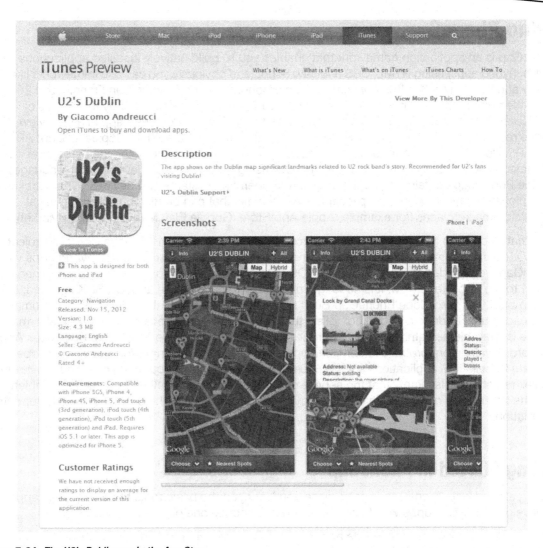

Figure 7-24. The U2's Dublin app in the App Store

Using Xcode to embed a web app in a native shell is, as you saw, a very easy process, but it is not the only way to create an hybrid app. You can also use a framework, whose most famous example is PhoneGap, that enables you to build applications for mobile devices using JavaScript, HTML5 and CSS3, instead of using Objective-C. The resulting applications are hybrid like the hybrid apps created using Xcode only. However, unlike Xcode, PhoneGap allows you to distribute hybrid apps not only for iOS but also for Android and other major mobile operating systems, so you are able to reach a wider audience using the same web app core. In the next section I will give an overview of PhoneGap and its main characteristics.

Using PhoneGap

PhoneGap is an application framework that enables you to build natively installed applications (that is, hybrid apps) using HTML, CSS and JavaScript (and obviously you can use frameworks like jQuery and jQuery Mobile). It was invented at an iPhoneDevCamp event in San Francisco in 2005. Since then, the framework has evolved and improved and is now being used by thousands of developers worldwide. Basically, PhoneGap allows you to include your web app in a web view so; the resulting app can have access hardware features through the PhoneGap JavaScript API. This API allows your web app to access location services, the accelerometer, the gyroscope, the compass, the camera, files. You build the app GUI using traditional web development languages and use the PhoneGap container to deploy to different operating systems and devices. When packaged for deployment, the PhoneGap application is a binary file that can be distributed by the usual application marketplaces (for example, Apple App Store, Google Play Market, Amazon Market).

Note that PhoneGap is completely open source since it is based on the Apache Cordova project: `http://incubator.apache.org/cordova`. At one time, if you wanted to realize iOS hybrid apps with PhoneGap, you needed to have Xcode and iOS SDK installed to compile the project in a binary to submit to the App Store. Now, it is no longer necessary to have Xcode and iOS SDK installed; in September 2012, the Adobe PhoneGap Build service was made available, allowing programmers to upload source code to a "cloud compiler" that generates apps for every supported platform. The service is available here: `https://build.phonegap.com`. However, since PhoneGap Build uses Apple's standard development process to compile applications, you must sign up for Apple's developer program to build iOS applications and you need a Mac to configure your certificate and provisioning profile. You should also know that the service offered by Adobe PhoneGap Build is not completely free; the price varies according to the typology of your apps. (Check the official website for updated information.)

Geting Started in PhoneGap

Getting started with PhoneGap is easy, since you just need the basic tools to develop web apps. To develop iOS hybrid apps with PhoneGap, you can choose one of two avenues:

- Use PhoneGap with Xcode and the iOS SDK environment. See official online tutorials here: `http://docs.phonegap.com/en/2.2.0/guide_getting-started_ios_index.md.html#Getting%20Started%20with%20iOS`. Note that if you want to distribute your apps in the App Store, you must also be enrolled in the iOS Developer Program.

- Use the Adobe PhoneGap Build online service to compile hybrid apps without needing Xcode. You will still need to be enrolled in the iOS Developer Program and you will also need a Mac computer to configure your certificate and provisioning profile, a task which is necessary to distribute your apps to the App Store. See more information here: `https://build.phonegap.com/docs/ios-builds`.

As for access to geolocation services, PhoneGap uses the same JavaScript objects of the W3C Geolocation API examined in the previous chapter, there is no need to change any syntax. Thus, you can implement the `getCurrentPosition()`, `watchPosition()`, and `clearWatch()` methods without any problem. The PhoneGap JavaScript API also offers many other methods and objects for accessing other device features such as the camera, compass and file system. See the documentation on the official website for detailed information.

Summary

In this chapter you learned how to build a native app that embeds a web app. An app of this kind is called a hybrid app. As I pointed out, it is not necessary to know Objective-C if you follow one of the two methods suggested: creating hybrid apps with Xcode or with the PhoneGap framework. I illustrated the main characteristics of every method, showing in detail how to develop a hybrid app using Xcode.

If you are enrolled in the iOS Developer program, you can submit the completed hybrid app to the App Store Board so that it can be reviewed and hopefully admitted to the App Store. Updating the hybrid app will then be a very easy process since you only need to modify web app files on the web server and on Fusion Tables (if you made use of this service), without having to submit updates through the App Store. Updates will be made immediately available, since the web view will simply access the new web page instead of the previous one.

Now you should know how to do the following:

- Create an Xcode project.
- Add a Web View (UIWebView) object to the project.
- Add a function to check Internet connection availability.
- Add a function to open links in external apps.
- Set icon and launch image for the app.
- Test the app in a simulator or real device.

Part 4

Native Apps with Apple Map Kit

Chapters 8–10 look at the new Apple Map Kit framework, which makes it possible to integrate mapping services in native iOS apps. To get the most out of these chapters, readers should have basic knowledge of the Xcode environment and Objective-C language.

Chapter 8

Introduction to the Core Location Framework

In chapters 2–7, I covered geo web apps and hybrid apps. This chapter introduces the third part of the book, in which I talk about native iOS geographic apps. There are two main ingredients for creating a native geo app in iOS: location services and maps. Location services are provided by the Core Location framework, which make available methods to obtain information about the user's location and direction. Maps are provided by the Map Kit framework, which until iOS 5.1, used the Google Mobile Maps service to provide map data. Starting with iOS 6, it uses the Apple Maps cartography recently introduced. (This is the same map data used by the Maps app in iOS 6.)

In this chapter I introduce you to the Core Location framework and in the following chapters we will focus on the Map Kit framework. As I explained in the overview in Chapter 1, to follow this and the next two chapters you need to have basic knowledge of Xcode, Objective-C, and iOS programming. I assume that you have installed Xcode and have correctly configured it on your computer. You do not need to be enrolled in the iOS Developer Program to follow the examples.

Main Core Location Services

The Core Location framework is a library (or API) that allows you to obtain location information from the device by using delegation. In addition to location information Core Location also reports Heading data (that is the direction in which a device is pointed). It also allows you to implement region monitoring, which lets you monitor boundary crossings for a region defined by geographical coordinates. Core Location can use all the geolocation methods the device makes available like A-GPS, Wi-Fi, Cell towers triangulation, etc. This is done in a way transparent to the API so that the developer cannot directly chose the method to use but can only specify the accuracy needed in a way similar to what happens with JavaScript W3C Geolocation API, which we examined in the first part of this book. Three services are available from Core Location:

- The *standard location service*: Named as such because it is available in all iOS devices and all iOS versions.

- The *significant-change location service*: Reports the current location and notifies the user of changes to that location with low-power consumption. This service is available in iOS 4.0 and later.

- The *region monitoring service*: Allows the developer to define geographic regions and monitor crossings of their boundaries. This service is available in iOS 4.0 and later.

Because geolocation is a power-consuming task, when you implement it in an app, you need to evaluate if you need only a one-shot position. For instance, to initially center a map, after which you can stop the geolocation task or if you need regular position updates. In this second case, you might prefer to use the less power-consuming *significant-change location service* instead of the *standard location service*. In the next section I will illustrate how to set the framework to use its services in your Xcode projects.

Setting Up the Framework

To use any of these Core Location services (standard location, significant-change location, or region monitoring) in an Xcode project, first you must import its framework. In Xcode 4.5 click on the project folder on the left in the Navigator area and then scroll down the Summary tab until you get to the Linked Frameworks and Libraries section (Figure 8-1). Here you will find all the frameworks used in the project.

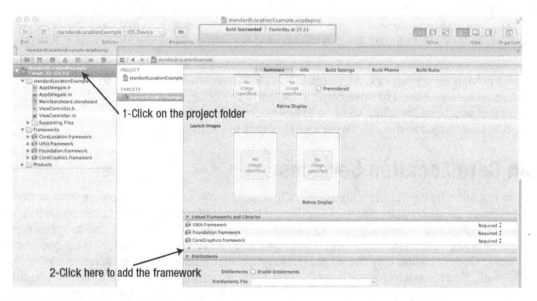

Figure 8-1. The Linked Frameworks and Libraries section

Click on the + sign below the framework list, select CoreLocation.framework (Figure 8-2), and then click on Add. The framework will be added to the project. To use the framework in a source file of your project, you also need to include an #import <CoreLocation/CoreLocation.h> statement at the top of the file (for instance, in the ViewController.h file).

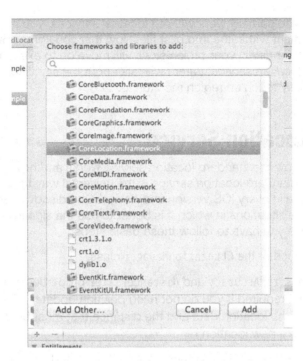

Figure 8-2.   Select CoreLocation.framework

If your app requires location services to function and cannot work without them, the official documentation recommends that you indicate this requirement in the app Info.plist file using the key UIRequiredDeviceCapabilities. Inside this key you need to signal the services that the app requires in order to function properly. This ensures that the App Store can read the information of this file and not allow devices lacking the required services to download and install the app. Within the UIRequiredDeviceCapabilities, required services and components must be indicated using a strings array. If the app requires location services, in general you can write:

```
<key>UIRequiredDeviceCapabilities</key>
<array>
    <string>location-services</string
</array>
```

If the app requires the specific presence of a GPS chip because it needs very accurate position data, you also need to add <string>gps</string>:

```
<key>UIRequiredDeviceCapabilities</key>
<array>

 <string>location-services</string>

<string>gps</string>
</array>
```

Note that if the app can also partially work without location services, you must not indicate the location services requirement within the Info.plist file. Now that you know how to set up the Core Location framework for use in your projects, we will move on to examining in detail how to implement the standard location service. Later I will talk about the significant-change location service and I will also briefly touch on region monitoring.

The Standard Location Service

In this section I illustrate how the standard location service works and how to implement it in an app. As I mentioned, the standard location service is the universal way to get location data on iOS devices since it is available in every iOS version and device. One disadvantage is that it consumes a lot of power, so there are situations in which it is better to use the significant-change location service. To use this service you have to follow these basic steps:

1. Create an instance of the `CLLocationManager` class.

2. Configure its `desiredAccuracy` and `distanceFilter` properties. Setting these properties is not required if you do not need position updates. (They indicate the accuracy of the location data and the distance that must be traveled before reporting a new location.)

3. Assign a delegate to the `CLLocationManager` instance and call the `startUpdatingLocation` method. Invoking this method causes the location manager to begin obtaining location data and notifying the delegate.

After starting location updates you can implement a method to continue receiving location updates, but, if you need only a one-shot position, you can just use the initial location data that is received. Note that, in this case, the first data that is received is not usually very accurate. In the next few sections I will show you how to build an app that, by implementing the standard location, generates a one-shot position (see section "Hello World Standard Location Service – One-Shot Position"). Then I will show you how to build an app that, using the same standard location service, continues updating position.

Hello World Standard Location Service: One-Shot Position

Here I will show you the steps to create a simple Hello World app that reveals the current position of the device. The app's interface is shown in Figure 8-3. As you can see, it is a single-view application, composed of a label, text fields, and a button that the user presses to show the current position. Once the user has pressed the button, the position is shown once but it is not updated automatically; in order to show a new position update, the user has to press the button again, which triggers the function another time.

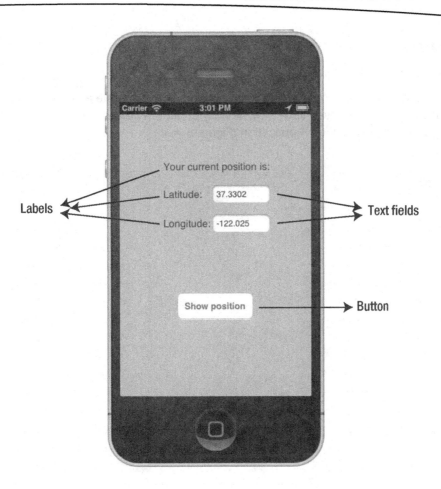

Labels

Text fields

Button

Figure 8-3. *The resulting Hello World app*

To create this Hello World app using the standard location method, you first build the UI of the app and connect the two text fields and the button to the view controller. You connect the two text fields as outlets and configure an action for the button. Then you implement the Core Location framework by declaring and creating an instance of CLLocationManager. After that, you start the location updates using the startUpdatingLocation method. Note that this method has been developed to notify a locationManager object delegate of the new location updates. However, in this example, you do not implement any delegate, therefore the app does not receive location updates – only a one-shot position. You can see this in action if you select in the simulator a changing position like Freeway Drive instead of a static one. (To learn how to do this, see the section Setting the Location in the iOS Simulator). You will see that, after tapping the Show position button, the coordinates do not change when the current position changes. To change them you need to tap the Show position button again. Later in this chapter I will show you how to implement a delegate of the locationManager object and a method to receive location updates and show them.

Setting Up the UI

Begin by setting up the UI as follows:

1. Open Xcode and in the Welcome to Xcode window click "Create a new Xcode project" (or choose File ➤ New ➤ New project). Within the iOS category select Single View Application (Figure 8-4).

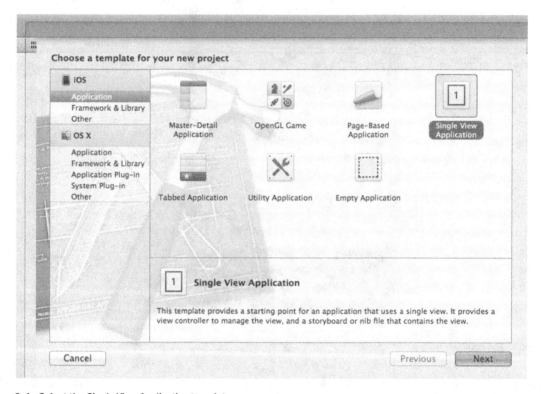

Figure 8-4. Select the Single View Application template

2. A new dialog appears that prompts you to name your app and choose additional options for your project (see Figure 7.2 in the previous chapter). Fill in the Product Name field, naming it Hello World Standard Location, and fill in the Organization Name field as well. In Devices, select iPhone. Make sure that the Use Storyboard and Use Automatic Reference Counting options are selected and that the Include Unit Tests option is unselected. Then click Next.

3. In the following window, indicate a location for your project (leave the Source Control option unselected), and then click Create. Xcode opens your new project in a new workspace window.

4. Now click on the file MainStoryboard_iPhone.storyboard and make sure that in the Utility area the Object library is displayed.

5. From the Object library, drag to the view one Label element and change its text to "Your current position is". Then add two labels below the first one and set their text to "Latitude:" and "Longitude:". Next to these two labels add two Text Field elements, which will be used to show the latitude value and the longitude value.

6. Finally, add a Round Rect button below the labels and set its text to "Show position". The UI should look like the one shown in Figure 8-5. In the example I have also set a green background color for the view.

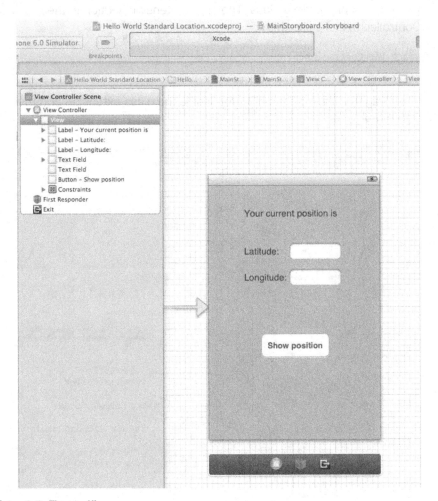

Figure 8-5. The app UI

Create an Action for the Button

Now we have to add the code to implement the geolocation function and connect it to the UI elements. First, let us take care of the button. When the user taps the Show position button, we want it to send a getLocation message (the action) to the view controller (the target). The view controller will respond to this message by starting the location service and showing the coordinate values in the text fields. These are the steps to follow:

1. Activate the Assistant Editor pane so as to show the MainStoryboard. storyboard on the left and on the right open the view controller's implementation file, which is ViewController.m.

2. On the view, Control-drag from the Show position button to the class extension section in ViewController.m. Remember that a class extension in an implementation file is a place where you can declare properties and methods that are private to a class. The class extension section in the ViewController.m. looks like this:

```
@interface ViewController ()
@end
```

You have to Control-drag the Show position button inside the class extension and then release the mouse button (Figure 8-6).

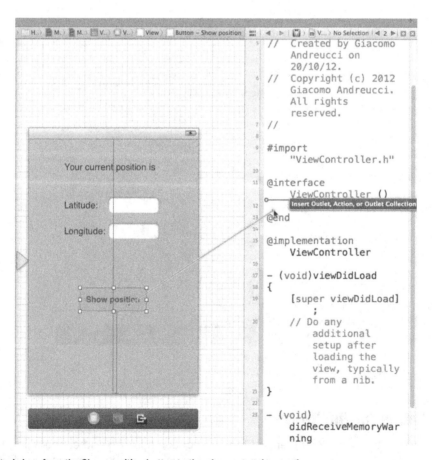

Figure 8-6. Control-drag from the Show position button to the class extension section

3. In the popover, set the following values (Figure 8-7):

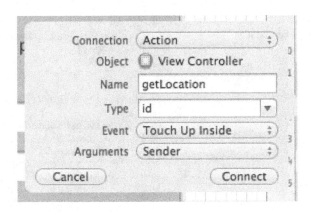

Figure 8-7. The values to be set for the popover

a. Connection: Action

b. Name: "getLocation": (be sure to include the colon)

c. Type: id

d. Event: Touch Up Inside

e. Arguments: Sender

4. After setting the values click on Connect in the popover. You will see that Xcode has added a stub implementation of the new getLocation: method. A filled-in circle to the left of the method indicates that the connection has been made between the button and the ViewController (Figure 8-8).

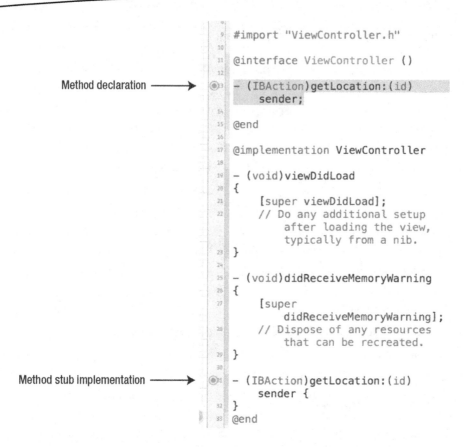

Method declaration

```
9  #import "ViewController.h"
10
11  @interface ViewController ()
12
13  - (IBAction)getLocation:(id)
       sender;
14
15  @end
16
17  @implementation ViewController
18
19  - (void)viewDidLoad
20  {
21      [super viewDidLoad];
22      // Do any additional setup
           after loading the view,
           typically from a nib.
23  }
24
25  - (void)didReceiveMemoryWarning
26  {
27      [super
           didReceiveMemoryWarning];
28      // Dispose of any resources
           that can be recreated.
29  }
30
31  - (IBAction)getLocation:(id)
       sender {
32  }
33  @end
```

Method stub implementation

Figure 8-8. A connection has been made between the button and the ViewController and a stub implementation of the method has been added

Create Connections Between the View Controller and the Two Text Fields

Now you have to create connections between the view controller and the two text field elements that will be used to show the coordinates. In this case, you will create two outlets:

1.   Control-drag the first text field to the class extension in the implementation file, as shown in Figure 8-9.

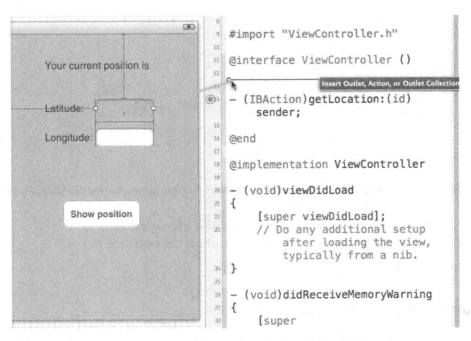

Figure 8-9. Control-drag the first text field to the class extension in the implementation file

2. When you release the mouse button, a popover is displayed in which you need to set the following parameters:

   a. Connection: Outlet

   b. Name: "latitudeField"

   c. Type: UITextField

   d. Storage: Weak.

3. After checking these settings, click on Connect. Xcode adds the declaration of the outlet to the class extension in the ViewController.h file and establishes the connection. (Note the filled-in circle to the left of the declaration shown in Figure 8-10.)

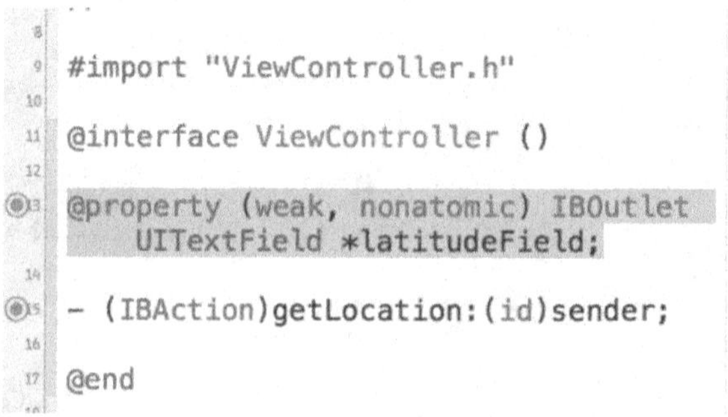

```
 8
 9  #import "ViewController.h"
10
11  @interface ViewController ()
12
13  @property (weak, nonatomic) IBOutlet
        UITextField *latitudeField;
14
15  - (IBAction)getLocation:(id)sender;
16
17  @end
```

Figure 8-10. Xcode added the declaration of the outlet to the class extension in the ViewController.h file

4. Repeat all these steps for the second text field but set its name to "longitudeField" because it will be used to show the longitude.

Now we need to implement the geolocation in the app.

Implementing the Geolocation

Here are the steps to implement geolocation in your app:

1. Include the following statement at the top of the ViewController.h file:

    ```
    #import <CoreLocation/CoreLocation.h>
    ```

2. Create an instance of the CLLocationManager class. This class allows you to configure the delivery of location and heading-related events to your application. As I will show you later in this chapter, you can use an instance of this class to establish the accuracy parameter of the location and when location and heading events should be delivered. By using an instance of this class, you can also start and stop the actual delivery of those events. In this first example, you will not set any parameters but you will use an instance of this class to start the standard location service and get position data. Declare an instance of the CLLocationManager class in the ViewController.h file:

    ```
    CLLocationManager *locationManager;
    ```

3. The ViewController.h file should look like the following:

    ```
    #import <UIKit/UIKit.h>
    #import <CoreLocation/CoreLocation.h>

    @interface ViewController : UIViewController
    {
        CLLocationManager *locationManager;
    }

    @end
    ```

4. Let us now move on to the ViewController.m file. Inside the viewDidLoad method, create and initialize the locationManager object we declared in the ViewController.h file:

    ```
    locationManager = [[CLLocationManager alloc] init];
    ```

5. Start the location update process using the startUpdatingLocation method:

    ```
    [locationManager startUpdatingLocation];
    ```

6. Implement the getLocation: method, which will be triggered when the user taps the Show position button. Inside the method you create a NSString object that captures the latitude value from the locationManager object. Note that the coordinate values are converted to a Double value by using the initWithFormat: set with the format specifier %g:

    ```
    NSString *latitudeFieldData = [[NSString alloc]initWithFormat:@"%g",
    locationManager.location.coordinate.latitude];
    ```

    Do the same thing to capture the longitude value inside the longitudeFieldData object:

    ```
    NSString *longitudeFieldData = [[NSString alloc]initWithFormat:@"%g",
    locationManager.location.coordinate.longitude];
    ```

7. Set the text property of the two text field UI objects using latitudeFieldData and longitudeFieldData:

    ```
    latitudeField.text = latitudeFieldData;
    longitudeField.text = longitudeFieldData;
    ```

    Here is the complete method implementation:

    ```
    - (IBAction)getLocation:(id)sender {

        NSString *latitudeFieldData = [[NSString alloc]initWithFormat:@"%g",
    locationManager.location.coordinate.latitude];
        NSString *longitudeFieldData = [[NSString alloc]initWithFormat:@"%g",
    locationManager.location.coordinate.longitude];
        latitudeField.text = latitudeFieldData;
        longitudeField.text = longitudeFieldData;
    }
    ```

Now the app code is complete but if you run it on the iOS simulator or on a real device you will get an error message (Figure 8-11). The error message appears because the project is not yet linked to the Core Location framework. It is not sufficient to add the `#import <CoreLocation/CoreLocation.h>` statement to the ViewController.h file; you also need to add the framework using the procedure shown at the beginning of this chapter (Figures 8-1 and 8-2).

Figure 8-11. The error message appears because of the missing Core Location framework

Once you have correctly added the framework, you can launch the application in the iOS simulator (or on a real device if you have one correctly configured). Note that the app asks for user permission for geolocation (Figure 8-12). You obviously need to give your permission to test the app.

Figure 8-12. When launched, the app asks the user for permission for geolocation

Setting the Location in the iOS Simulator

If you use the iOS simulator, you then need to set a Location. When the simulator is displayed, in the File menu click on Debug ➤ Location and select a location (otherwise you can set a custom location), as shown in Figure 8-13. The list shows you some static locations (choose Apple, for instance), but it is also possible to select the simulation of a changing location with different speeds (City Bicycle Ride, City Run, Freeway Drive). For now, select a static location.

Figure 8-13. How to set a simulated location

Once you have set a simulated location (or you are using real device location), you can test the app by tapping the Show position button. The current location coordinates will be shown in the respective text fields (Figure 8-14).

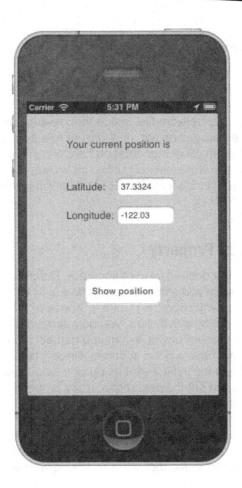

Figure 8-14. *The app at work*

Receiving Location Updates

I want to show you how to create a method for receiving location updates and showing them to the user. Note that this method can be used to receive location updates both with the standard location service as we are doing here and with the significant-change location service, which I will talk about later. Since location updates will be notified by the locationManager object to the locationManager:didUpdateLocations: method of its delegate, it is necessary to implement the CLLocationManagerDelegate protocol. Add <CLLocationManagerDelegate> to the previous Hello World standard location's ViewController.h file . Your ViewController.h file should look like the following:

```
#import <UIKit/UIKit.h>
#import <CoreLocation/CoreLocation.h>

@interface ViewController : UIViewController <CLLocationManagerDelegate>
```

```
{
    CLLocationManager *locationManager;
}
```

@end

Now let us move on to the ViewController.m file. Inside the viewDidLoad method you need to set some properties of the locationManager object. (If you want to a complete description of the properties available, consult the official documentation here: http://developer.apple.com/library/ios/#documentation/CoreLocation/Reference/CLLocationManager_Class/CLLocationManager/CLLocationManager.html#//apple_ref/occ/instp/CLLocationManager/.) The properties to set are desiredAccuracy and distanceFilter.

Set the desiredAccuracy Property

This property allows you to set the desired level of accuracy. Before setting the accuracy, you have to be aware that the more accuracy you set, the more power (and time) the device will consume. Thus, you should select the accuracy according to the purpose of the app. For instance, if a location with an error-margin of 1 KM is sufficient, you do not need to set the best accuracy level and can avoid consuming unnecessary power. When you request high-accuracy location data, the initial event delivered may not have a good accuracy since it takes time to receive accurate data. The location service delivers the initial event as quickly as possible and then continues to get more accurate data. You can set the desiredAccuracy property only when you use the standard location service: It will not work with the significant-change location service. The values that you can set for the property are the following (the names are self-explanatory). Note that kCLLocationAccuracyBestForNavigation should be used only in navigation apps, since it provides the highest possible accuracy combining it with additional sensor data, consuming this way a lot of energy. For this reason it is recommended that you use this value only if the device is meant to be plugged in.

- kCLLocationAccuracyBestForNavigation
- kCLLocationAccuracyBest
- kCLLocationAccuracyNearestTenMeters
- kCLLocationAccuracyHundredMeters
- kCLLocationAccuracyKilometer
- kCLLocationAccuracyThreeKilometers

In our Hello World app, inside the viewDidLoad method, set the desiredAccuracy property to kCLLocationAccuracyBest. Then you have to set the other property, distanceFilter.

Setting the distanceFilter Property

The distanceFilter property defines the minimum distance a device has to move horizontally before an update event is produced. The distance is measured in meters and is relative to the previously delivered location. If you want the app be notified of all movements, use the value kCLDistanceFilterNone. Note that this property can be used only with the standard location service. In the example app set the property to three meters:

```
locationManager.distanceFilter = 3;
```

Now that the location manager is fully configured, let us move on to implementing the method that will receive position updates.

Implementing the Receiver Method

The method I explain here can be used to receive position updates both from the standard location service and from the significant-change location service. In the example here, the method is used to receive updates from the standard location service.

Before implementing the receiver method, you must set the delegate of the locationManager object. In this case, you set the locationManager object as a delegate of itself by writing:

```
locationManager.delegate = self;
```

Now the viewDidLoad method will look like the following:

```
- (void)viewDidLoad
{
    [super viewDidLoad];
    locationManager = [[CLLocationManager alloc] init];
    locationManager.delegate = self;
    locationManager.desiredAccuracy = kCLLocationAccuracyBest;

    locationManager.distanceFilter = 3;
}
```

Now you need to move on to the getLocation: method that is triggered when the Show position button is tapped. Inside this method you need to leave only the line [locationManager startUpdatingLocation]; that starts the standard location service. You will understand the reason soon. The getLocation: method should look like the following:

```
- (IBAction)getLocation:(id)sender {

    [locationManager startUpdatingLocation];
}
```

Let us add the implementation of the method for receiving the location updates. Whether you use the standard location service or the significant-change location service to get location events, the way you receive those events is the same. In iOS 6 the location manager notifies location update events to the locationManager:didUpdateLocations: method of its delegate when they are available. Here is the structure of the method:

```
- (void)locationManager:(CLLocationManager *)manager didUpdateLocations:(NSArray *)locations
```

You can see that two parameters are requested: manager, which is the locationManager object that generated the update event, and locations, which is an array of objects of type CLLocation containing the location data. (See the section dedicated to the CLLocation class later in this chapter.) The array might contain more than one element in case multiples events arrive without being delivered yet. Regardless, the array always contains at least one object indicating the current location. Note that the objects in the array are ordered from the older to the most recent so the freshest location update is found at the end of the array. In the following code I show you how to implement this method in the example app:

```
- (void)locationManager:(CLLocationManager *)manager
    didUpdateLocations:(NSArray *)locations {
    CLLocation* location = [locations lastObject];
    NSString *latitudeFieldData = [[NSString alloc]initWithFormat:@"%g",
location.coordinate.latitude];
    NSString *longitudeFieldData = [[NSString alloc]initWithFormat:@"%g",
location.coordinate.longitude];
    latitudeField.text = latitudeFieldData;

    longitudeField.text = longitudeFieldData;
}
```

The part of the code inside the braces will be executed every time a new location update event is reported. This way, the text fields will be updated with the new position data every time it becomes available according to the distanceFilter property value you set, which, in this case, is every three meters of linear distance covered from the previous position reported. Here is the complete ViewController.m code (Listing 8-1).

Listing 8-1. The complete ViewController.m code

```
#import "ViewController.h"

@interface ViewController ()

@property (weak, nonatomic) IBOutlet UITextField *latitudeField;
@property (weak, nonatomic) IBOutlet UITextField *longitudeField;

- (IBAction)getLocation:(id)sender;

@end

@implementation ViewController
@synthesize latitudeField;
@synthesize longitudeField;

- (void)viewDidLoad
{
    [super viewDidLoad];
    locationManager = [[CLLocationManager alloc] init];
    locationManager.delegate = self;
    locationManager.desiredAccuracy = kCLLocationAccuracyBest;
```

```objc
    locationManager.distanceFilter = 3;
}

- (void)didReceiveMemoryWarning
{
    [super didReceiveMemoryWarning];
}

- (IBAction)getLocation:(id)sender {

    [locationManager startUpdatingLocation];
}

- (void)locationManager:(CLLocationManager *)manager

    didUpdateLocations:(NSArray *)locations {
    CLLocation* location = [locations lastObject];
    NSString *latitudeFieldData = [[NSString alloc]initWithFormat:@"%g",
location.coordinate.latitude];
    NSString *longitudeFieldData = [[NSString alloc]initWithFormat:@"%g",
location.coordinate.longitude];
    latitudeField.text = latitudeFieldData;
    longitudeField.text = longitudeFieldData;
}

@end
```

Now run the app in the simulator. Once the simulator is started, click on Debug ➤ Location ➤ Freeway Drive. This way, changing location updates will be simulated. Next, click on the Show position button in the app. You will see that the coordinates in the text fields will change quickly according to the parameters set (Figure 8-15).

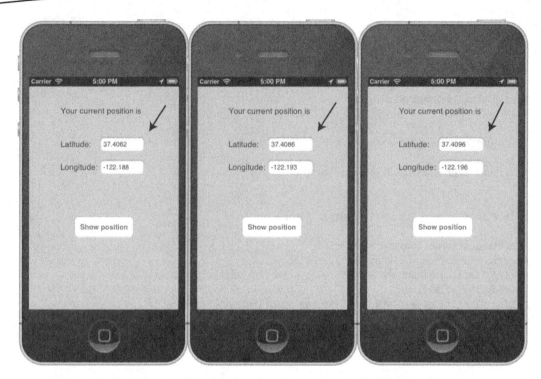

Figure 8-15. The app is at work in the simulator: notice the location updates shown in the text fields

Improving Freshness of Location Data

When implementing the locationManager:didUpdateLocations: method, you might want to perform a check of the freshness of the location data you use and select only the most recent data. The reason for this check is that the location manager object sometimes returns cached events. Because it can take time to obtain a location fix, the old cached data might be used to report the last known location. To avoid using old cached data, you can implement a freshness check by looking at the timestamp property of the location object. Here is the modified implementation of the locationManager:didUpdateLocations: method, which checks the freshness of location update events and refuses events older than 5 seconds:

```
- (void)locationManager:(CLLocationManager *)manager

    didUpdateLocations:(NSArray *)locations {

CLLocation* location = [locations lastObject];

    NSDate* eventDate = location.timestamp;

    NSTimeInterval howRecent = [eventDate timeIntervalSinceNow];

    if (abs(howRecent) < 5.0) {
```

```
    // If the event is less than 5 seconds older display the coordinates
    NSString *latitudeFieldData = [[NSString alloc]initWithFormat:@"%g",
location.coordinate.latitude];
    NSString *longitudeFieldData = [[NSString alloc]initWithFormat:@"%g",
location.coordinate.longitude];
    latitudeField.text = latitudeFieldData;
    longitudeField.text = longitudeFieldData;

    }

}
```

Stopping the Standard Location Service

Now you need to know how to stop a standard location service process, since it will allow the device to save power when geolocation is no longer necessary. You can do this using the stopUpdatingLocation method. When the method is invoked, the geolocation hardware (for instance, a GPS chip) is disabled, thereby saving power. If you then want to restart the location process, you can simply invoke the startUpdatingLocation method again. To put this method in practice, I will show you how to substitute the Show position button we implemented in the previous section with a Switch control that allows the user to start or stop the location process. Here are the steps:

1. Remove the Show position button from the MainStoryboard.storyboard file, add a Switch element, taking it from the Object library and, in the Attributes Inspector, set the element state to Off so that when the app is launched its state is Off (Figure 8-16).

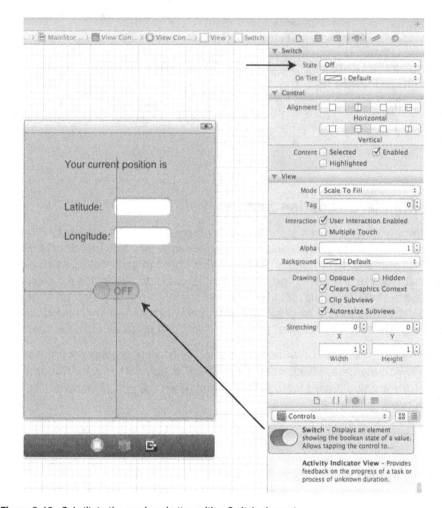

Figure 8-16. *Substitute the previous button with a Switch element*

2. Now Control-drag the Switch element to the class extension in the
    ViewController.m file. Release the mouse button and in the popover set the
    following parameters:

    ▪ Connection: Outlet

    ▪ Name: "onOffSwitch"

    ▪ Type: UISwitch

    ▪ Storage: Weak

3. After checking these settings, click on Connect. Xcode adds the declaration
    of the outlet to the class extension in the ViewController.h file and establishes
    the connection. This new declaration appears:

```
@property (weak, nonatomic) IBOutlet UISwitch *onOffSwitch;
```

4. Now Control-drag the Switch element to the class extension in the ViewController.m file, connecting the Switch element to the already existing method declaration (this is to connect the action):

```
- (IBAction)getLocation:(id)sender;
```

5. Add some code to the getLocation: implementation to check the state of the Switch. If the state is On, then you need to start the location process using the startUpdatingLocation method. Otherwise (if the status is Off), you need to stop the location process using the stopUpdatingLocation method. In the following code I show you the implementation of the method. Note that if the Switch status is Off, besides stopping the location, the code also clears the two text fields:

```
- (IBAction)getLocation:(id)sender {

    if(onOffSwitch.on) {
        [locationManager startUpdatingLocation];
    }

    else {

        [locationManager stopUpdatingLocation];
        latitudeField.text = @"";
        longitudeField.text = @"";
    }

}
```

6. Now test the app. You can see that by switching it to On, the location process starts, and by switching to Off, it stops clearing the text fields (Figure 8-17).

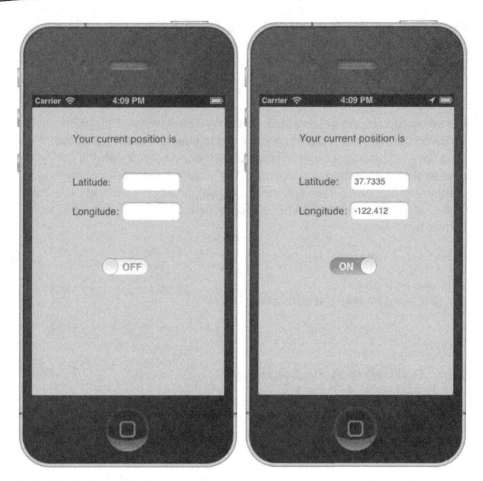

Figure 8-17. The Switch element at work

Handling Location Errors

The receiver method I showed you earlier can also implement (and I recommend you implement it) a method to handle errors in case the user did not allow location services to be used by the app or it is not possible to get location data. If an error occurs when trying to get the location, the location manager calls the locationManager:didFailWithError: method of its delegate. By implementing this method, we can handle the errors and show appropriate messages to the user. This method takes two arguments: the locationManager object that reported the error while retrieving the location and the error object containing the reason why the location (or heading, as this method reports heading errors as well) could not be retrieved. The most common error codes reported are listed below. (You can find the complete list in the documentation here: http://developer.apple.com/library/ios/#documentation/CoreLocation/Reference/CoreLocationConstantsRef/Reference/reference.html#//apple_ref/c/econst/kCLErrorLocationUnknown.)

- ▨ kCLErrorLocationUnknown: Reported if the location service is unable to get a location. Note that the location service keeps trying, thus in a situation of this kind, the user can simply ignore the error and wait for a new event.

- ▨ kCLErrorDenied: Reported if the user denies permission for the app to use location services. If the app receives such an error, you should stop the location service.

- ▨ kCLErrorNetwork: Reported if the network is unavailable or a network error has occurred.

In the following code (Listing 8-2) to be added to the ViewController.m file, I show you how to implement error handling in the Hello World standard location app. In case of error, an alert window will be displayed, reporting an appropriate message according to the error code. Note that if the user denies location permission, an appropriate alert window will be shown, the location service will be stopped, and the switch will be set to Off.

Listing 8-2. The error-handling locationManager:didFailWithError: method

```
- (void)locationManager:(CLLocationManager *)manager didFailWithError:(NSError *)error
{

    switch([error code])
    {
        case kCLErrorLocationUnknown://The location manager was unable to obtain a location
value right now.
        {
            UIAlertView *alert = [[UIAlertView alloc] initWithTitle:@"Location error"
message:@"It is not possible to obtain current location" delegate:self cancelButtonTitle:@"Ok"
otherButtonTitles:nil, nil];

 [alert show];

        }
            break;

        case kCLErrorDenied://Access to the location service was denied by the user.
        {
            UIAlertView *alert = [[UIAlertView alloc] initWithTitle:@"Error: permission denied"
message:@"User has denied permission to use location services. Go to Settings > Privacy >
Location and enable Location Services for the app." delegate:self cancelButtonTitle:@"Ok"
otherButtonTitles:nil, nil];
            [alert show];
            [locationManager stopUpdatingLocation];
            onOffSwitch.on = NO;

        }
            break;

        case kCLErrorNetwork: //The network was unavailable or a network error occurred.
```

```
        {
                UIAlertView *alert = [[UIAlertView alloc] initWithTitle:@"Network error" message:@"Make
sure your network connection is activated or that you are not in Airplane Mode" delegate:self
cancelButtonTitle:@"Ok" otherButtonTitles:nil, nil];
                [alert show];

        }
                break;

    }

}
```

To test the error handling method, run the app in the simulator, and then try to deny location permission or set the location to None (Debug ➤ Location ➤ None). Check to see if the appropriate error message is displayed (Figure 8-18).

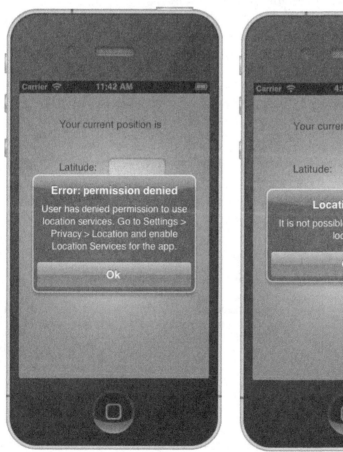

Figure 8-18. Error messages shown by the app

The Significant-Change Location Service

As I explained at the beginning of the chapter, the Core Location framework offers a second type of location service, called the significant-change location service, which can save power when it is not necessary to get accurate location data. This service reports location updates only when a significant location change has occurred. It monitors the cell tower associated with the device, so as the user moves to another location and therefore changing cell towers, a new location update is reported. The location data generated by this method is not very accurate due to the method itself, the margin of error might be 100 meters or more, but the accuracy it provides is good enough for most apps. This service can also wake up an app that is currently suspended or not running to report new location data. Using this service is very easy. You start it with the `startMonitoringSignificantLocationChanges` method without needing to set any `desiredAccuracy` or `distanceFilter` properties. To stop the service you call the `stopMonitoringSignificantLocationChanges` method. To receive location updates, you use the `locationManager:didUpdateLocations:` method – the same method used for the standard location service – and to handle errors, you use the `locationManager:didFailWithError:` method.

The `CLLocation` class

In the receiver method I showed you previously in this chapter, you saw that location data is stored in an array of objects of type `CLLocation`. You also saw that I used the `coordinate` property of a `CLLocation` object to get the coordinates of the location. A `CLLocation` object represents the location data generated by a `CLLocationManager` object and contains geographical coordinates, altitude information, and other useful location-related data. There are a number of properties you can use to access this data, as listed here:

`altitude`: Indicates the altitude measured in meters (read-only). Positive values indicate altitudes above sea level while negative values indicate altitudes below sea level. Here follows the definition:

```
@property(readonly, NS_NONATOMIC_IPHONEONLY) CLLocationDistance altitude
```

`coordinate`: Indicates the geographical coordinates of the location (read-only). Here follows the definition:

```
@property(readonly, NS_NONATOMIC_IPHONEONLY) CLLocationCoordinate2D coordinate
```

`course`: Indicates the direction in which the device is moving. Its values are measured in degrees starting at due north and continuing clockwise following the compass. North is 0 degrees, east is 90 degrees, south is 180 degrees, and so on. Note that these values may not be available on all devices. A negative value means that the direction is invalid. Here follows the definition:

```
@property(readonly, NS_NONATOMIC_IPHONEONLY) CLLocationDirection course
```

`horizontalAccuracy`: Indicates the radius of uncertainty for the location, measured in meters (read-only). The center of the circle is defined by the location's coordinates. A negative value means that the location's latitude and longitude are invalid. Here follows the definition:

```
@property(readonly, NS_NONATOMIC_IPHONEONLY) CLLocationAccuracy horizontalAccuracy
```

speed: Indicates the current speed of the device in meters per second in the direction it is currently heading. A negative value means an invalid speed. Here follows the definition:

```
@property(readonly, NS_NONATOMIC_IPHONEONLY) CLLocationSpeed speed
```

timestamp: Indicates the time at which this location was determined (read-only). Here follows the definition:

```
@property(readonly, NS_NONATOMIC_IPHONEONLY) NSDate *timestamp
```

verticalAccuracy: Indicates the accuracy of the altitude value expressed in meters (read-only). Note that the value indicated by the altitude property could be plus or minus the value indicated by this property. A negative value means that the altitude value is invalid. Here follows the definition:

```
@property(readonly, NS_NONATOMIC_IPHONEONLY) CLLocationAccuracy verticalAccuracy
```

Region Monitoring and Direction-Related Events

iOS Core Location allows you not only to obtain and use current location data but also to implement other functions, for instance, region monitoring and getting direction-related events. Region monitoring lets you define geographical regions and then monitor their boundary crossings. For instance, you can implement a function in an app that alerts users as soon as they enter a city area, and displays events occurring there that day. For more information about region monitoring, consult the guide Monitoring Shape-Based Regions in the official documentation here: http://developer. apple.com/library/ios/#documentation/userexperience/conceptual/LocationAwarenessPG/ CoreLocation/CoreLocation.html#//apple_ref/doc/uid/TP40009497-CH2-SW13.

Direction-related events are determined by the heading and course information. Heading indicates the orientation of the device relative to true north, while course indicates the direction the device is moving in. You can use the heading and course information especially for augmented reality apps, for instance to show information about the objects around the user's current position. To implement direction-related events, check the official documentation here: http://developer.apple.com/ library/ios/#documentation/userexperience/conceptual/LocationAwarenessPG/GettingHeadings/ GettingHeadings.html#//apple_ref/doc/uid/TP40009497-CH5-SW1.

What Happens When Location Services Are Disabled?

The Hello World standard location app I showed you in this chapter is an app that requires location services to function. It cannot work without them. You need to know how the app behaves when location services are disabled, either for all the apps on the device or for a single app. Also, the user could have given initial permission to the app to use location services but then could have disabled them. Just a reminder: iOS 6 location services can be enabled or disabled by opening Settings ➤ Privacy ➤ Location (Figure 8-19).

Figure 8-19. Location services settings

In Figure 8-19 you can see that besides enabling and disabling location services, you can also select which apps can use them. If Location Services is switched to Off, the sample app cannot function, so a message must be displayed to the user indicating that Location Services must be switched to On. Luckily, iOS takes care of this by displaying an alert window prompting the user to set Location Services to On when the startUpdatingLocation or startMonitoringSignificantLocationChanges methods are started again (Figure 8-20).

Figure 8-20. The alert prompting the user to set Location Services to On

However, if the user has set Location Services to On but has disabled the location services only for our single app (Figure 8-21), the message shown in Figure 8-20 will not be displayed.

Figure 8-21. The user has disabled location services only for the Hello World standard location app

In this case, the error message appears, indicating that the user has denied permission as we saw earlier in this chapter (Figure 8-18, left example).

Summary

In this chapter I introduced you to using location services in a native iOS app. You've begun to familiarize yourself with the Core Location framework and now you should be able to do the following:

- Import Core Location framework in a project.

- Configure and start the standard location method.

- Configure and start the significant-change location method.

- Implement the `locationManager:didUpdateLocations:` method to receive location updates and use them.

- Handle errors with the method `locationManager:didFailWithError:`.

Chapter 9

Introduction to Apple Maps and the Map Kit Framework

In the previous chapter I walked you through the two basic ingredients for creating native geo apps for iOS : location services, which is managed through the Core Location framework, and Apple Maps cartography, which is managed through the Map Kit framework. In this chapter I illustrate the basic procedures to integrate Apple Maps into your native apps. I demonstrate two ways to perform the procedures: using the Xcode Storyboard interface and] coding them directly. In the chapter I show you how to: Link the Map Kit framework to your project. Create a map view using the storyboard. Set the map type, enable and disable pan and zoom, and show user location using the storyboard. Create a map view using the MKMapView class. Set the map type, enable and disable pan and zoom, and show user location.Center the map on a given set of coordinates and set its zoom level. MapKit was based on Google Maps through iOS 5.1. Starting with iOS 6, Apple Maps took the place of Google Maps, so let's start with a quick look at the change.

Apple Maps vs. Google Maps

When iOS 6 was officially released in September 2012, the substitution of Google Maps with Apple Maps generated criticism against Apple's choice because Apple Maps services had many flaws and limitations compared to Google Maps (cartography errors, scarcity of map data, fewer overlays available, to name a few). At the time of writing, Apple Maps cartography is less accurate and offers less richness of data compared to Google Maps. In Figure 9-1 I show a simple example: an area of Dublin (Grand Canal Docks) mapped in Google Maps (left) and in Apple Maps (right). You can clearly see the differences between the two maps in terms of level of detail and information. The Apple map is less rich in detail (for example, no building outlines are drawn, streets and roads are not well differentiated, etc.).

Figure 9-1. Grand Canal Docks area (Dublin)

The difference in quality between the two services is quite understandable since Google has been implementing its maps services for almost 7 years, putting all together an amount of specialists, expertise and geographic data unrivaled until now (just think about the street level photo coverage made available in the Street View function and not available in Apple Maps). Although Google Maps would have been a better cartographic base to use for developing native apps, because Apple substituted it with Apple Maps, we have no choice but to use this service. However, if you do not need to create native apps, you can refer back to the part of the book where I explain how to develop geo web apps taking full advantage of the power and richness of data provided by Google Maps through its JavaScript API.

In the following sections I will show you how to add a map view to your app and how to set its basic properties and controls. Note that since we are developing for iOS 6, Map Kit will use Apple Maps, but if you are developing for iOS 5 or earlier, you can still set up Map Kit to use Google Maps. You will need to agree to the Google Mobile Maps terms of service at http://code.google.com/apis/maps/iphone/terms.html.

Getting Started with Map Kit

The official documentation of the Map Kit framework and its related classes and protocols is available here: http://developer.apple.com/library/ios/#documentation/MapKit/Reference/ MapKit_Framework_Reference/_index.html. Keep the documentation as a reference point when developing with Map Kit. If you want to use the Map Kit framework in an app, first you must add it to the Xcode project as follows:

1. Open Xcode and, in the Welcome to Xcode window, click "Create a new Xcode project" (or choose File ➤ New ➤ New project). Within the iOS category, select Single View Application.

2. A new dialog appears that prompts you to name your app and choose additional options for your project. Fill in the Product Name field, naming it "Map Kit Hello World," and fill in the Organization Name field as well. In Devices, select iPhone. Make sure that the Use Storyboard and Use Automatic Reference Counting options are selected and that the Include Unit Tests option is unselected, and then click on Next. In the following window indicate a location for your project (leave the Source Control option unselected), and then click Create. Xcode opens your new project in a new workspace window.

3. To use Map Kit in an Xcode project, you must import its framework. In Xcode 4.5 click on the project folder on the left in the Navigator area, and then scroll down the Summary tab until you get to the section Linked Frameworks and Libraries. Here you will find all the frameworks used in the project (Figure 9-2).

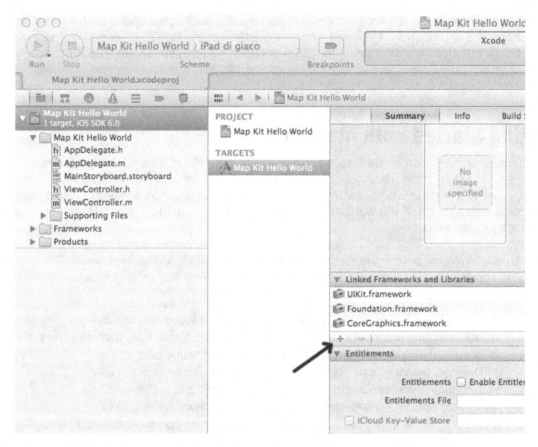

Figure 9-2. *The frameworks used in the project*

4. Click on the + sign below the framework list and select MapKit.framework (Figure 9-3), and then click on Add. The framework will be added to the project.

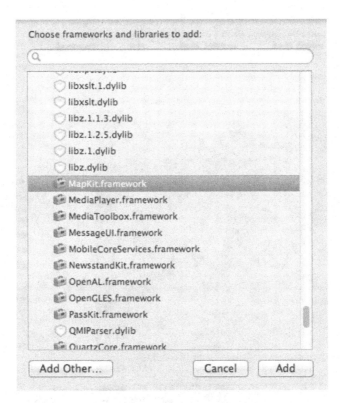

Figure 9-3. Select the MapKit.framework and add it to the project

5. To use the framework classes in your project you need to also add an
    #import <MapKit/MapKit.h> statement at the top of the header files – for
    instance, to the ViewController.h file. (For this Hello world it is not necessary,
    but I mention it to you now for the next apps we will look at.)

Once the Map Kit framework is added to the project, you can easily use it to display a map view.

Adding a Map View to the Project

In this section I show you how to display a simple map view using the Storyboard instrument, which
is an Xcode tool that allows you to design the UI of your app and its views without directly writing
code. Then I will illustrate how to configure some properties of the map view using the Attributes
Inspector window. Here are the steps:

1. Click on the MainStoryboard_iPhone.storyboard file and make sure that the
    Object library is displayed in the Utility area. From the Object library, drag a
    Map View (that is, a MKMapView object) onto the view and place it so that it fills
    all the available space (see Figure 9-4).

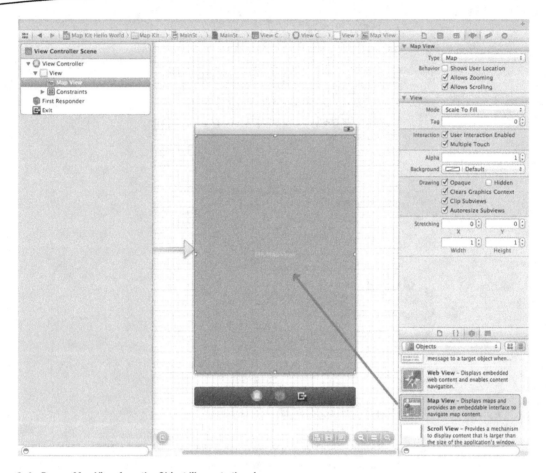

Figure 9-4. *Drag a Map View from the Object library to the view*

2.   Click Run to execute the app in the simulator or on a real device. You will get
     a result similar to what is shown in Figure 9-5.

Figure 9-5. *The app running in the simulator*

Now you can try to pan and zoom the map. (If you are using the simulator to emulate pinch zoom, hold the Option key down and click on the map with the mouse: The position of the two fingers will appear so that you can easily zoom in and out.)

As you can see, it is very easy to add a map view to an app using the storyboard.

Setting Some Basic Properties of the Map

You can also set some properties of the map view through the Attributes Inspector. Let's look at that now. Select the Map View object in the storyboard and then display the Attributes Inspector on the right (Figure 9-6).

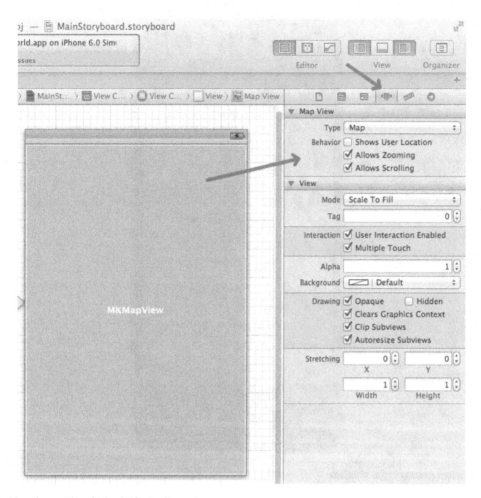

Figure 9-6. Map view settings in the Attributes Inspector

The first property you can set is the map type. Three options are available: Map, Satellite, and Hybrid. They are very similar to the Google Maps JavaScript API map types. Map is the standard map type, Satellite shows aerial and satellite images, and Hybrid overlays labels and other information on the Satellite map type (Figure 9-7).

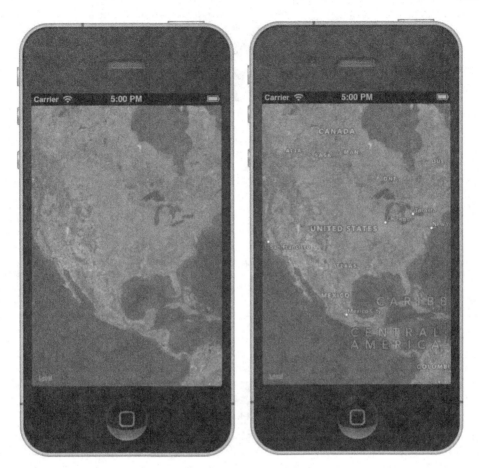

Figure 9-7. Satellite (on the left) and Hybrid (on the right) map types

To test a different map type, stop the previous application if it is running, and then run it again after selecting a different map type in the Attributes Inspector.

The next option you encounter in the Attributes Inspector is Show User Location, which allows you to show or hide the user position. If you enable Show User Location, a built-in location function based on Core Location is activated and the user position is shown through a marker (annotation) on the map (see Figure 9-8). Note that when the user location moves out of the currently displayed portion of map, the map does not re-center automatically to show the location marker.

Figure 9-8. The current location shown on the map

In the Attributes Inspector there are still two options for configuring the Map View to enable or disable zooming and panning by simply selecting or unselecting the respective fields (see Figure 9-6). It is generally recommended that you keep panning and zooming enabled, but in some circumstances you might want disable these options. For instance, if you want the user stay focused only on a portion of the map without wandering around on the map, you may disable panning.

As you have just seen, it is possible to create and basically configure a map view without writing a single line of code. However, to have wider control of the map view and integrate it in your application, you need to use code for some of its elements.

Controlling Your Map View Using Code

The basic Map Kit Framework class that allows you to create a map view is MKMapView. By using this class you can create a map object to embed in your apps. You can center the map, zoom in, and add elements (called annotations) on it that get stuck to the map itself so that, when panned, they are panned as well. You can also assign a delegate object to the map that allows you to handle user interactions with the map. The map view reports all relevant interactions to its delegate.

In this section I illustrate how to create an instance of the `MKMapView` class. Then I show you how to set the map type of the map. You will learn how to build a map type control that allows the user to select the map type (Standard, Satellite, or Hybrid). Later in the section you will learn how to center the map on a given set of coordinates, setting its zoom level as well. I will also show how to enable and disable zoom, pan, and display user location.

The `MKMapView` Class

To create and add a map view using code, you need to create an instance of the `MKMapView` class, initialize it by using the `initWithFrame:` method, and add it as a subview to your view hierarchy.

Note that because the map is a view, you can manipulate it in the same way you manipulate other views. Let us now try to create a map with code, without using the storyboard:

1. Create a new project, giving it the name "Map Kit Hello World 2". Link the project to the Map Kit Framework.

2. Open the ViewController.h file and add the `#import <MapKit/MapKit.h>` directive.

3. Declare an instance variable of the `MKMapView` class, and then declare it as an outlet. Now the content of the ViewController.h file should look like the following:

   ```
   #import <UIKit/UIKit.h>
   #import <MapKit/MapKit.h>

   @interface ViewController : UIViewController {
   MKMapView *mapView;
   }
   @property (nonatomic, retain) IBOutlet MKMapView *mapView;
   @end
   ```

Let us now move on to the implementation file (ViewController.m). First, add the `@synthesize mapView;` directive. Then, inside the `ViewDidLoad` method, initialize the `MKMapView` object using the `initWithFrame:` method, setting it to fill all the available space:

```
mapView = [[MKMapView alloc] initWithFrame:self.view.bounds]
```

4. Add the `MKMapView` object as a subview of the view hierarchy:

   ```
   [self.view addSubview:mapView];
   ```

5. Run the code in the simulator or on a real device. The map view will be created and displayed.

Now you can turn to configuring the map properties.

Configuring Map Properties Using Code

You can configure the same map properties using code as the ones you set using the storyboard, for instance, the map type, pan and zoom. First, I will show you how to work with the map type by building a map type control that will allow the user to select the desired map type. Then I will show you how to set a center and a zoom level for the map. Let's look at that now.

Changing Map Type

To change the map type, you need to set a constant for the `mapType` property of the map view. The available map type constants are:

- `MKMapTypeStandard`
- `MKMapTypeSatellite`

`MKMapTypeHybrid` For example, if you want to change the Standard map type to Satellite, inside the `ViewDidLoad` method, you can write:

```
mapView.mapType = MKMapTypeSatellite;
```

Note that, when you change the map type, the app has to load new map content (for instance, satellite imagery when switching from the Standard to the Satellite map type) and this can take some time depending on the available Internet band. Also, if you do not specify a map type, the standard one is set by default.

Since I want you to practice a little bit with map types, in the next section you will build an app equipped with a control to change map type.

Building a Map Type Control

Here is how to create a simple control for a map-based app that allows you to change map type choosing among three options: Standard, Satellite, and Hybrid. The initial map type will be Standard (which is set by default so you do not need to do anything for it). The resulting app is shown in Figure 9-9.

Figure 9-9. *The complete app*

To build the app you need to create a new iPhone Single View application project and then build a map view. To do this, follow the steps I illustrated in the "Adding a map view to the project" section.

Call the project Map Type Control and create the map view using a storyboard so that the hierarchy of the views is managed through the storyboard. Once you have created the map view, check to make sure that its properties are set the same way as in Figure 9-10, and then run it to check that it is properly working.

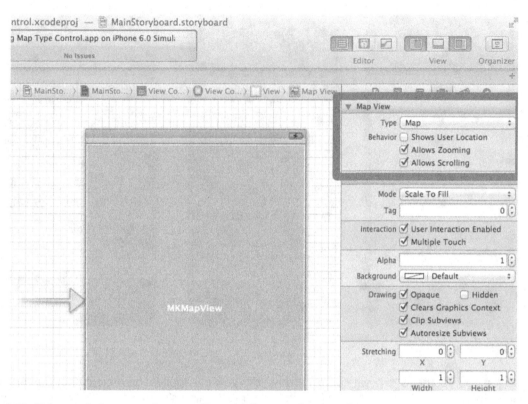

Figure 9-10. Make sure that your map view properties match the properties shown here

Adding a Segmented Control

Now display the Objects library and drag a Segmented Control (UISegmentedControl) object onto the map, as shown in Figure 9-11. Note that the segment covers part of the map. This is not a problem but be careful not to cover the Legal link in the lower-left corner of the map.

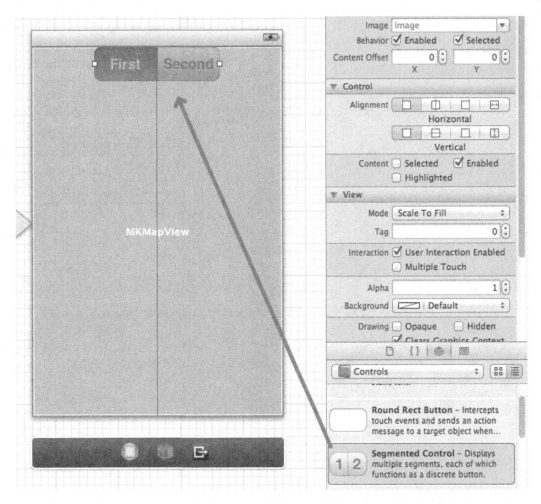

Figure 9-11. *The Segmented Control placed on the map*

In the Attributes Inspector, change the properties of the Segmented Control so that is composed of three segments, and then name the three segments Standard, Satellite, and Hybrid, respectively. Stretch the segment control so that the segments' names are properly displayed, as shown in Figure 9-12.

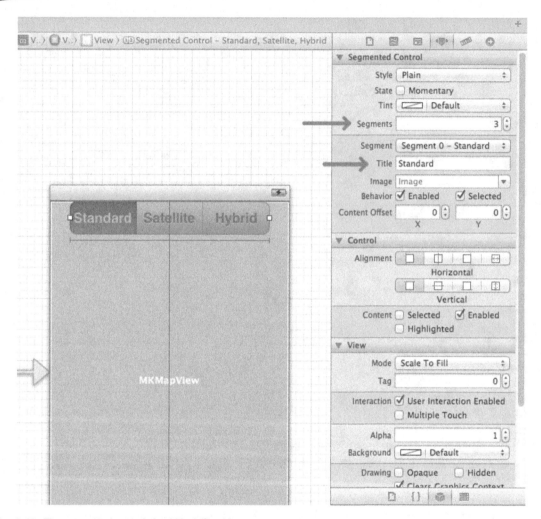

Figure 9-12. *The segmented control should look like this*

Creating the Outlets

Open the ViewController.h file and add the #import <MapKit/MapKit.h> directive if it is not already present, and then save the files. Now display the Assistant Editor so that the storyboard appears on the left and the ViewController.m file appears on the right (Figure 9-13).

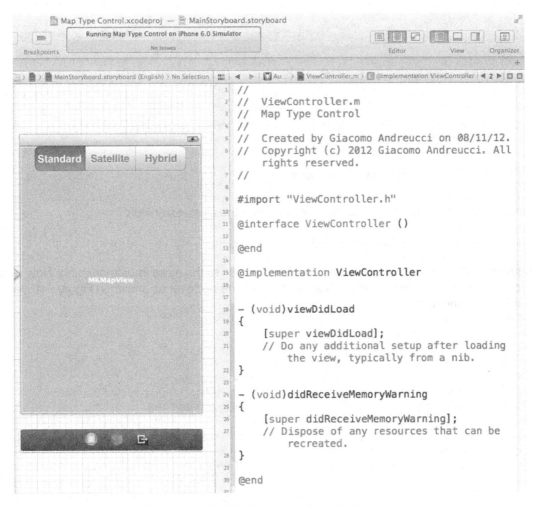

Figure 9-13. Display the Assistant Editor and open the ViewController.m file on the right

In the class extension of the implementation file (that is, the space within @interface
HellowWorldViewController() and its @end directive), you have to create two outlets, one for the
map view and one for the map type control, so that you can programmatically manipulate them
later using code. From the storyboard Ctrl drag the map view to the class extension. A popover will
appear. Fill its fields as shown in Figure 9-14, and then click on Connect.

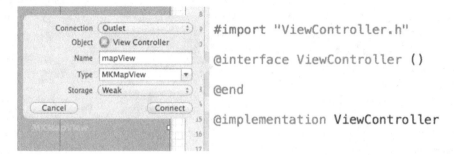

Figure 9-14. Configure the popover for the map view outlet

Now the declaration of the map view outlet is added to the class extension:

```
@property (weak, nonatomic) IBOutlet MKMapView *mapView;
```

The respective @synthetize directive has also been added to the class implementation. Now repeat this procedure with the segmented control, configuring the popover as shown in Figure 9-15, and then click on Connect.

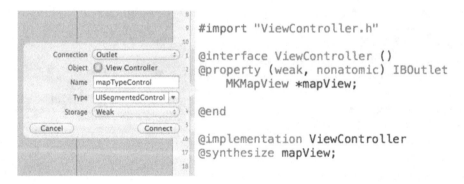

Figure 9-15. Configure the popover for the segmented control

Now the declaration of the map type control has been added to the class extension (and the respective @synthetize directive to the class implementation):

```
@property (weak, nonatomic) IBOutlet UISegmentedControl *mapTypeControl;
```

Creating the Action and the Method

Now we have to create an action so that, when the user taps a segment of the control, an action message is sent to the view controller, which, in turn, performs a method (in this case, a method to change the map type). To do this, again Ctrl drag the segmented control on the class extension, but this time, set the fields in the popover as follows (Figure 9-16), and then click on Connect.

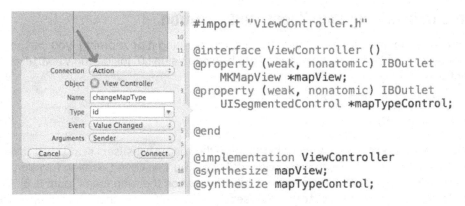

```
 9  #import "ViewController.h"
10
11  @interface ViewController ()
 2  @property (weak, nonatomic) IBOutlet
        MKMapView *mapView;
 3  @property (weak, nonatomic) IBOutlet
        UISegmentedControl *mapTypeControl;
 5
    @end
 5
    @implementation ViewController
18  @synthesize mapView;
19  @synthesize mapTypeControl;
```

Figure 9-16. Configure the popover for the action connected to the segmented control

You can see that the action method has been declared in the class extension:

```
- (IBAction)changeMapType:(id)sender;
```

A stub method implementation has also been added to the implementation section:

```
- (IBAction)changeMapType:(id)sender {
}
```

Now if you tap the segmented control, the changeMapType: method is triggered but it does not do anything since we still have to fully implement it. Let us modify the method as shown here:

```
-

(IBAction)changeMapType:(id)sender {
    if ([mapTypeControl selectedSegmentIndex] == 0){
        mapView.mapType = MKMapTypeStandard;
    }
    else if ([mapTypeControl selectedSegmentIndex] == 1)
    {
        mapView.mapType = MKMapTypeSatellite;

    }

    else if ([mapTypeControl selectedSegmentIndex] == 2)
    {
        mapView.mapType = MKMapTypeHybrid;

    }
}
```

As you can see in the code, the method checks which part of the segmented control has been selected and then sets the appropriate map type. Now run the app. Tapping on a segment will load the respective map type (see Figure 9-9 above). In the next section you will see how to enable and disable pan, zoom, and the display of user location using code, without using the storyboard.

Enabling and Disabling Pan, Zoom, and Location

If you do not want the user to interact with the map by panning it or zooming, you can set the map properties zoomEnabled and scrollEnabled to the boolean value NO. Inside the ViewDidLoad method you can write:

```
mapView.zoomEnabled=NO;
mapView.scrollEnabled=NO;
```

Map Kit also has a property to show user location on the map: showsUserLocation. It takes a boolean value; if you set it to YES, the map view will use a built-in Core Location function to find the current location and then show it by drawing a blue marker on the map (see Figure 9-8). Inside the ViewDidLoad method try to add mapView.showsUserLocation=YES; and then run the app. The current location (or the location set in the simulator) will be shown and updated. As long as this property is set to YES, the map view continues to track and update the user's location.

Centering and Zooming the MapI have shown you how to create a map view and set some of its basic properties. There is still one very important thing you need to know: how to center a map and set its initial zoom level. When using the Google Maps JavaScript API it is very easy to center and set the zoom level: You simply set the center and zoom properties of the map object, giving appropriate values to them. Map Kit uses a slightly different method. The visible area of the map is defined through a property of the MKMapView class called region. This property contains an MKCoordinateRegion structure defined as follows:

```
typedef struct {*-

    CLLocationCoordinate2D center;

    MKCoordinateSpan span;

} MKCoordinateRegion;
```

If you look at the structure, you see that the center field is of type CLLocationCoordinate2D. To center the map on a location, you can assign a set of coordinates, latitude and longitude, to center. For instance, if you want to center the map on New York city (lat: 40.716667°; long: -74°), add the following lines to the ViewDidLoad method:

```
MKCoordinateRegion region;
region.center.latitude = 40.716667;
region.center.longitude = -74;
[mapView setRegion:region animated:YES];
```

As you can see, first you create the region object, then you set its latitude and longitude properties, and finally you set the map view to the new region using the setRegion:animated: method. (Note that you can specify YES to animate the transition to the new region; otherwise, set NO if you want the map to be centered on the specified region immediately.) Doing this centers the map on the desired location but still does not set a specific zoom level. The maximum zoom-in level is applied by default, as shown in Figure 9-17.

Figure 9-17. The map is centered on New York City with the maximum zoom-in level

How to Set a Zoom Level

To set a zoom level, you need to define a value for the second property of region, which is span. A region object is defined by its center (center property) and by horizontal and vertical distances (span property). In other words, span defines the width and height of the map rectangle using map coordinates and adopting as units of measure degrees, minutes, and seconds. If you specify a large span, you can show a wide map area to the user, therefore setting a low zoom level. If you define a smaller span, you show a smaller area to the user and therefore the zoom level increases. The main distinction from the Google Maps JS API is that in Map Kit you do not set a zoom level. Instead, you define the extension of the portion of map to be displayed in the space made available for the map view.

Since span values are expressed in degrees, you need to know that one degree of latitude is equivalent to 111 kilometers (approximately) while the equivalence between one longitude degree and meters varies based on the current latitude: at the equator, one degree of longitude is equivalent is about 111 kilometers and at the poles this value is zero. To define the span values you must set its latitudeDelta (amount of north-to-south distance measured in degrees) and longitudeDelta (amount of east-to-west distance measured in degrees) properties. Note that it is sufficient to set just one of the two properties to define a span. Try to add region.span.latitudeDelta =1; to the previous code so that the ViewDidLoad method is modified the following way:

```
- (void)viewDidLoad
{
    [super viewDidLoad];

    MKCoordinateRegion region;
    region.center.latitude = 40.716667;
    region.center.longitude = -74;
    region.span.latitudeDelta =1;
    [mapView setRegion:region animated:YES];
}
```

Run the code. On a standard iPhone, you will get a map like the one shown in Figure 9-18. You will see that New York City is still at the center of the map but a span has been added, making the map height 1°. The width of the map has been automatically set based on the defined height and center and the map has been zoomed out (see differences with respect to Figure 9-17).

Figure 9-18. A north-south span has been added to the map

Now try to add a value also for the longitudeDelta property of span. Set the value to "3" (region.span.longitudeDelta =3;) and run the app. You will get a map like the one shown in Figure 9-19.

Figure 9-19. *An east-west span has been added to the map as well*

Looking at Figure 9-19, you notice that the latitude span has also changed. The map view chooses the zoom level that allows the region defined by latitudeDelta and longitudeDelta to be fully visible while still filling as much of the screen as possible. Note that you can also specify the span in meters using the MKCoordinateRegionMakeWithDistance function, which allows you to create a new MKCoordinateRegion with span values expressed in meters. Here is the function:

```
MKCoordinateRegion MKCoordinateRegionMakeWithDistance(
    CLLocationCoordinate2D centerCoordinate,
    CLLocationDistance latitudinalMeters,
    CLLocationDistance longitudinalMeters
);
```

If you want to set a latitudinal span of 100,000 meters and a longitudinal span of 50,000 meters, you can write:

```
region = MKCoordinateRegionMakeWithDistance(region.center, 100000, 50000);
```

Summary

In this chapter I introduced you to the Map Kit Framework, the library that allows you to implement Apple Maps cartography in a native iOS app. Before you move on to the next chapter, you should now know how to do the following:

- Link the Map Kit Framework.
- Create a map view using a storyboard.
- Set the map type, enable and disable pan and zoom, and show user location using the storyboard.
- Create a map view with code, using the `MKMapView` class.
- Set the map type, enable and disable pan and zoom, and show user location.
- Center the map on a given set of coordinates and set its zoom level.

Displaying Objects on the Map

Map Kit allows you to display objects of different types on the map. You can represent *annotations*, which are points to which an icon and a balloon are associated (elements that in the Google Maps JavaScript API were called marker and info window) and *overlays*, which are objects defined by several coordinates, such as lines and polygons. In this chapter I show you different methods to create annotations and overlays, and I demonstrate ways to customize them.

Working with Annotations

Annotations (which in the Google Maps JavaScript API are called "markers" and in Google Earth are called "placemarks") allow you to represent a point primitive, which is an object anchored to the map in one point identified by a set of coordinates (latitude and longitude). An annotation is represented by an icon that can be customized and, when clicked, open a balloon (here called a "callout") containing a title and other elements (see Figure 10-1).

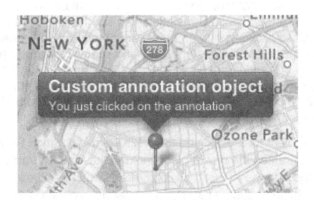

Figure 10-1. Example of an annotation

Map Kit facilitates working with annotations (and overlays as well) by keeping the associated data (coordinates, title, and other content of the callout) separate from their visual presentation on the map, in a way that somewhat resembles the way CSS works. With this approach, you can better manage hundreds of annotations (or overlays) without excessively slowing the app's performance. To add annotations to a map, you need to implement two elements:

- An object that will store the annotation content (the annotation object); this object must conform to the MKAnnotation protocol.

- A view, derived from the MKAnnotationView class that will be used to present the annotation on the map surface (the annotation view).

You can build an annotation object in one of two ways:

1. Using the MKPointAnnotation class to quickly create a simple annotation to display a callout provided with a title and a subtitle.

2. Building a custom object that conforms to the MKAnnotation protocol. This gives you more flexibility in defining the appearance of the annotation and its callout.

Regarding the presentation of the annotation object on the map, Map Kit provides some standard annotation views. You can also define custom annotation views.

In the next section I show you how to build annotations by defining an MKPointAnnotation annotation object and then using a standard annotation view to display it on the map. Later I will illustrate how to build custom annotation objects using the MKAnnotation protocol.

Creating an Annotation Object Using the MKPointAnnotation Class

The quickest way to create an annotation object is to use the MKPointAnnotation class. This class allows you to create simple annotations, with a title and a subtitle like the one shown in Figure 10-1. The MKPointAnnotation class allows you to create an annotation object whose properties are coordinate (of type CLLocationCoordinate2D), title, and subtitle; the last two properties are set with strings containing the title and subtitle text of the callout. In the following procedure I show you how to display an annotation positioned on New York City (latitude: 40.664167; longitude: -73.938611). The title of the callout will read "New York City," while the subtitle will read "New York is the most populous city in the USA". Here are the steps:

1. Create a new project for iPhone and call it MKPointAnnotation Example. Once you have created the new project, include the Map Kit framework in your project and add the #import <MapKit/MapKit.h> directive inside your ViewController.h file (see explanations in the previous chapter). Next, create a map view using the storyboard. (For more information, see the previous chapter.) Once the map view is created, set up the Assistant Editor to display the ViewController.h file on the right of the storyboard. Ctrl-drag the map view

from the storyboard inside the @interface declaration of ViewController.h
to declare its relative property. You should also declare an instance variable
of the class MKPointAnnotation, which will be the annotation object:
MKPointAnnotation *annotation;. Now the ViewController.h file should look
like the following:

```
#import <UIKit/UIKit.h>
#import <MapKit/MapKit.h>

@interface ViewController : UIViewController {
MKPointAnnotation *annotation;
}

@property (weak, nonatomic) IBOutlet MKMapView *mapView;

@end
```

2. Now let us move on to the ViewController.m file. Inside the viewDidLoad
   method, allocate and initialize the annotation instance variable:

   ```
   annotation = [[MKPointAnnotation alloc]init];
   ```

   Then set the title and subtitle properties with the appropriate strings:

   ```
   annotation.title =@"New York City";
   annotation.subtitle =@"New York is the most populous city in the USA";
   ```

3. Now create a variable of type CLLocationCoordinate2D that will contain the
   set of coordinates to be used to position the annotation, set the appropriate
   coordinate values, and assign the CLLocationCoordinate2D variable to the
   coordinate property of annotation:

   ```
   CLLocationCoordinate2D NewYorkCoords;
   NewYorkCoords.latitude = 40.664167;
   NewYorkCoords.longitude = -73.938611;
   annotation.coordinate = NewYorkCoords;
   ```

4. Finally, use the addAnnotation: method to add the annotation object to the
   map view:

   ```
   [_mapView addAnnotation:annotation];
   ```

You probably noticed that we did not declare an instance variable for the map view but only its
property and we did not explicitly @synthesize it in the ViewController.m file. Xcode 4.5 automatically
generates an instance variable with the same type (and, under ARC, ownership qualification) as the
declared property. The instance variable name will be an underscore (_) followed by the declared

property name, in this case _mapView. This allows you to save time while coding. You could also explicitly @synthesize the property and declare the instance variable in the traditional way. Here is the complete code of ViewController.m:

```objc
#import "ViewController.h"

@interface ViewController ()
@end

@implementation ViewController

- (void)viewDidLoad
{
    [super viewDidLoad];
    annotation = [[MKPointAnnotation alloc]init];
    annotation.title =@"New York City";
    annotation.subtitle =@"New York is the most populous city in the USA";
    CLLocationCoordinate2D NewYorkCoords;
    NewYorkCoords.latitude = 40.664167;
    NewYorkCoords.longitude = -73.938611;
    annotation.coordinate = NewYorkCoords;
    [_mapView addAnnotation:annotation];
}

- (void)didReceiveMemoryWarning
{
    [super didReceiveMemoryWarning];

}

@end
```

Now run the app. The annotation will be displayed on the map and you will be able to open its callout by clicking on it (Figure 10-2).

Figure 10-2. The annotation created

Displaying Current Location Using an MKPointAnnotation Annotation

As I showed you in the previous chapter, you can easily show user location by using the built-in function that you can directly activate in the Attributes Inspector of the map view. However, using this built-in function, you do not have much control over the Core Location service or over the appearance of the annotation, which is automatically generated with a default title and no subtitle. Thus, I want to explain here how to manually implement a location manager and use a MKPointAnnotation object to show the current location. I will also show you how to add a function that automatically centers the map view on the current location so that the annotation cannot disappear outside the map when its position changes (as it would do by default). We will take the code of the previous example and make some changes to it. Here are the steps:

1. Open the previous project. Since you will also use the Core Location framework, import it into your project, and then add the #import <CoreLocation/CoreLocation.h> directive to the ViewController.h file.

2. Inside the ViewController.h file declare the `<CLLocationManagerDelegate>` protocol since location updates will be reported to it (see Chapter 8). Inside the same file also declare two instance variables, one of type `CLLocationManager`, which will be the location manager object, and one of type `CLLocation`, which will contain the current location coordinates:

```
CLLocationManager *locationManager;
CLLocation *location;
```

Now the ViewController.h file should look like the following:

```
#import <UIKit/UIKit.h>
#import <MapKit/MapKit.h>
#import <CoreLocation/CoreLocation.h>

@interface ViewController : UIViewController <CLLocationManagerDelegate> {
MKPointAnnotation *annotation;
CLLocationManager *locationManager;
CLLocation *location;
}

@property (weak, nonatomic) IBOutlet MKMapView *mapView;

@end
```

3. Let us now move on to the ViewController.m file. Inside the `viewDidLoad` method allocate and initiate the location manager, and then the view controller as its delegate. Finally, activate location by using the `startUpdatingLocation` method. (See Chapter 8 for more information.) The code is as follows:

```
locationManager = [[CLLocationManager alloc] init];
locationManager.delegate = self;
[locationManager startUpdatingLocation];
```

4. Now change the `title` and `subtitle` strings of the annotation since it will no longer be centered on the New York City coordinates but instead will display your current location. You should also set the annotation's `coordinate` property to the `location.coordinate` value (location is the object that we use to store the current position coordinates and that we declared in the ViewController.h file).

```
annotation.title =@"Your current position";
annotation.subtitle =@"This annotation shows your current position";
annotation.coordinate = location.coordinate;
```

Then assign the current position coordinates to regionCenter:

```
CLLocationCoordinate2D regionCenter = location.coordinate;
```

5. Now let us move on to the locationManager:didUpdateLocations: method, which receives position updates (see Chapter 8 for more information), and add an instruction to it to update the annotation coordinate property to the current location coordinates contained in the location object:

```
annotation.coordinate = location.coordinate;
```

This way, at every location update, the annotation position is updated on the map as well.

6. We also want the map to change its center when the annotation changes position, so as to keep the annotation at the center of the map. To do this, you use the setCenterCoordinate:animated: method:

```
[_mapView setCenterCoordinate:location.coordinate animated:TRUE];
```

Here is the complete code of ViewController.m:

```objc
#import "ViewController.h"

@interface ViewController ()

@end

@implementation ViewController

- (void)viewDidLoad
{
    [super viewDidLoad];
    //Allocate and initialize the location manager, then start position updates
    locationManager = [[CLLocationManager alloc] init];
    locationManager.delegate = self;
    [locationManager startUpdatingLocation];

    //Set the properties of the annotation and add this to the map
    annotation = [[MKPointAnnotation alloc]init];
    annotation.title =@"Your current position";
    annotation.subtitle =@"This annotation shows your current position";
    annotation.coordinate = location.coordinate;
    [_mapView addAnnotation:annotation];

    //Define the region of the map
    CLLocationCoordinate2D regionCenter = location.coordinate;
    MKCoordinateRegion region = MKCoordinateRegionMakeWithDistance(regionCenter, 400, 400);
    [_mapView setRegion:region animated:TRUE];

}
```

```
    //Receive current position updates and based on them change the position of the annotation and
set the center of the region
- (void)locationManager:(CLLocationManager *)manager

    didUpdateLocations:(NSArray *)locations {
    location = [locations lastObject];
    annotation.coordinate = location.coordinate;
    [_mapView setCenterCoordinate:location.coordinate animated:TRUE];
}

- (void)didReceiveMemoryWarning
{
    [super didReceiveMemoryWarning];

}

@end
```

Now the code is complete and you can run the app. If you use the simulator, try the Freeway Drive simulation. You will see the annotation position changing and the map being simultaneously re-centered so as to keep the annotation in its center (Figure 10-3).

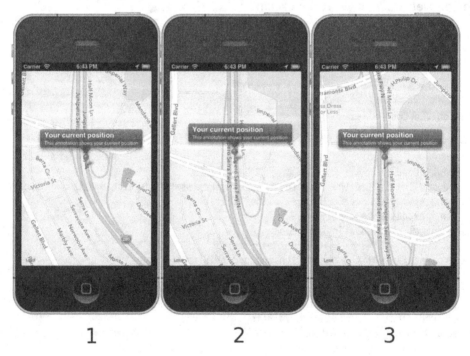

Figure 10-3. The position of the annotation changes as does the visible portion of the map

Creating Custom Annotation Objects

Custom annotation objects give you more flexibility compared to a `MKPointAnnotation`, but their creation is a bit more complex. The steps I show you in this section will make things quite easy for you:

1. Create a new project (of the Single View Application type, for iPhone devices) and name it Custom Annotation Object Example. Add the MapKit.framework to it and add the `#import <MapKit/MapKit.h>` directive to the ViewController.h file.

2. Create a map view using the storyboard. Once the map view is created, activate the Assistant Editor so as to display the ViewController.h file on the left and the storyboard on the right. Ctrl-drag the map view from the storyboard inside the `@interface` declaration of ViewController.h to declare its relative property:

    `@property (weak, nonatomic) IBOutlet MKMapView *mapView;`

    As in the previous example you do not declare an instance variable for the map view but only its property and you do not explicitly `@synthesize` it in the ViewController.m file. The instance variable name will therefore be an underscore (_) followed by the declared property name, in this case _mapView. You could also explicitly `@synthesize` the property and declare the instance variable in the traditional way. Now run the app to make sure it works.

3. Now you must create a new class for the custom annotation object. In Xcode click on File ➤ New ➤ File and select Objective-C class (Figure 10-4).

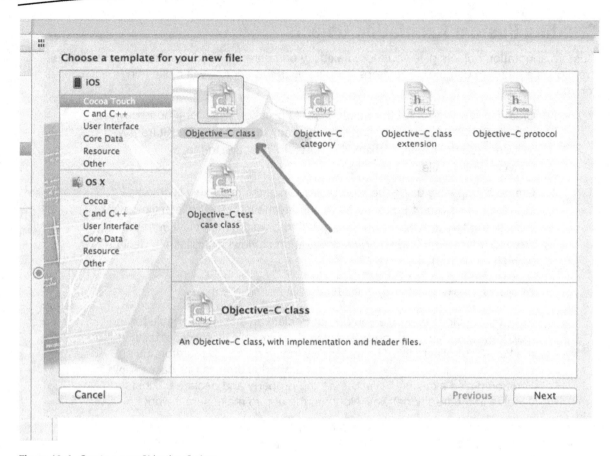

Figure 10-4. Create a new Objective-C class

4. Name the class CustomAnnotation and make sure it is a subclass of NSObject (Figure 10-5). Click on Next and create the class.

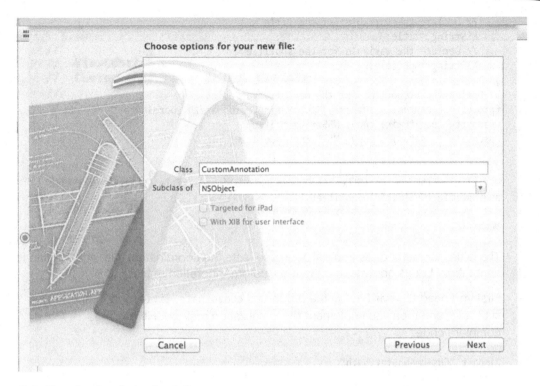

Figure 10-5. Name the class CustomAnnotation

5. Now open the file CustomAnnotation.h of the newly created class. First add the #import <MapKit/MapKit.h> directive to it. A custom annotation object must conform to the MKAnnotation protocol, so declare it:

```
@interface CustomAnnotation : NSObject <MKAnnotation>

@end
```

6. A custom annotation object consists of a set of a set of coordinates and whatever other data you want to associate with the annotation. The MKAnnotation protocol provides a coordinate property that you must declare. Therefore, add the property declaration to the CustomAnnotation.h file and the declaration of its instance variable. You should also declare a variable for the title and subtitle as well as for the method that will be used to initialize the annotation. Here is the complete code of CustomAnnotation.h: >

```
#import <UIKit/UIKit.h>
#import <MapKit/MapKit.h>

// The class must conform to the MKAnnotation protocol
@interface CustomAnnotation : NSObject <MKAnnotation> {
    // Declare the coordinate variable
    CLLocationCoordinate2D coordinate;
```

```
    // Declare the variable for the title
    NSString *title;
    // Declare the variable for the subtitle
    NSString *subtitle;
}
// Define the properties for the declared variables
@property (nonatomic, readonly) CLLocationCoordinate2D coordinate;
@property (nonatomic, copy) NSString *title;
@property (nonatomic, copy) NSString *subtitle;

//Declare the initialization method
- (id)initWithLocation:(CLLocationCoordinate2D)coords title:(NSString *)aTitle
andSubtitle:(NSString*)aSubtitle;

@end>
```

The initializer method, as you will soon see, sets the coordinates, title, and subtitle for the annotation. Let us now move on to the CustomAnnotation.m file.

7. First you need to @synthesize the properties coordinate, title, and subtitle, and then you implement the initialization method. Here is the complete code:

```
#import "CustomAnnotation.h"

@implementation CustomAnnotation

@synthesize coordinate, title, subtitle;

//Implement the initialization method

- (id)initWithLocation:(CLLocationCoordinate2D)coords title:(NSString *)aTitle
andSubtitle:(NSString*)aSubtitle

{
    self = [super init];
        coordinate = coords;
    title = aTitle;
        subtitle = aSubtitle;
    return self;
}

@end
```

8. Now the custom annotation class is complete. Thus, let us move on to the ViewController.m file. You need to import the CustomAnnotation class, so add the following to the top of the file: #import "CustomAnnotation.h". Since the map must be centered on New York City and the annotation must be centered

on it as well, inside the `viewDidLoad` method define the region and a span for it, and then set it to the map view (if the span is set to 10,000 meters):

```
CLLocationCoordinate2D regionCenter;
regionCenter.latitude = 40.664167;
regionCenter.longitude = -73.938611;
MKCoordinateRegion region = MKCoordinateRegionMakeWithDistance(regionCenter, 10000, 10000);
[_mapView setRegion:region animated:TRUE];
```

9. Now create an instance variable of the class `CustomAnnotation`, allocate it, and initialize it with the initialization method defined in the `CustomAnnotation` class. In this case, pass to the method the set of coordinates used to center the region object, since we want the annotation to be displayed at the center of the map view:

```
CustomAnnotation *annotation = [[CustomAnnotation alloc]initWithLocation: regionCenter
                                            title: @"Custom annotation object"
                                        andSubtitle:@"You just clicked on the
annotation"];
```

10. Finally, to add the annotation to the map view, use the `addAnnotation:` method, which will add the annotation using a standard annotation view. (Later I will talk about custom annotation views.)

```
[_mapView addAnnotation:annotation];
```

Here I show you all the code for the ViewController.m file:

```
#import "ViewController.h"
#import "CustomAnnotation.h"

@interface ViewController ()
@end

@implementation ViewController

- (void)viewDidLoad
{
    [super viewDidLoad];
        CLLocationCoordinate2D regionCenter;
    regionCenter.latitude = 40.664167;
    regionCenter.longitude = -73.938611;
    MKCoordinateRegion region = MKCoordinateRegionMakeWithDistance(regionCenter, 10000, 10000);
    [_mapView setRegion:region animated:TRUE];
    CustomAnnotation *annotation = [[CustomAnnotation alloc]initWithLocation: regionCenter
                                            title: @"Custom annotation object"
                                        andSubtitle:@"You just clicked on the annotation"];

        [_mapView addAnnotation:annotation];
}
```

```
- (void)didReceiveMemoryWarning
{
    [super didReceiveMemoryWarning];

}
```

@end

Now run the app. If all goes well, you should get an annotation like the one in Figure 10-6.

Figure 10-6. *The running app*

Creating Custom Annotation Objects Using a `for` Loop

Let us create another example to help you get comfortable with the custom annotation objects. We will modify the code of the previous example to generate 10 random annotation instances and display them on the map. From the previous code you need to remove (or comment) the part where a new CustomAnnotation instance is created and then displayed on the map. In its place, add a for loop that, at every cycle, creates an instance of CustomAnnotation, and set random generated values for its coordinates (within a specified range). Here are the steps:

1. Inside the viewDidLoad method create a CLLocationCoordinate2D randomCoord variable that will contain the random generated values which will be used to create the coordinates:

    ```
    CLLocationCoordinate2D randomCoord;
    ```

2. Write the for loop that will be used to create the 10 annotations and display them on the map:

    ```
    for(int i = 0; i < 10; i++) {

        CGFloat latDelta = (arc4random() % 10)  * 0.01;
        CGFloat longDelta = (arc4random() % 10) * 0.01;
        randomCoord.latitude = regionCenter.latitude + latDelta;
        randomCoord.longitude = regionCenter.longitude + longDelta;

        CustomAnnotation *annotation = [[CustomAnnotation alloc]initWithLocation: randomCoord
                                                                title:
    @"Custom annotation object"
                                                                andSubtitle:@"You just
    clicked on the annotation"];

        [_mapView addAnnotation:annotation];

    }
    ```

Note that the code creates random numbers using arc4random():. The function creates random numbers within the range 0 to 10, and then they are multiplied by 0.01 so as to limit their values. The numbers are then added to the coordinates of regionCenter so that the annotations are positioned within the New York City area. Note that fewer than 10 annotations may sometimes be displayed since the function might repeat the same random number two or more times. This is a well-known issue with random generated numbers, but for the purpose of this exercise, it does not matter. You should just know about this in case you see less than ten annotations displayed. Once you have written the code, run the app and you will see results similar to what is shown in Figure 10-7.

Figure 10-7. The 10 random generated annotations

Now that you know how to create custom annotations, you might display data on the map from external sources, like public databases, with a little effort.

Working with Annotation Views

Until now, we have focused on the first element necessary to display an annotation – that is, the annotation object. Now it is time to move to the second element: the annotation view, which is a view derived from the MKAnnotationView class used to present the annotation on the map surface. As you noticed, we were able to show annotations on a map without implementing any annotation view. When a map view needs an annotation view, the map view invokes the mapView:viewForAnnotation: method of its delegate object. If you do not implement this method, the map view then uses the default red pin annotation view. If you want to display annotation views other than the default ones, you need to override the method and create your views. Here is the structure of the mapView:viewForAnnotation: method:

```
- (MKAnnotationView *)mapView:(MKMapView *)mapView viewForAnnotation:(id < MKAnnotation >)annotation
```

The parameters the method takes are *mapView*, which is the map view that requested the annotation view, and *annotation*, which is the annotation object to be displayed on the map, as discussed in the previous sections. The method returns the view associated with the indicated annotation object. If the method returns nil, a standard annotation view is displayed. To better understand the use of the method, I include an example based on the code of the app examined in the previous section, which displays random located annotations on the map. To the existing ViewController.m file add the mapView:viewForAnnotation: method that we are going to implement:

```
-(MKAnnotationView *)mapView:(MKMapView *)theMapView viewForAnnotation:(id <MKAnnotation>)annotation
```

Now let us implement the method. You are going to use an instance of the MKPinAnnotationView class, which is a subclass of MKAnnotationView. This class provides an annotation view that displays a standard pin icon but lets you configure the color of the pin and other options. It does not give you a complete customization of the annotation (for instance it is not possible to change the image used for the pin), but it gives you more options than the standard red pin. For a more complete customization of the annotation view, see the Annotation Views with Custom Icons section later in this chapter. Here are the steps to implement the mapView:viewForAnnotation: method:

1. Since the mapView:viewForAnnotation: method is a delegate's method, declare the MKMapViewDelegate protocol in the ViewController.h file.

2. Create a MKPinAnnotationView object, and then allocate and initialize it using the initWithAnnotation:reuseIdentifier: method. This method takes as arguments the annotation object to associate with the view and a string to identify the view. This last parameter is optional; you can pass nil, but, as I cover more extensively later, if you set a string identifier, you will be able to reuse the view, saving memory resources. Here is the code:

    ```
    MKPinAnnotationView*    pinView = [[MKPinAnnotationView alloc]
    initWithAnnotation:annotation reuseIdentifier:@"ViewIdentifier"];
    ```

3. Once the MKPinAnnotationView object is created, allocated, and initialized, you can set some properties for it. You can set the color of the pin using the pinColor property that takes one of the following constants: MKPinAnnotationColorRed, MKPinAnnotationColorGreen, and MKPinAnnotationColorPurple. To set the color of the pin to green, you write:

    ```
    pinView.pinColor = MKPinAnnotationColorGreen;
    ```

Note that the iOS documentation assigns different meanings to the colors:

- Red pins indicate destination points on the map.

- Green pins indicate starting points on the map.

- Purple pins indicate user-specified points on the map.

I recommend you respect the meaning associated with each color, however you are free to give them the meaning that best suits your purposes.

4. Another property you can set for the view is animatesDrop, which takes a boolean value indicating whether the annotation view should be animated by making the pin appear to drop onto the map at its target point. To enable the animation for the pin, write:

    ```
    pinView.animatesDrop = YES;
    ```

Note that the animation may not work properly in iOS 6 if the annotation is added to the map inside the viewDidLoad method. To make it work, you need to move it inside the viewDidAppear method.

These two properties, pinColor and animatesDrop, belong to the MKPinAnnotationView class. Besides these, there are other properties that belong to the MKAnnotationView parent class that allow you to further customize the annotation view, as I will illustrate later in this chapter. Here I will just show you the canShowCallout property, which allows you to decide whether a callout is shown or not when the user clicks on the annotation. If you do not set the property, the callout is not shown by default. The property takes a boolean value, so to display the callout, you write:

```
pinView.canShowCallout = YES;
I now show you the complete code to implement the mapView:viewForAnnotation: method in the
ViewController.m file:
-(MKAnnotationView *)mapView:(MKMapView *)theMapView viewForAnnotation:(id <MKAnnotation>)annotation
{
    MKPinAnnotationView*    pinView = [[MKPinAnnotationView alloc] initWithAnnotation:annotation
reuseIdentifier:@"ViewIdentifier"];

    pinView.pinColor = MKPinAnnotationColorGreen;

    pinView.animatesDrop = YES;

    pinView.canShowCallout = YES;

    return pinView;
}
```

Now run the code. You will see that standard green pins are animated when shown on the map (Figure 10-8).

Figure 10-8. The pins appear in green and are animated when added to the map

Dequeueing Annotations

The official documentation recommends that, before creating a new annotation view inside the mapView:viewForAnnotation: method, you check if an annotation view already exists. The map view may have cached unused annotation views that it is no longer using. When this happens, the map view makes the unused views available from the dequeueReusableAnnotationViewWithIdentifier: method. If this method returns a value other than nil, meaning that an annotation view already exists, you should reuse the annotation view by updating its attributes and then returning it. If the method returns nil, you can create a new instance of the annotation view. Dequeueing an annotation view allows you to save time and memory resources. This is the structure of the method dequeueReusableAnnotationViewWithIdentifier:

```
- (MKAnnotationView *)dequeueReusableAnnotationViewWithIdentifier:(NSString *)identifier
```

The method takes *identifier* as parameter. This is a string identifying the annotation view that you want to reuse. Note that this string is the same one you specify when initializing the annotation view using the initWithAnnotation:reuseIdentifier: method. The method returns a reusable annotation view identified by its identifier. In the following code listing I show you how to implement the method by modifying the code illustrated in the previous paragraph. If an existing pin annotation view is present, this method associates the annotation object with that view. If no existing annotation view is found, the method creates a new one, setting up the basic properties of the view. Here is the code:

```
-(MKAnnotationView *)mapView:(MKMapView *)theMapView viewForAnnotation:(id <MKAnnotation>)annotation
{
    // Try to dequeue an existing pin annotation view first.
    MKPinAnnotationView*    pinView = (MKPinAnnotationView*)[theMapView dequeueReusableAnnotationVie
wWithIdentifier:@"ViewIdentifier"];

    // If an existing pin view annotation is not available create one and set its properties.
    if (pinView==NULL){

    MKPinAnnotationView*    pinView = [[MKPinAnnotationView alloc] initWithAnnotation:annotation
reuseIdentifier:@"ViewIdentifier"];

    pinView.pinColor = MKPinAnnotationColorGreen;

    pinView.animatesDrop = YES;

    pinView.canShowCallout = YES;

    return pinView;

    }

    //If an existing pin annotation view is available associate it to the annotation object and then
return it
    else {
    pinView.annotation = annotation;
    return pinView;}
}
```

Removing Annotations

You can remove an annotation from the map view using the removeAnnotation: method. Here is an example:

```
[_mapView removeAnnotation:annotation];
```

Note that if the annotation is currently associated with an annotation view that has a reuse identifier, this method removes the annotation view and queues it internally for reuse. You can then retrieve queued annotation views using the dequeueReusableAnnotationViewWithIdentifier: method, as explained in the previous section. You can also remove an array of annotations from the map using the removeAnnotations: method, which takes as parameter an NSArray containing the annotations.

Annotation Views with Custom Icons

While designing maps, choosing the right symbols is very important. The standard icons for annotations that Map Kit makes available are not always the most suitable for representing information on the map. To display the location of restaurants, a more specific icon could be better than the standard pin. Different icons allow you to display different categories of information on the map without confusing the user. For instance, you can have one symbol for restaurants, one for bars, and one for fast food joints, according to the different typologies of data. Luckily, Map Kit allows you to define custom annotation icons very easily. All you need is an image to be used as an icon. You create a MKAnnotationView object and then assign your custom image to the image property of the object. Let us look at an example that modifies the code of the previous section Working with Annotation Views.

1. First you need an image. You can create one yourself or you can find a free one online, I suggest you have a look at the very extensive gallery of free icons for Google Maps here: http://mapicons.nicolasmollet.com. The icons can be used in Map Kit as well. When you have found the icon you want, you must save it in a folder (right-click on the image and then click to Save the image), and then drag it on to your project folder in Xcode. Next, the Choose options for adding these files window appears. Select Copy items into destination group's folder (if needed) and in Add to target make sure your project is selected (see Figure 10-9). Then click on Finish to add the image. In the example, the starIcon.png file has been added to the project (Figure 10-10).

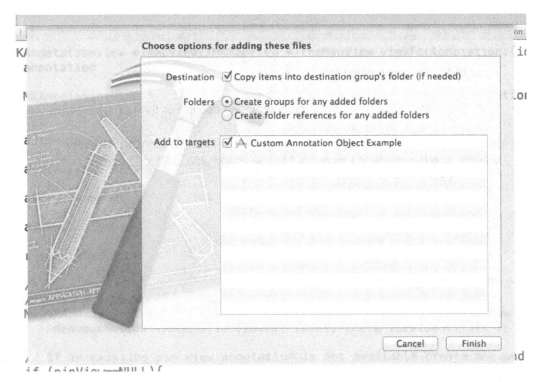

Figure 10-9. The settings to select when adding the image to the project

Figure 10-10. The image has been added to the project

2.   Once the image is added to the project, you can use it. For the
      example, I chose an image taken from
      http://mapicons.nicolasmollet.com/category/markers/tourism/place-to-see/.
      You can see the image in Figure 10-11. The image size is 32 x 37 pixels.

Figure 10-11. The image to be used as a custom icon for the annotation view

3. From the starting example, remove the implementation previously made of the mapView:viewForAnnotation: method so as to start with the following lines:

    ```
    -(MKAnnotationView *)mapView:(MKMapView *)theMapView viewForAnnotation:
    (id <MKAnnotation>)annotation
    ```

4. This time we are going to instantiate inside the method the MKAnnotationView class instead of its subclass MKPinAnnotationView:

    ```
    MKAnnotationView *aView = [[MKAnnotationView alloc] initWithAnnotation:annotation
    reuseIdentifier:@"ViewIdentifier"];
    ```

5. Once the annotation view is created, allocate, and initialized (we are not going to implement a method to dequeue an existing pin), you can set its image property to give the annotation view a custom icon. In the example, I use an image named starIcon.png, so I write:

    ```
    aView.image = [UIImage imageNamed:@"starIcon.png"];
    ```

6. Note that, by default, the center point of an annotation view is placed at the coordinate point of the associated annotation. You might need to reposition the annotation view, depending on the shape of the icon. For instance, if you consider the image used in the example (Figure 10-11), you might want to position it so that its bottom pointed end indicates the coordinate point. To reposition the icon, you set the `centerOffset` property of the annotation view. X and Y offset values are measured in pixels. You use positive offset values to move the annotation view down and to the right, and you use negative values to move it up and to the left. In the example, to get a better positioning for the image, I set:

```
aView.centerOffset = CGPointMake(0, -19);
```

7. You also need to decide whether or not to show a callout associated with the annotation. In this case, I set:

```
aView.canShowCallout = YES;
Now I show the complete code of the method:
-(MKAnnotationView *)mapView:(MKMapView *)theMapView viewForAnnotation:(id
<MKAnnotation>)annotation
{
    MKAnnotationView *aView = [[MKAnnotationView alloc] initWithAnnotation:annotation
reuseIdentifier:@"ViewIdentifier"];

    aView.image = [UIImage imageNamed:@"starIcon.png"];

    aView.centerOffset = CGPointMake(0, -19);

    aView.canShowCallout = YES;

    return aView;
}
```

The result is shown in Figure 10-12. You can see the custom icon for the annotation view correctly displayed.

Figure 10-12. The custom icon for the annotation view has been applied

The MKAnnotationView class includes other properties that can be used to customize annotation views. For instance, you can define the callout offset by setting the calloutOffset property, and you can make draggable annotations by setting the draggable property. For more information, I suggest you thoroughly read the explanations offered in the MKAnnotationView Class Reference available here: http://developer.apple.com/library/ios/#documentation/MapKit/Reference/MKAnnotationView_Class/Reference/Reference.html#//apple_ref/occ/cl/MKAnnotationView.

Working with Overlays

In addition to annotations, overlays are another kind of object that you can display on a map and anchor to it. While annotations are always positioned by defining a single coordinate point on the map, overlays are typically defined by multiple coordinates. You can use overlays to draw lines, polylines, polygons, circles and other shapes. Overlays can be filled or stroked with color. You can use overlays to define areas like for instance the boundaries of a country, to draw routes. They are an essential ingredient for realizing map-based apps.

Similar to what happens with annotations, Map Kit tries to facilitate working with overlays by keeping the data associated to an overlay (like coordinates, title, and other content) separate from their visual presentation on the map. To add an overlay to a map, you must implement two elements:

1. An object that will store the overlay content (called an overlay object); this object must conform to the MKOverlay protocol.

2. A view, derived from the MKOverlayView class that will be used to present the overlay on the map surface (called annotation view).

You can build an overlay object using one of the following basic methods:

- Using the MKCircle, MKPolygon, or MKPolyline class to quickly create circle, polygon, or polyline overlays.

- Subclassing MKShape or MKMultiPoint to create overlays with custom shapes.

- Creating custom overlay objects using an existing class from your app and making it conform to the MKOverlay protocol.

Once you have created an overlay object, you display it on the map using one of the following options:

- For polygons, polylines, or circles, use the MKPolygonView, MKPolylineView, or MKCircleView overlay views.

- For custom shapes descended from MKShape you must define an appropriate subclass of MKOverlayPathView.

- For all other custom shapes and overlays, subclass MKOverlayView and implement your custom code.

Similar to what happens with annotations, to display an overlays view you must implement the mapView:viewForOverlay: method of your map view delegate and add your overlay to the map view using the addOverlay: method.

While annotations are not scaled when the map is zoomed, overlays are automatically scaled because they are used to define areas, roads, and other content that gets scaled when zooming. You can also define Z-ordering of overlays in a map to make sure that specific overlays are always displayed on top of others.

In the next section, I will show you how to realize a polyline overlay using the MKPolyline and MKPolylineView classes.

Creating and Displaying a Polyline Overlay

In this project we are going to draw a line connecting four points in New York City. The points will be represented using annotations, while the polyline will be an overlay. In Figure 10-13 I show the four points represented by placemarks in Google Earth.

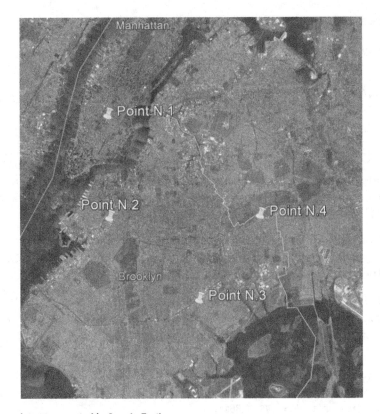

Figure 10-13. The four points represented in Google Earth

Here are the steps to follow:

1. Create a new Xcode project for iPhone and name it "Polyline Example". Add the Core Location and Map Kit frameworks to it.

2. Create a map view, and then, from the Assistant Editor, Ctrl-drag the map view on to the ViewController.h file to declare it as an outlet. In the same file, declare the <MKMapViewDelegate> protocol and an instance variable of type MKPolyline and its relative property. The MKPolyline class allows you to draw a geometry consisting of one or more line segments that connects points end-to-end in the order they are provided. The complete code of the ViewController.h file is as follows:

```
#import <UIKit/UIKit.h>
#import <MapKit/MapKit.h>
#import <CoreLocation/CoreLocation.h>
```

```
@interface ViewController : UIViewController <MKMapViewDelegate>
{
    MKPolyline *polyLine;
}
@property (weak, nonatomic) IBOutlet MKMapView *mapView;
@property(nonatomic, retain) MKPolyline *polyLine;

@end
```

3. Add to the project a custom Objective-C class called CustomAnnotation that will be the class for the custom annotation object. (To build the class, repeat the same steps explained in the previous section Creating custom annotation objects.)

4. Now let us move on to the ViewController.m file. Add the #import "CustomAnnotation.h" directive so that you can use the CustomAnnotation class. Then add the @synthesize polyLine; directive.

5. Inside the viewDidLoad method set the view controller as delegate for the map view, and then define and set a region showing the New York City area (it is the same region we used in the previous examples):

```
[_mapView setDelegate:self];
CLLocationCoordinate2D regionCenter;
regionCenter.latitude = 40.664167;
regionCenter.longitude = -73.938611;
MKCoordinateRegion region = MKCoordinateRegionMakeWithDistance(regionCenter, 10000,
10000);
[_mapView setRegion:region animated:TRUE];
```

6. Now we want to assign data to the MKPolyline instance. We can use the polylineWithPoints:count: class method to do this. The method takes two arguments: the array of map points defining the polyline and the number of items contained in the array. We have to build the array containing the four map points that we want to connect with a polyline. Map points are objects of type MKMapPoint and are built using the MKMapPointForCoordinate function. This function takes as argument a CLLocationCoordinate2D object that we create using the CLLocationCoordinate2DMake function. Here is the code for creating the array:

```
MKMapPoint * pointsArray = malloc(sizeof(CLLocationCoordinate2D)*4);
pointsArray[0]= MKMapPointForCoordinate(CLLocationCoordinate2DMake(40.730742,-73.992257));

pointsArray[1]= MKMapPointForCoordinate(CLLocationCoordinate2DMake(40.677762,-73.985409));

pointsArray[2]= MKMapPointForCoordinate(CLLocationCoordinate2DMake(40.639047,-73.918120));

pointsArray[3]= MKMapPointForCoordinate(CLLocationCoordinate2DMake(40.685396,-73.880044));
```

7. Once you created the array you must assign it to the MKPolyline instance by using the polylineWithPoints:count: method, then you add it to the map view using the addOverlay: method:

```
polyLine = [MKPolyline polylineWithPoints:pointsArray count:4];
[_mapView addOverlay:polyLine];
free(pointsArray);
```

8. To show the overlay, we also have to implement the mapView:viewForOverlay: method of the map view delegate. Here is the structure of the method:

```
- (MKOverlayView *)mapView:(MKMapView *)mapView viewForOverlay:(id < MKOverlay >)overlay
```

9. The method takes as parameters *mapView*, which is the map view that requested the overlay view, and *overlay*, which is the overlay object that you want to display. The method then returns the overlay view to be used to display the specified overlay object. If nil is returned, no view is displayed for the specified overlay object. In the implementation of the method, first an instance of the MKPolylineView class is created. This class provides the overlay view for an MKPolyline overlay object. The overlay view generated by this class strokes the path represented by the polyline but does not fill the area enclosed by the path. It is possible to change the color, the width, and other visual attributes of the polyline by modifying the properties inherited from the MKOverlayPathView class of which MKPolylineView is a subclass. For more information on the class, see: http://developer.apple.com/library/ios/#documentation/MapKit/Reference/MKPolylineView_class/Reference/Reference.html. Here is the implementation of the mapView:viewForOverlay: method:

```
- (MKOverlayView *)mapView:(MKMapView *)theMapView viewForOverlay:(id )overlay

{

    MKPolylineView * polyLineView = [[MKPolylineView alloc] initWithPolyline:polyLine];

    polyLineView.strokeColor = [UIColor redColor];

    polyLineView.lineWidth = 3;

    return polyLineView;

}
```

10. Now run the code. You will get a picture similar to what shown in Figure 10-14.

Figure 10-14. The polyline is displayed on New York City

11. Now we can add four annotations to the map to indicate the points that
     define the polyline. To do this we use the CustomAnnotation class we
     created previously and add the following code to the viewDidLoad method.
     To extract the coordinates from the array of MKMapPoint map points, the
     MKCoordinateForMapPoint function is used. Here is the code:

```
for (int i = 0; i<4; i++) {
    CustomAnnotation *annotation = [[CustomAnnotation alloc]initWithLocation: MKCoor
dinateForMapPoint(pointsArray[i]) title: [NSString stringWithFormat:@"Annotation N. %i",
i] andSubtitle:[NSString stringWithFormat:@"This is annotation N. %i", i]];
        [_mapView addAnnotation:annotation];
    }
```

12. Now run the code. The annotations will be added to the map and their
     callouts will indicate their respective positions in order (Figure 10-15).

Figure 10-15. *The annotations have been added to the map. Here is the complete code of the ViewController.m file*

```
#import "ViewController.h"
#import "CustomAnnotation.h"

@interface ViewController ()

@end

@implementation ViewController
@synthesize polyLine;
@synthesize showHideSwitch;

- (void)viewDidLoad
{
    [super viewDidLoad];
    [_mapView setDelegate:self];

    //Set the region shown in the map view
        CLLocationCoordinate2D regionCenter;
    regionCenter.latitude = 40.664167;
```

```
        regionCenter.longitude = -73.938611;
        MKCoordinateRegion region = MKCoordinateRegionMakeWithDistance(regionCenter, 10000, 10000);
        [_mapView setRegion:region animated:TRUE];

        //Create the array of map points
        MKMapPoint * pointsArray = malloc(sizeof(CLLocationCoordinate2D)*4);
        pointsArray[0]= MKMapPointForCoordinate(CLLocationCoordinate2DMake(40.730742,-73.992257));

        pointsArray[1]= MKMapPointForCoordinate(CLLocationCoordinate2DMake(40.677762,-73.985409));

        pointsArray[2]= MKMapPointForCoordinate(CLLocationCoordinate2DMake(40.639047,-73.918120));

        pointsArray[3]= MKMapPointForCoordinate(CLLocationCoordinate2DMake(40.685396,-73.880044));

        //Pass the array to the MKPolyline instance and add the overlay to the map view
        polyLine = [MKPolyline polylineWithPoints:pointsArray count:4];
        [_mapView addOverlay:polyLine];

        for (int i = 0; i<4; i++) {

            CustomAnnotation *annotation = [[CustomAnnotation alloc]initWithLocation:
MKCoordinateForMapPoint(pointsArray[i]) title: [NSString stringWithFormat:@"Annotation N. %i", i]
andSubtitle:[NSString stringWithFormat:@"This is annotation N. %i", i]];
            [_mapView addAnnotation:annotation];

        }

        free(pointsArray);

}

- (MKOverlayView *)mapView:(MKMapView *)theMapView viewForOverlay:(id )overlay

{

    MKPolylineView  * polyLineView = [[MKPolylineView alloc] initWithPolyline:polyLine];

    polyLineView.strokeColor = [UIColor redColor];

    polyLineView.lineWidth = 3;

    return polyLineView;

}

- (void)didReceiveMemoryWarning
{
    [super didReceiveMemoryWarning];
    // Dispose of any resources that can be recreated.
}

@end
```

Removing Overlays

I have shown you how to add overlays to a map, but it can also be very useful for you to know how to remove them. You might want to give the user the possibility to show or hide different overlays. To do this, MapKit makes available the removeOverlay: method. Let us add to the previous app a switch control to show or hide the polyline overlay.

1. Open the storyboard, resize the map view, and add a toolbar and a UISwitch object accompanied by a text label (see Figure 10-16).

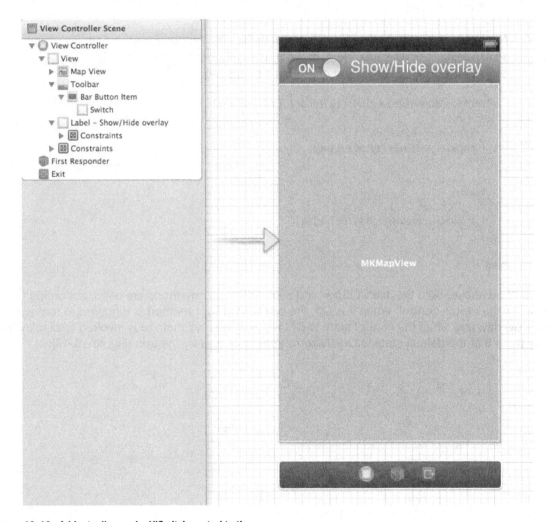

Figure 10-16. Add a toolbar and a UISwitch control to the map

2. Open the Assistant Editor and Ctrl-drag the UISwitch on to the ViewController.h file. Declare it as an outlet, naming it showHideSwitch to get:

    ```
    @property (weak, nonatomic) IBOutlet UISwitch *showHideSwitch;
    ```

3. Ctrl-drag the UISwitch object on to the ViewController.h again, but this time in the popup, select Connection: Action and give the action the name showHideOverlay to get the following method declaration:

    ```
    - (IBAction)showHideOverlay:(id)sender;
    ```

4. Now let us move on to the ViewController.m file and add the @synthesize showHideSwitch; directive. Next, move to the stub implementation of the showHideOverlay: method and complete it by adding:

    ```
    - (IBAction)showHideOverlay:(id)sender {

        if(showHideSwitch.on) {
        [_mapView addOverlay:polyLine];
        }

        else {

        [_mapView removeOverlay:polyLine];
        }
    }
    @end
    ```

In the method above, both the addOverlay: and removeOverlay: methods are used, according to the state of the switch control. When it is Off, the removeOverlay: method is triggered to remove the present overlay, and when the control state is On, the addOverlay: method is invoked to display the overlay (note that the default state is On). Now run the code and try the app (Figure 10-17).

Figure 10-17. The switch control allows the user to remove or display the polyline overlay

Displaying a Polygon

In the previous section I illustrated a particular type of overlay: an MKPolyline object. Another type of overlay that is frequently used is the MKPolygon class. This class allows you to draw a shape consisting of one or more points that define a closed polygon. The first and last points are connected to each other to close the polygon. To display a polygon, you use a polygon view of the MKPolygonView class. The way to implement a polygon is very similar to the way to implement a polyline. In this next example, by modifying the code of the previous app, a polygon is drawn instead of a polyline. Here are the steps:

1. Open the ViewController.h file and substitute the line MKPolyline *polyLine; with MKPolygon * polygon;. Substitute the property declaration @property(nonatomic, retain) MKPolyline *polyLine; with @property(nonatomic, retain) MKPolygon *polygon;.

2. Move on to the ViewController.m file and, instead of @synthesize polyLine;, write @synthesize polygon;.

3. Inside the `viewDidLoad` method instead of the lines

    ```
    polyLine = [MKPolyline polylineWithPoints:pointsArray count:4];
    [_mapView addOverlay:polyLine];
    ```

    write

    ```
    polygon = [MKPolygon polygonWithPoints:pointsArray count:4];
    [_mapView addOverlay:polygon];
    ```

    As you can see, the method polygonWithPoints:count: is quite similar to polylineWithPoints:count: as it takes as arguments an array of map points and the number of elements in the array.

4. Now let us move on to the `mapView:viewForOverlay:` method implementation and modify it in the following way:

    ```
    - (MKOverlayView *)mapView:(MKMapView *)theMapView viewForOverlay:(id )overlay

    {

        MKPolygonView  * polygonView = [[MKPolygonView alloc] initWithPolygon:polygon];

        polygonView.fillColor = [UIColor colorWithWhite:0.2 alpha:0.5];

        polygonView.strokeColor = [UIColor redColor];

        polygonView.lineWidth = 3;

        return polygonView;

    }
    ```

    Run the code. A polygon will be displayed, defined by the four points that, in the previous example, were connected by the polyline (Figure 10-18).

Figure 10-18. *The switch control allows the user to remove or display the polyline overlay*

Summary

In this chapter I illustrated the basics of creating elements to be overlaid on the map. Now you should be able to display geometric primitives, points, lines, and polygons on the map and associate data to them, like a callout with a title and other data. You now have the basic knowledge to further explore and understand official Map Kit documentation to create complex representations of data on the map and to display data from external sources as well. In particular, you should now be able to do the following:

- Create annotations objects using `MKPointAnnotation` objects.
- Create annotations objects using custom annotation objects.
- Display annotations using standard annotation views.

- Display annotations of type `MKPinAnnotationView`.
- Display annotations using annotation views of type `MKAnnotationView` to display custom icons.
- Create and display annotations using `for` loops.
- Create overlays objects of type `MKPolyline` and `MKPolygon`.
- Display overlays using overlay views of type `MKPolylineView` and `MKPolygonView`.

Understanding the Terms Of Service

This appendix provides an overview of the main documents and topics concerning the terms of service (TOS) of the platforms I discussed in the previous chapters. It is very important that you know how to legally use the previously mentioned technologies and also legally profit from them. There are some documents that I invite you to read carefully and in their entirety and whose main points I will comment on in the next pages. The documents to be familiar with concerning the first part of the book, which is about developing web apps using Google Maps services, are:

- Google Maps/Google Earth APIs Terms of Service and their connected documents: `https://developers.google.com/maps/terms`.

- Google Maps FAQ: `https://developers.google.com/maps/faq`. In particular, consider the sections "Understanding the Terms of Service", "Usage limits", and "Advertising on your Map".

In addition to these documents, it important to be familiar with the End User TOS of Google Earth/Maps (`http://www.google.com/intl/en-us/help/terms_maps.html`), which every user of the software and its services must accept. These TOS and their connected documents can be reached from within the maps itself, since the link to them must be explicitly displayed in every Google Maps implementation (Figure A-1).

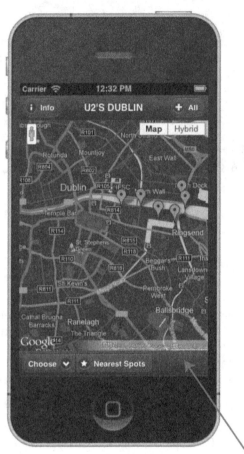

Link to End User TOS

Figure A-1. *How to reach the End User TOS from within the map itself*

If you use jQuery and jQuery Mobile, you also need to agree to the framework license here (http://jquery.org/license). For the second part of the book (hybrid apps) and the third (native apps), you need to read and accept the Xcode License Agreement (Xcode ➤ About Xcode ➤ License Agreement). If you want to be enrolled in the iOS Developer Program you first need to register as an Apple Developer and agree to the terms and conditions of the Registered Apple Developer Agreement (https://developer.apple.com/programs/terms/registered_apple_developer_20100301.pdf), then you need to read and agree to the iOS Developer Program License Agreement (https://developer.apple.com/membercenter/index.action#agreements). If you create hybrid apps, you also need to know and agree to the Google Maps API TOS and related documents. In the following sections I will illustrate the most important points from these documents, however I recommend you read them in their entirety.

TOS for Developing Web Apps with Google Maps API

First, you need to know that the terms are composed of the Google Maps/Google Earth APIs Terms of Service (https://developers.google.com/maps/terms), The Legal Notices (http://www.google.com/intl/en-us/help/legalnotices_maps.html), and the Privacy Policy document (http://www.google.com/policies/privacy). You should read every one of these documents.

The basic take-away from the Google Maps API TOS is that you can use the API in a web app as long as your Maps API implementation is free and publicly accessible (Section 9.1 of Maps/Google Earth APIs TOS); otherwise, you need to use the Google Maps API for Business. So, for example, you cannot make an API implementation accessible only to members of an intranet or to people who registered for a site with a fee. However, and this is of the greatest interest to us, if you develop a mobile app, this rule does not apply (Section 9.1.2). You can sell a Google Maps-based hybrid app in the Apple App Store. This last exception was added in 2011 (see http://googlegeodevelopers. blogspot.it/2011/04/updates-to-google-maps-apigoogle-earth.html) and was clearly meant to encourage the use of Google Maps API in mobile app development.

If you want to make a web app accessible to both desktop computers and mobile devices by selling it in the App Store, you must keep the desktop version freely accessible. Among the requirements for using the Google Maps API, I would like to highlight the requirement to show the link on the map to the End User Terms (see Figure A-1) and to show the proper attribution to Google and other third-party content providers (trade names, trademarks, service marks, logos, domain names, and other distinctive brand features). You must be careful not to hide the information in the bottom part of the map (Figure A-2), otherwise this may result in a violation of the TOS.

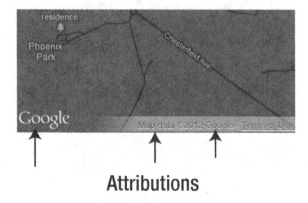

Figure A-2. You must not hide the attributions of Google and other content providers

Another important point concerns a user's privacy and geolocation privacy. As I mentioned throughout the book, before using user location data, you must get the user's permission and your app must let the user revoke consent at any time.

These are some of the main points to know, but I strongly recommend you to read the TOS in their entirety. I also suggest you consult the FAQs here: https://developers.google.com/maps/faq. The "Usage limits" section explains the limits of the free Google Maps API (as well as the Google Maps JavaScript API, which I talked about in this book). The current limit is fixed at 25,000 map loads per day. If you are lucky enough to exceed this maximum, you need to enroll in automated billing of excess map loads in the Google APIs Console or purchase a Maps API for Business license. You can find more information in the FAQ. Note that there are also usage limits for geocoding if you intend to use this functionality.

In addition to the FAQ, you can consult the Permission Guidelines which includes a tool (Permissions Tools) that asks you questions about the content you plan to use and then displays the usage requirements and guidelines (Figure A-3). I did not find the tool so useful because it offers a very limited number of scenarios, but you can try it out here:
http://www.google.com/permissions/geoguidelines.html.

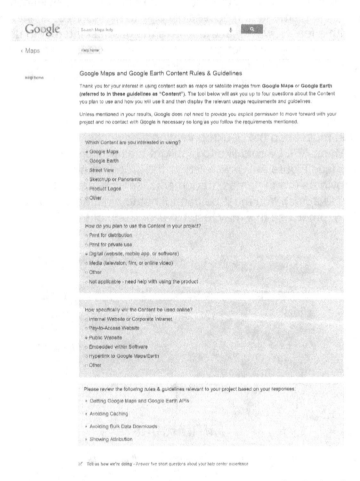

Figure A-3. The Permission Tool helps you understand the usage requirements for your Google Maps implementation

Advertising on the Maps

When using the Google Maps API, be aware that Google reserves the right to include advertising in the maps images and in the Places search results. (See Google Maps/Google Earth APIs Terms of Service, Section 4.3). As of November 2012, the service does not include advertising on the map images (perhaps they do not want to drive away users in this period of competition following the introduction of its rival Apple Maps). However, it is possible that in the near future advertising on map tiles will become effective. If you do not want advertising on the maps (if and when such a practice should become effective), you can contact the Google Maps API for Business sales team to obtain a Google enterprise license, which will allow you to avoid advertising.

In addition to advertising by Google, you can also monetize your maps through your AdSense account (if you own one). The Google Maps JavaScript API offers an AdSense Library, allowing you to put advertising on your Google maps, either in a web app or in a hybrid app. The section of the official documentation dedicated to the AdSense library is available here:

`https://developers.google.com/maps/documentation/javascript/advertising`

As you can see, the library is very simple to use and you can display advertising in many different formats (see Figure A-4).

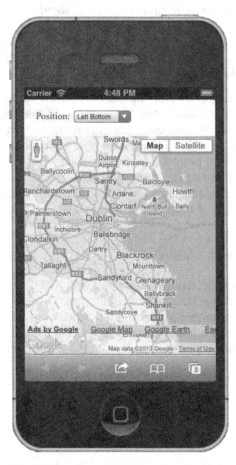

Figure A-4. Some ads displayed through the AdSense library. With this tool you can get a preview of different types of ad formats: `https://google-developers.appspot.com/maps/documentation/javascript/examples/ads-adunit`

If you decide to release an app for free on the App Store and you still want to generate revenue, you could simply implement advertising on the map through the AdSense library.

TOS for Developing Hybrid and Native Apps with Xcode

Before you begin developing hybrid or native apps, you must agree to the Xcode License Agreement (Xcode ➤ About Xcode ➤ License Agreement). Within that agreement, which you should read in its entirety, Section 2 (Permitted License Uses and Restrictions), subsection F Location Services, states, "Subject to these terms and conditions, you may only use such Location APIs and services to enable applications you develop ("Applications") to access location data (for example, the real-time geographic location of a user's computer) from users who consent to such access."

As I mentioned earlier in the book, it is necessary ask the user for location permission: By default, iOS asks the user for permission when a geolocation function is triggered. Whether you use the W3C Geolocation API or the Core Location library, you must be careful not to bypass or alter this default behavior. If you want to be enrolled in the iOS Developer Program, you need to register as an Apple developer and agree to the terms here: `https://developer.apple.com/programs/terms/registered_apple_developer_20100301.pdf`. Then, you must agree to the iOS Developer Program License Agreement: `https://developer.apple.com/membercenter/index.action#agreements` (You need to be enrolled to view the documents.) In the last document you can find many references to how you can use location services and Apple Maps.

At the beginning of the document, in Section 1.2 Definitions, the Apple Maps service itself is defined as "the mapping platform and Map Data provided by Apple via the MapKit API for iOS version 6 or later and for use by You only in connection with Your Applications". In that section, pay particular attention to points 3.3.14 to 3.3.17. With the apps we deal with in this book, Apple Maps and Core Location usage are regulated. Note point 3.3.17, which states that using MapKit on devices running iOS 6 and later versions means that Apple Maps will be used and you must follow the present agreement. Otherwise, for apps created using MapKit on devices running a previous version of iOS, Google Maps will be used instead of Apple Maps and you will have to agree to the Google Maps TOS for iPhone SDK here:

`https://developers.google.com/maps/iphone/terms`

If you want to distribute your app on devices equipped with iOS 6 as well as on devices with earlier iOS versions, you must agree to the TOS for both platforms. The iOS Developer Program License Agreement also includes an attachment (Attachment 6. Additional Terms for the use of the Apple Maps Service) that contains additional terms regulating the use of the Apple Maps service. You should be aware of this when you create apps with the MapKit library.

Index